NORTHWEST
WINES & WINERIES

CHUCK HILL

Speed Graphics

Seattle, Washington

About the Author

Chuck Hill has been involved with the Northwest wine industry since 1976, following the rapid development of Washington, Oregon and Idaho wineries. In this ever-changing environment he has found a challenge in keeping the consumer informed about the best in Northwest wines and the most enjoyable of winery visits.

Chuck is a regular contributor to Northwest food and wine periodicals and is co-author, with Gilda Barrow-Zimmar, of the cookbook *Food and Wine Northwest Style*. The exciting emergence of food and wine pairing as a popular culinary exercise continues to provide new avenues for the exploration of the best wines from the region.

As Vice President and member of the Board of Directors of the Enological Society of the Pacific Northwest, Seattle Chapter, Chuck contributes to the ongoing goal of the Society to learn and enjoy the realms of wine and food. He is the editor of Northwest Enographic, the Seattle Chapter's monthly newsletter and wine columnist for *Seattle Downtown News*.

Credits
Cover illustration by Colin Hayes
Original illustrations by Colleen Higgins.

Accolades
To the Wandering Winelover, Steve Gaddis for his devotion to this project and his assistance in traveling the "Wine Trail."

Printed in the United States of America • ISBN 0-9617699-4-7

To
My Mother, Ina Hill

*Thanks for your patience,
perseverence, and love.*

Special Thanks
to Some Great Wine Tasters

To complete the task of judging over 600 Northwest wines for the Best of the Northwest wines section of this book, I called upon friends and colleagues in the wine and hospitality fields. Concensus in judging wine is critical and I feel that this way I was able to bring to you the most accurate evaluations of Northwest wines. Panelists in alphabetical order:

Monique Barbeau, *Executive Chef, Fullers Restaurant*

Pat Campbell, *Winemaker, Elk Cove Vineyards*

Brian Carter, *Winemaker, Washington Hills Cellars*

Stan Clarke, *Wine Writer, Yakima Herald Republic*

Maurice & Dale Collada, *Wine Enthusiasts, Salem, OR*

Greg Finger, *Winery Representative, Ste. Chapelle Winery*

Stephen Gaddis, *Wine Enthusiast, Enological Society*

Kerry Godes, *Winery Representative, Columbia Crest*

Jeff Hill, *Wine Enthusiast, Salem, OR*

Lane Hoss, *Marketing Manager, Anthony's Restaurants*

David Lake, M.W., *Winemaker, Columbia Winery*

Cindy Lewis, *Chef, Duke's Restaurants*

Steve & Martha Lind, *Wine Enthusiasts, Salem, OR*

Greg & Gayle Lundmark, *Wine Enthusiasts, Salem, OR*

Karen Matson, *Wine Enthusiast, Ballard Bratsberg, Inc.*

Dan McCarthy, *Wine Retailer, McCarthy & Schiering*

Doug McCrea, *Winemaker, McCrea Cellars*

Michael Mercer, *Wine Wholesaler, K & L Wines*

Teri Moore, *Wine Wholesaler, G. Raden & Sons*

Emile Ninaud, *Restaurateur, Le Tastevin*

Dixie Pintler, *Wine Enthusiast, Enological Society*

Jeff Prather, *Sommelier, Ray's Boathouse*

Tom Schaeffer, *Wine Wholesaler, Western Wash. Beverage*

Tom Stockley, *Wine Writer, The Seattle Times*

Walt Sumner, *Wine Retailer, Larry's Markets*

Brooks Tish, *Wine Writer, Pacific Northwest Magazine*

TABLE OF CONTENTS

NORTHWEST WINE COUNTRY

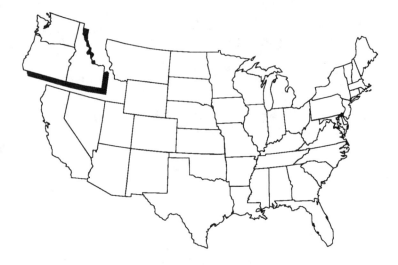

The wineries of the Pacific Northwest are producing some of the finest wine in the United States. Whether you are counting gold medals won in prestigious competitions or consulting chefs from the nation's finest restaurants, you will find that Northwest wines are world class enological efforts.

The wines of the Northwest have evolved with the number of wineries and the sophistication of the consumer. Winemakers have learned to work with Mother Nature to produce better wines from every vintage, and vineyardists have expanded the number of planted varietals to provide new choices at the wine shop. New vineyards are being developed by Northwesterners and by investors from California, the Midwest and abroad.

Wine touring in the Northwest affords the opportunity to experience not only the fruits of the vineyards but the fruits of orchard and field as well. Mountain peaks, towering evergreens, vast waterways and welcoming, livable cities are additional attractions. While the wine scene in the Northwest has not conglomerated to the extent of the Napa Valley, you can still find wineries clustered in small numbers around the vineyard areas of Oregon and Washington. Urban centers such as Seattle and Portland have attracted a number of winemakers who prefer the closeness of their major customers to the closeness of the grapevine.

You can join in tours at major facilities in mid-season if you choose, or you can visit the smaller wineries on chilly spring weekdays to have a few private moments of conversation with the winemaker. Enjoy the variety of winery sizes and the diversity of winery personalities.

This book is designed to provide the wine tourist with enough information to travel, tour, eat and sleep without additional references. Experiences are genuine and recommendations are sincere. A state highway map is a useful addition to the touring knapsack, along with a chunk of cheese, some flavorful bread and, of course, a corkscrew!

Imbibing beverage alcohol and getting behind the wheel of a car is dangerous. Wine is beverage alcohol and wine touring is getting behind the wheel of a car. It doesn't take a rocket scientist to figure out that something's wrong with this picture. Bring along a friend who agrees not to drink wine on the tour and reward him with a bottle of wine to take home afterwards. This designated driver idea has saved hundreds of lives and hopefully will save many more. If you choose not to designate, then spit (this is a ne-tested custom for those who truly want to evaluate

Remarks

e maps in this book are oriented so north is up, west is left, ok right side up and you should be just fine. Landmarks have re necessary and some mileage distances are given when e your odometer, trip meter or trip computer to figure out

ine country you'll find that your travels often begin on a ir-laner and end up on dusty gravel. That's the way it's I don't think a change is coming any time soon. Dings on e no fun so drive carefully and be considerate of the guy

eeping

nd lodging suggestions are provided for most touring re-ies with hundreds of motels, hotels and B & Bs are missing s listings but have lots of restaurant suggestions. Smaller e only one restaurant worth trying but finding a clean, m requires more listings of overnight accommodations. hotels are listed mainly for the convenience of those children. Most recommendations have a pool and other he younger set. Bed & Breakfasts in the Northwest have nore than a "home stay." Rooms often have private baths d breakfasts take on proportions that eliminate the need for I have recommended are clean, well-run and savvy to the he tourist.

lishments have been chosen – at least partly – with their Northwest wine industry in mind. You won't find a HIS book that serves a majority of cheap California plonk at s. Many of the suggestions for dining have expansive rthwest bottlings at fair prices, as well as Northwest wines

MORE ABOUT WINE TOURING

For Parents Only

Those who travel with children have special needs that non-parents sometimes find hard to understand. Clean places to change diapers, food that's inexpensive and kid-oriented places for running around and letting off steam are the bare necessities of jaunting with junior.

The Pacific Northwest is home to some of the world's best family activities. Most towns have interesting museums, parks and historic sites. Community pools, beaches and sport fields provide recreation, exercise and fresh air. Listings for the best of these areas are included. I have taken a lot of flack over the last few years for continuing to recommend McDonald's for kiddie dining. I insist on doing so for their kid-calming selections, clean restrooms and quick service.

Winery Listings

The almost 200 wineries listed in this book are arranged alphabetically within the touring region section. The regions have been determined by geographic common sense and by clustering of wineries open for touring.

It is essential that a guidebook of this type provide more than just a few lines about a place along with the address and phone number. Winery listings include:

Statistics such as address, phone number, size of facility and winemaker;
Winery History encapsulated into a few accurate sentences;
A Visit to the Winery with hours, amenities, navigation aids, etc.
The Wines describes the winemaking style and currently available choices
Special Events offers dates and times of wine-related events and regional special events

Wine Label Terminology

Vintage Year - by federal law, 95% of the grapes had to be harvested in the year specified on the label

Winery Name -(a winery may substitute a proprietary name)

Appellation /Viticultural Area - These terms inform the consumer of the origin of the grapes that went into the wine. All viticultural areas that appear on wine labels in the United States must be approved by BATF (Federal Bureau of Alcohol, Tobacco and Firearms). Washington has three: Columbia Valley, Yakima Valley and Walla Walla Valley. Oregon also has three: Columbia Valley (extending across the border from Washington), Willamette Valley and Umpqua Valley. To use the appellation name on the label, 85% of the grapes must originate in that area.

Grape Variety - If a varietal is named on the label, at least 75% of the wine must be of the named variety. In Oregon, their tougher state law requires that 90% of the wine must be from the named grape.

Producer Information - This line tells the consumer if the wine was actually fermented at the named winery or just bottled there.

Alcohol Content - The percentage of alcohol in the wine as measured by volume. Must be accurate to ± 1.5%.

NORTHWEST WINE EVENTS

Annual Wine Events
Throughout the Pacific Northwest

January
    Pasco Winter Wine Fair

April
    Hood River Blossom Festival
    Yakima Valley Barrel Tasting (last weekend)

May
    Walla Walla Hot Air Balloon Stampede &
        Winery Open House (first weekend)
    Yamhill County Wineries Match Made in Heaven
        (Memorial Day weekend)
    Eola Hills/Polk County Wineries Memorial Day Tour

June
    Southern Oregon Wine Festival

July
    July 4th Open House - Washington County Oregon

August
    Enological Society Northwest Wine & Food Festival
        (1st Saturday)
    International Pinot Noir Celebration, McMinnville, OR
        (Phone 503-472-8964)

September
    Walla Walla Wineries Open House
        (weekend after Labor Day)
    Tri-Cities Wineries "Catch the Crush" (last weekend)

October
    Capitol Food & Wine Festival - Olympia (St. Martins Col.)

November
    Wine Country Thanksgiving: Yakima Valley, Washington,
        Washington County, Oregon, Yamhill County, Oregon
    Great American Cookbook Show - Columbia Winery
    Tri-Cities Wine Festival - 509-375-0211

December
    Woodinville Wineries Open House (first weekend)

THE GRAPES OF NORTHWEST WINE

Whether you prefer red wines or white, there is a varietal produced in the Northwest just for you. From deep-colored, tannic Cabernet Sauvignons to the most delicate Rieslings and Chenin Blancs, the Northwest states produce a variety of styles to please the most discriminating wine lover.

Cabernet Sauvignon (*cab air nay saw veen yawn*) is the major red wine grape of the Bordeaux region in France. Like many famous French chateaux, some of Washington's small wineries are staking their futures on this varietal alone. Two distinct styes of Cabernet exist in the Northwest, a fresh, intensely fruity version and a fruity-with-plenty-of-oak version. Winemakers claim consumers love the oaky style but wine critics are becoming increasingly skeptical. Pair up your cabernet with beef, veal, richly sauced pastas and, for some, chocolate desserts.

Cabernet Franc (*cab air nay frahnc*) is one of the main blending grapes in French Bordeaux and has become popular for the same purpose in the Northwest. Varietal bottlings of Cabernet Franc have been produced by several wineries with mixed reception.

Chardonnay (*shar doe nay*) is the queen of white grapes in the Burgundy region of France and it has found a home in Eastern Washington and the Willamette Valley of Oregon. A trend toward barrel-fermented wines (most often "reserves") finds rich, buttery, toasty, mouthfilling chardonnays that are quite remarkable. A leaner style is also popular clinging to the tenet that "food wines" don't need all that oak but should have crisp acidity. Oakier chardonnays don't do well with light fish dishes but make a delightful companion to smoked fish and shellfish.

Chenin Blanc (*shen in blahnc*) is less well-known as a varietal wine these days but several wineries carry the torch with good results. Dry versions have come into vogue as lightly flavored quaffs similar to Italian Frascati. The best off-dry styles continue to offer delicate aromas of pear and vanilla with a lightly sweet palate. A good sipper for a hot afternoon.

Gewürztraminer (*gaverts trah meener*) is a difficult grape to grow successfully and a difficult wine to make in a marketable style. The most varietally-true examples are still off-dry sipping wines. Dry style gewurztraminers have been attempted in recent years with some success. The natural finish of this varietal is slightly bitter (due to the ripeness of the grape required to achieve the spicy character) and a slightly sweet palate helps to overcome this problem. Dry styles should, therefore, be accompanied by food.

Grenache (*gray nasch*) has found a couple of new champions in the Northwest industry and promises to have a future as a Rhone-style medium-bodied red wine instead of the rosés of the past. Blended with 10% to 30% merlot, it takes on a quality not unlike pinot noir but with a unique character all its own. Small production means the wines will be in short supply.

Johannisberg Riesling (See White Riesling)

THE GRAPES OF NORTHWEST WINE

Lemberger is a red variety that is grown primarily in Washington State and offers ripe zinfandel-like wines with berry fruit and a simple plummy-cherry palate.

Merlot *(mare-low)* is another red grape originating in Bordeaux, France. Often used to soften wines made from Cabernet Sauvignon, this variety produces a rich and plummy wine that is gentle on the palate. Light black cherry and herbal aromas make Merlot a great accompaniment to sharp cheeses and flavorful meats.

Müller Thurgau *(mooler ter gow)* is a German grape used mostly in that country to produce Liebfraumilch. In the Northwest, it produces a fragrant, light wine enjoyable by itself or with light foods.

Muscat is widely grown in Italy where it is the major component in Asti Spumante among other wines. Excellent Northwest varieties include both off-dry sipping wines and sweet late-harvest styles.

Pinot Noir *(pee noh nwah)*, the great red grape of Burgundy, has taken root in the Northwest with many Oregon producers beating the French at their own game. Complex, smoky aromas of cherry and herbs complement chicken, duck and other meats.

Pinot Gris (pee noh gree) has been highly touted recently by Oregon winemakers as the perfect food wine for many Northwest seafoods. The best examples have a flinty-yet-fruity character in the aroma and flavor. The aroma of overripe bottlings tends to favor banana!

Sauvignon Blanc *(saw veen yawn blahnc)* The white grape relative of Cabernet Sauvignon, this is also the variety that, when aged in oak, becomes Fumé Blanc. Much improved versions of this variety are surfacing as more wineries blend in small amounts of Sémillon to soften the herbaceous character.

Sémillon *(say me on)* A major white grape of the Bordeaux region of France, this variety is grown successfully in Washington where it is just coming into its own as a popular food wine. The melon and apple aromas and flavors complement lighter meats and cheeses, as well as a wide variety of lighter seafoods.

Syrah *(sir ahh)* comes to the Northwest via France's Rhone Valley. The small plantings here have produced spicy, full-bodied red wines that promise good things for the future.

White Riesling *(reez ling)* Although Oregon's state wine law prohibits the use of this variety's other name (Johannisberg Riesling), Washington and Idaho use the names interchangeably. A convention of usage has evolved where wines labeled 'White Riesling' are often sweeter versions and those labelled 'Johannisberg Riesling' are dry or off-dry. With thousands of acres in Washington alone, this prolific producer has contributed to the success of this state's wine industry. Dry rieslings offer aromas of apples and pears and a crisp palate begging for food accompaniment. Sweeter, late harvest versions lean toward peach and apricot aromas and flavors.

WINE EVALUATION (TASTING)

Take a look . . .

1. Appearance & Color - The appearance of wine is very important to your enjoyment of it. Fortunately, modern winemaking technology has made bright, sediment-free wines the rule rather than the exception. Your wine should be free from floating particles and should have no visible cloudiness.

White wines often range in color from almost water-clear to golden yellow. Most Northwest whites are somewhere in-between and are described as 'pale straw' in color.

Red wines can be anywhere from dark ruby to pale garnet in hue. Lighter colored wines often have lighter flavor and less tannin.

Take a sniff . . .

2. Aroma & Bouquet - Swirl the wine in your glass and take a deep sniff to appreciate the smell of the grape (aroma) and the smell of the aging and treatment (i.e. oak, etc.) of the wine (bouquet). Together the two sensations can tell you much about the quality of the wine and its origin. Professional wine tasters often make most of their judgements based on a wine's smell rather than on the taste of the wine.

Take a sip . . .

3. Flavor & Balance - Take a small amount of wine in your mouth and swirl it around your tongue. The flavor of a good quality wine will often echo the aroma and bouquet. Additional factors influencing "mouthfeel" include acidity, sweetness and alcohol content of the wine. The balance between acidity (sour) taste and sugar (sweet) taste is very important to high-acid Northwest wines. Most rieslings, chenin blancs and other 'sipping' wines have residual sweetness left in the wine to balance the acidity and thus provide a 'refreshing' feeling on the palate. The finish is the combination of tactile sensations and flavors you encounter after swallowing. Lingering fruitiness and toasty vanilla from barrel fermentation are often encountered.

A WINE TASTING GLOSSARY

Acidity - the major acid present in grapes and wine is tartaric acid. The puckery sensation on the sides of the tongue give the taster the impression of how much acid is present and whether it is in balance with the other components of the wine.

Alcohol - Ethyl alcohol fermented naturally by wine yeast is present in all wines. Excessive alcohol leaves a burning sensation on the palate.

Balance - When the acidity, alcohol, sugar and tannin of a wine are in correct proportion, the wine is said to have good balance.

Body - The sensation of viscosity on the palate. A wine that gives a watery impression is thin in body. A wine that is thick or syrupy is heavy in body. High alcohol tends to make a wine heavy in body.

Bouquet - The smell of the wine relating to aging and to the handling of the wine. Oak aging adds a certain 'bouquet' and wines with considerable bottle age often exhibit smells referred to as 'bottle bouquet'.

Dry - In wine tasting terms, the opposite of sweet. If a wine has been fermented so that little or no sugar is left over, it is said to be 'bone dry.'

Fermentation - The process whereby wine yeast converts grape sugar to alcohol and carbon dioxide. Slow, cool fermentations produce fruity, light-flavored wines while warmer (70°F or higher) fermentations are used to produce full-bodied, flavorful red wines.

Finish - After the wine is swallowed, the sensation left on your palate. Often reflects the flavor of the wine, but can be alcoholic, bitter or tart.

Floral - The natural 'bouquet' of many riesling wines that is reminiscent of fresh cut flowers.

Fruit, Fruity - A catch-all term describing a pleasant sensation of the flavor or aroma of a particular wine. Most useful when indicating the intensity of aroma or flavor, i.e. 'light fruit in the nose' or 'intensely fruity flavor.'

Must - Unfermented grape juice or a combination of juice and crushed grapes.

Nose - The term used for the overall olfactory sensation of a wine. This can include subjective comments relating to the aroma AND bouquet.

Oak - The wood from which wine-aging barrels are constructed. Many oak barrels from France are made from selected species of the wood. The term can also refer to the flavor or smell of oak as it is found in wine.

Oxidation - The chemical reaction of the alcohol in wine turning first into acetaldehyde (sherry odor) and then into vinegar.

Sweet - The opposite of dry. A wine with high levels of residual sugar and/or low levels of balancing acidity.

Tannin - The polyphenolic substances present in all wines but most obvious in reds where they provide a textural astringency on the palate that cuts through fatty foods. This is part of the tradition of red wines accompanying red meats which contain high levels of animal fat.

Judging and Selection
of the Best Northwest Wines

Judging and rating of over 600 Northwest wines was accomplished through a series of comprehensive tastings where wine writers, winemakers, restaurant wine experts, wine retailers and well-informed wine consumers participated (panelists are listed on page 4). All wines were presented blind in flights of 6 wines of like varietal. Panels were asked to score each wine on a scale of one to ten and to record tasting notes describing color, aroma, flavor and palate feel, and finish. Following each tasting session the wines were sampled with an appropriate meal to evaluate their "food friendliness." The author compiled the following reviews through examination and correlation of his tasting notes and those of the other panelists.

Your Guide to the Wine Reviews

Many wine reviews simply point out the virtues of particular wines by a numerical score. While it was obvious in many cases which of the wines were the very best, it is important to recognize that you as a consumer may seek different qualities in a wine than the average assessment by a group of panelists. For this reason, wines are presented with descriptive reviews that you can use to evaluate a particular wine's suitability to your palate and purpose. Where appropriate, comments are included on a wine's particular affinity to food or potential for extended aging.

Presentation of the Selected Wines

The wines chosen for review in Northwest Wines and Wineries were selected for commercial acceptibility (no outstanding technical flaws), distinct varietal character, and above-average quality in balance and structure. Wines listed as the "Very Best" were judged by the panelists to be outstanding examples of the particular varietal, exhibiting distinct varietal character, complexity in aroma and flavor, and excellent candidates for consumption with approriate foods and/or for further aging. "Very Best" wines are listed in the order of the average of the panelists' scores. "Other Top-Rated Wines" are listed alphabetically by winery name.

Wines judged for this review were current releases in late 1992. With the exception of the "Very Best" wines, vintage dates of the wines have been omitted. Most wineries whose wines appear in the reviews have consistent track records for the reviewed varietals and a consumer would be safe in selecting the reviewed wine (same appellation and vineyard designation) from any vintage. Realizing the wines listed as the "Very Best" will be highly sought after, the vintage is included at the end of the review along with a brief comment about availability.

Cellaring the Wines

Now that you've chosen the best of the Northwest, how long can you (or *should* you) cellar the wines for optimum enjoyment? Put away most Cabernets and Merlots for two to three years maximum.. The very best of these varietals can handle much longer aging – ask your trusted wine merchant. Most Pinot Noirs likewise stop improving after two to three years aging. For the rare exceptions (the very best) check with a trusted wine professional.

CABERNET SAUVIGNON

As a group, the Cabernet Sauvignon panel found the wines to be of extremely high quality and stylistically varied. There was a tendency of several wineries to overoak their wines (the panel's concensus) due at least partially to consumer demand fueled by reviews in popular wine periodicals. While  some Northwest Cabernets can handle long barrel aging in new oak, most would be more true to varietal style if the fruit were allowed to show through the splinters. Aging Cabernets for a year or two (or more) after purchase rounds out the balance between fruit and oak.

The Very Best Cabernets

Leonetti Cellar Cabernet Sauvignon - Deep ruby - ripe berry aroma with toasty American oak - cherry, plum and currant on palate - closed, short finish - good structure - 1989 tasted, extremely rare due to high quality and very limited supply

Columbia Winery Cabernet Sauvignon Yakima Valley-David Lake-Otis Vineyard - Herbal aromas of tea, bell pepper, tobacco - excellent mouth feel with long flavorful finish - astringent - 1988 tasted, widely available in Northwest and at winery

The Hogue Cellars Cabernet Sauvignon - Medium garnet - classic Northwest aroma of cherry and vanilla (oak) - medium-bodied palate exhibits layered flavors of berries and cassis with toasty oak - clean finish - great short term red - 1989 tasted, widely available

Other Top-Rated Cabernets

Andrew Will Cabernet Sauvignon - Light ruby - ripe cherry aromas, tight structure on palate, closed and firm, promising future

Chateau Ste. Michelle Cabernet Sauvignon Columbia Valley - Deep ruby - mature aroma of spice and herbs - sweet berry fruit and oak comes through on palate - pleasant lingering finish - enjoy now for excellent affinity for food, age for 3 - 5 years for more complexity

Columbia Winery Cabernet Sauvignon Yakima Valley-Red Willow Medium ruby - light minty nose - full bodied palate, rich fruit of plums and cherries - good structure for aging

Elk Cove Vineyards Cabernet Sauvignon Commanders Willamette Valley - Medium ruby - youthful aromas of plums, berry and spice - full bodied with ample tannins - complex finish - limited availability

French Creek Cellars Cabernet Sauvignon - Medium ruby - light aroma of vanilla and dill - herbaceous flavors and medium body - a pleasant, lighter style

Girardet Wine Cellars Cabernet Sauvignon Oregon - Medium garnet - fresh cherry aroma - clean cherry and plum flavors with hint of oak - simple finish, good lighter style

Continued on next page

Other Top-Rated Cabernets, *cont'd.*

Henry Estate Cabernet Sauvignon Umpqua Valley - Medium ruby - smoky/earthy nose with distinctive American oak - well-structured palate shows oak and fruit - short finish - needs age

Kiona Vineyards Winery Cabernet Sauvignon Tapteil Vnyd., Yakima Valley - Medium ruby - simple cherry and oak aroma - medium-bodied palate with flavors of cherry and cassis - lighter style

Preston Wine Cellars Cabernet Sauvignon - Reserve - Medium brick/ruby - mature aroma of berry, oak and toffee - soft plummy palate - oaky finish - hearty style will easily handle medium term aging

Quilceda Creek Vintners Cabernet Sauvignon - Deep ruby - rich berry fruit with anise and black currant - complex vanilla and oak on palate - long finish with astrigent component - excellent aging potential

Soos Creek Winery Cabernet Sauvignon - Deep ruby - toasty oak aromas dominate with background of cassis and cherry - plum and cherry on palate with astringent finish - age for 3 - 5 years

Staton Hills Winery Cabernet Sauvignon - Medium ruby, brick edge - mature aromas of cassis, eucalyptus and spice "Bordeaux-like" - medium-bodied palate - astringent finish - enjoy now or in a year

Stewart Vineyards Cabernet Sauvignon Columbia Valley - Medium garnet - spicy, herbal nose - cherry, chocolate and tea flavors - light palate - excellent lighter style

Cabernets Judged: 55   Cabernets chosen for review: 16

Food and Wine Pairing with Cabernet Sauvignon

Grown in the Northwest, Cabernet Sauvignon rarely takes on the extreme vegetative character common to some California versions. The resulting wines (as evidenced by the reviews above) offer cherry, berry and herbaceous aromas, with complex nuances related to oak and bottle aging. This fruitiness (in young wines especially) offers both opportunities and challenges to the wine lover chef.

Full-blown Northwest Cabs usually have enough tannin and oak to stand up to the richest meats – beef, lamb, venison – those with hearty flavors and textures in abundance. The adage of red wine with red meat applies here as the tannin in the wine cuts through the animal fat in the meat. Prepare simply and let the powerful pairing show its stuff.

Medium to lighter Cabernets tend tothe fruity end of the spectrum and suggest a more varied apporach to matching with food. Fruit-based sauces, glazes and accompanying savory condiments are the easist way to find harmony in a dish paired with Cabernets of this style. Pork with berry or cherry glaze is great – even better if you use a little of the wine in the preparation. Berry chutneys and herbal tomato sauces are other potentials.

Herbs that tend to complement Cabernet Sauvignon are dill, coriander, mint and rosemary. Garlic is a popular ingredient that works with Cabernet to enhance flavors especially when matched with fresh basil.

PINOT NOIR

The Pinot Noir tasting panel enjoyed sampling a wide range of wines from almost 40 producers. Styles varied from fresh, light berry-flavored wines to earthy, meaty, complex Pinots crying out for paté, chevre and herbed crostini! While the panel agreed that the best wines prevailed, it was obvious that blind tasting hurt some wines whose romantic attachments to the tasters were masked by the brown bag.

The Very Best Pinot Noirs

Ponzi Vineyards Pinot Noir Reserve Willamette Valley - Medium ruby - cherry/berry aromas along with smokiness - big fruit on palate, balanced - plummy finish with medium tannins and noticeable acidity - 1989 tasted, a superb example but very limited availability

Broadley Vineyards Pinot Noir Reserve - Medium deep ruby - forward fruit with earth, new oak and bright berry notes - complex flavors on palate of berry and smoke - lengthy complex finish, 1989 tasted, available in Northwest only

Elk Cove Vineyards Pinot Noir Willamette Valley Wind Hill Vineyard Deep ruby - strong varietal aroma with complex toast and earth - smooth palate with complex flavors "varietally true" - excellent balance and long, complex finish - "definitive Burgundian style" - 1989 tasted, available in selected markets across U.S.

Other Top-Rated Pinot Noirs

Adams Vineyard Winery Pinot Noir Reserve Polk County - Medium ruby - ripe berry nose, closed - rich, full palate with astringent finish - good aging potential - one of Oregon's most consistent producers

Adams Vineyard Winery Pinot Noir Willamette Valley - Deep ruby - ripe grapy aroma with earth and black cherry - oak and cherry palate with moderate tannins - pleasant finish

Amity Vineyards Pinot Noir Winemaker's Reserve Willamette Valley - Medium garnet with ruby edge - shy nose with hints of prune and herb - good berry notes on palate, well balanced, wood shows through

Autumn Wind Vineyard Pinot Noir - Medium ruby - rich aroma of earth and fruit with coffee undertones - delicate flavors of berry and barrel toast - long finish with moderate astringency - ageable

Bethel Heights Vineyard Pinot Noir Willamette Valley - Medium garnet - simple aromas of cherry, berry and spice - toasty notes on palate round out berry flavors - good length and food affinity

Broadley Vineyards Pinot Noir - Medium ruby - straightforward berry and light toast on nose - more complex palate shows wood and earth - short, clean finish - needs age to round out finish

Callahan Ridge Pinot Noir Umpqua Valley - Medium garnet - fresh berry aroma "Beaujolais-like" - light bodied with pretty flavors of candy and strawberry - spicy finish - nice style for red-wine sipping

Continued on next page

Other Top-Rated Pinot Noirs, cont'd.

Cameron Pinot Noir Reserve - Abbey Ridge Vineyard - Medium ruby - dusty new oak nose, earthy and spicy, fresh cherry flavors and light palate - light finish - "elegant" style for lighter, complex meals

Chateau Benoit Pinot Noir Reserve - Medium ruby - closed aroma yields raspberry, cooked cherry notes - "big fruit," ripe style shows through, spicy finish - medium tannins - enjoy with hearty foods

Domaine Drouhin Oregon Pinot Noir - Medium ruby, purple edges - Smoky-toasty aroma with berry fruit and earth in background - vanilla, berry and oak on palate - "simple but true" - clean finish - this highly touted wine shows its best with fine cuisine

Elk Cove Vineyards Pinot Noir Willamette Valley - Medium purple/ruby - candy cherry aroma, odd herbal notes - palate shows smoky toast of new oak - tannic finish - needs grilled meats to really shine

Elk Cove Vineyards Pinot Noir Willamette Valley Dundee Hills Vnyd. Medium ruby - toast and bing cherry fruit on nose - chewy cherry and earth on palate - soft finish - a good complement for lighter fare

Elk Cove Vineyards Pinot Noir Willamette Valley Estate Vnyd. - Deep ruby - distinctive Pinot aroma of berry, spice and earth - good acidity and strawberry flavors - long finish - age or enjoy now

The Eyrie Vineyards Pinot Noir Willamette Valley - Light garnet - strawberry/cherry aromas with light wood - toasty mature palate, complex flavors - long finish with little tannin - enjoy the complexity

Knudsen Erath Pinot Noir Vintage Select Willamette Valley - Medium garnet - light aroma of candy cherry and clove - "youthful palate will mellow" - overripe notes - balanced and structured for aging

Oak Knoll Winery Pinot Noir Oregon Willamette Valley - Medium garnet - oak and cherry aromas dominate - medium body and good mouthfeel, cherry flavors with oak - pleasant finish

Panther Creek Pinot Noir Reserve Oregon - Deep ruby - black cherry and chocolate on nose - "Gevrey Chambertin-like" - nice balance of big fruit and tannin on palate

Rex Hill Vineyards Pinot Noir Willamette Valley - Medium ruby - cherry aromas with herbs and medicinal notes - full palate with pleasing flavors of cherry and toast - long, clean finish

Salishan Vineyards Pinot Noir Washington State - Light ruby - earthy barnyard aroma with toasty strawberry notes - currant jelly flavors on palate - slightly astringent finish - enjoy with rich cheeses and meats

Pinots judged: 66   Pinots chosen for review: 22

Food and Wine Pairing with Pinot Noir

The Northwest style of Pinot Noir is still emerging with influences from France shaping the direction of many producers. Vinification techniques and aging regimens are producing wines of great complexity and interest. No longer will you find "Cabernet styled" Pinots. In fact, the International Pinot Noir Celebration recently offered a seminar titled "Just Say No to Cabernet!"

While eschewing Cabernet totally may be a bit extreme, the allure of Pinot Noir as a food wine is unequaled. Matching everything from salmon to steak, cheeses to charcuterie, Pinot promoters have made a career in recent years of pointing out this varietal's strong vino-culinarial suit.

To enjoy the glories of Pinot Noir with a meal, choose a complex preparation with herbs and butter-rich sauce – red wine will save you from cholesterol. Bare-bones presentations just don't provide this varietal with a wide enough playing field to show its stuff. Go for it!

Mussels, salmon, anything with tarragon, veal with herb sauce, pheasant, duck, quail, pesto-and-pasta . . . it seems like almost anything is a good idea. Oysters . . . NOT! Oh well, everything in life has its limits.

MERLOT

Merlot from Washington's Columbia Valley has become a nationwide phenomenon for its easy drinking style and forward, luscious fruit. The panel found a slightly disturbing trend toward over-oaking wines that just didnt have the fruit to handle the wood. For a wine that should be consumed in the moderately short term, too much oak takes away the fresh and fruity appeal of this popular wine.

The Very Best Merlots

Chinook Wines Merlot Washington - Medium ruby - quintessential Northwest Merlot nose of black cherry, plums and toast - rich berry fruit on palate framed by complex oak and mature notes of violets and chocolate - 1989 vintage tasted, limited availability, but every vintage is worth seeking out - annual release date is in May/June

Steven Thomas Livingstone Wine Cellars Merlot Columbia Valley - Deep ruby/purple - Candy cherry nose, American oak aromas - chewy palate with oak and cherry dominating - astringent finish - good aging potential - 1990 vintage tasted, available in Spokane, Seattle area wine shops

Other Top-Rated Merlots

Adelsheim Vineyard Merlot Oregon - Deep ruby - aromas of cherry, and slight vegetative notes - good mouthfeel and acid balance, flavors of Bing cherry and barrel toast - astringent finish, needs rich food

Andrew Will Merlot - Deep ruby - toasty oak nose with ripe plum and cherry - astringent, closed palate with underlying rich fruit and oak - short, tannic finish - needs age

Continued on next page

Other Top-Rated Merlots, cont'd.

Arbor Crest Merlot Columbia Valley - Medium ruby - complex aroma of cherry, tobacco and toast - ripe flavors with hint of vanilla - great balance on palate, long finish

Barnard Griffin Merlot - Medium ruby - Toasty nose with hints of American oak and cherry - rich, complex palate with flavors of plum and cherry - toasty oak finish - a favorite with lamb

Chateau Ste. Michelle Merlot Columbia Valley - Ruby - spice and herbal/floral nose - balanced palate of vanilla and berry with herbal flavors - good mouthfeel and finish - age for one to two years

Columbia Crest Merlot Columbia Valley - Ruby with brick edge - plum/blackberry nose with strong vanilla - firmly structured palate with good acidity - pleasant finish - enjoy now with hearty fare

Columbia Winery Merlot Yakima Valley-Milestone-Red Willow Vnyd. Ruby with garnet edge - Bing cherry nose with light toast - simple fruity palate of cherry and oak - good mouthfeel and structure - ample tannins for aging

Covey Run Vintners Merlot Reserve Yakima Valley - Medium ruby with brick edge - Light aromas of herbs, cherry and bell pepper - toasty oak shows through on palate with earthy flavors reminiscent of French Bordeaux - complex finish - feature the wine, not the food

Facelli Winery Merlot - Deep ruby with garnet edge - coffee, tobacco and candied cherry aromas - cherry and herbal flavors on palate - tight structure and closed finish

Hyatt Vineyards Merlot Columbia Valley - Ruby with violet edge - "berry- chocolate-meaty aroma" - cherry and dusty flavors on palate - long finish - enjoyable with a wide range of foods

L 'Ecole No 41 Merlot - Medium ruby - herbal aromas with hints of bell pepper and spice - rich palate of plum and cherry with edge of oak - long complex finish

Leonetti Cellars Merlot - Deep ruby - Spicy cherry aroma, but new oak aromas dominate - rich cherry and vanilla on palate - tannic, closed finish - needs time to incorporate the wood into the complexity

Quarry Lake Vintners Merlot - Deep ruby - toasty aroma with hints of berry - black cherry and oak flavors on palate - ample tannins

Valley View Vineyards Merlot Rogue River Valley - Medium ruby with amber edge - toasty oak nose dominates, light cherry - good fruit in middle palate - mature, complex finish - feature the wine

Waterbrook Merlot Columbia Valley - Deep ruby with purple rim - toasty new oak on nose with plum and cherry aromas - "good mouthfeel with black cherry on palate" - balanced tannins and rich finish - enjoy now or age for several years

Merlots judged: 33   Merlots chosen for review: 17

Food and Wine Pairing with Merlot

Most Northwest Merlots are made in a feminine style that favors the cherry-berry-plum fruit and supple tannins. This style tends to place the wine in the background at meal time, serving as a flavor enhancer and palate refresher. Simple preparations of pork, veal and poultry are well-complenented by Merlot, as are rich pasta dishes where a background wine to the food is needed.

The more expensive Merlots often have some Cabernet blended in and are treated to a little more oak. These few wines (see reviews) can handle many of the same preparations as Cabernet and Pinot Noir.

LEMBERGER

A charming varietal that has adopted by Washington vintners, Lemberger offers many of the attractions of Zinfandel although lighter in body and more round in flavor. The panel had mixed feelings about whether Lemberger should be light and Beaujolais-like, or rich and powerful like a Cabernet.

Covey Run Vintners Lemberger Yakima Valley - Light Beaujolais style with cherry aroma and mild palate

Hoodsport Winery Lemberger - Forward cherry fruit, slightly disjointed

Kiona Vineyards Winery Lemberger Columbia Valley - Rich, full-bodied style with full tannin and tobacco, coffee flavors

Thurston Wolfe Lemberger Reserve Yakima Valley - Hearty style as above with cherry tobacco fruit

Lembergers judged: 5   Lembergers chosen for review: 4

BORDEAUX BLENDS

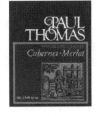

Cabernet and Merlot blended together in a simple 50/50 or 60/40 ratio has been an ongoing production method for few Northwest wineries. Recently, this combination has taken a firm hold on the local market. The California "Meritage" blends (which include Cabernet Franc, Petit Verdot and Malbec) have inspired some to produce high-priced blends with toasty oak and rich comlexity. Others have joined the 50/50 bandwagon to compete in a more popular price category of around $10.

The Very Best Bordeaux Blends

Chateau Ste. Michelle Chateau Reserve Red- Columbia Valley - Deep ruby - complex aroma shows cassis, plums and spice, very French - palate is more simple cherry/berry/coffee with ample tannins - 1989 tasted available primarily at the winery

Paul Thomas Winery Cabernet-Merlot Columbia Valley - Ruby - hearty cherry aroma with hints of coffee and tobacco - palate yields plummy/ berry notes and light tannins - very good with salmon - 1990 tasted, widely available

21   *Continued on next page*

Other Top-Rated Bordeaux Blends

Hedges Cellars Cabernet-Merlot Columbia Valley - Medium ruby - aromas of cherry and cassis mingle with earthy notes and hints of chocolate - simple palate of cherry/berry with ample tannins - good food wine

Worden Winery Cabernet-Merlot - Garnet - Vegetative notes frame a base aroma of berry and spice - light, fresh palate with moderate tannins - good with food

Bordeaux Blends judged: 8   Bordeaux Blends chosen for review: 4

OTHER RED BLENDS & RED VARIETALS

Innovations among the makers of Northwest red wines include varieties popularized in California, true varietals somehow lost in the shuffle of original plantings and cool-weather varietal crosses. Oregon's champion of Gamay Noir a Jus Blanc, Myron Redford has led the charge in establishing this true grape of Beaujolais. Doug McCrea uses the Rhone varietal Grenache in his Mariah. Larry Preedy of Airlie has succeeded with Marechal Foche.

Top-Rated Red Blends and Red Varietals

Amity Vineyards Gamay Noir - Medium garnet - strawberry and tar on nose, earthy - fruity palate with finishing notes of tobacco and coffee - excellent choice for light meats or red wine sipping

Airlie Winery Marchal Foche Willamette Valley - Deep garnet - jammy nose with background of spicy oak - blackberry and grape flavors on palate - needs food

Eola Hills Wine Cellars Gamay Noir - Ruby - spicy, heavy pinot fruit - black pepper and cherry, tannic finish - would benefit from aging

Girardet Wine Cellars Vin Rouge - Medium ruby - smoky/toasty aroma with light berry fruit - balanced palate with very little tannin

McCrea Cellars Mariah 100% Grenache - Garnet - floral/berry nose reminiscent of Pinot Noir, oaky notes - spice and berry on palate - fruity finish - good with lighter meats and casseroles

Zillah Oakes Grenache - Medium garnet - raspberry and toasty oak on nose - chewy palate of berry and oak - light tannic finish - nice lighter red with pasta

Red Blends judged: 13   Red Blends chosen for review: 6

CHARDONNAY

A daunting task for the Chardonnay panel: decide which of 85 wines were the Northwest's finest. Over 60 producers were represented with styles ranging from voluptuous, barrel-fermented powerhouses to lean, apple-scented sippers. Power was not the criterion for deciding the best. The finest examples showed balance, structure and varietal character. Use these reviews to choose the style you like. Barrel-fermented reserves tend to be more expensive that the more moderately flavored regular bottlings.

The Very Best Chardonnays

Tualatin Vineyards Chardonnay Barrel Fermented - Willamette Vly. - Pale gold - creamy aromas of pear, toast and tropical fruit-balanced, long vanilla finish - a big style - 1989 tasted, available in NW

Apex Chardonnay Yakima Valley - Bright gold/straw, earthy nose, toast, pineapple, figs -long palate of toast and apple/pear fruit - lengthy finish of vanilla with slightly bitter note - good complement to rich chicken or fish preparations - 1989 tasted, available in NW

Ste. Chapelle Chardonnay Idaho - Reserve - Medium straw - attractive apple and oak on nose, with notes of pear - balanced palate with flavors of crisp apple and citrus - vanilla and toast on finish - good food wine - 1988 tasted, limited availability nationally

Waterbrook Reserve Chardonnay - Medium gold - toasty, citrus nose with hint of clove - citrus, apple flavors on palate - nicely balanced structure with distinct vanilla finish and crisp acidity - good sipper or serve with light meats or pastas - 1990 tasted, limited availability

Latah Creek Wine Cellars Feather Chardonnay - Straw color - intense tropical fruit aromas, light toast - well-balanced palate, 1991 tasted

Other Top-Rated Chardonnays

Arbor Crest Chardonnay Columbia Valley - Bright gold - tropical fruit aromas with butterscotch notes - creamy, vanilla/butterscotch palate - balanced acidity and slight tannic bite - good food wine

Autumn Wind Vineyard Chardonnay - Pale gold - apple and vanilla aromas with slight spicy notes - mild apple palate with crisp acidity

Bridgeview Vineyards Chardonnay Barrel Select - Medium straw with green edge - apple and toast nose, fruit cocktail - vanilla, fresh fruit palate with light acidity - good sipping wine

Chinook Wines Chardonnay - Medium gold - toast and tropical fruit on nose, hints of pineapple, light banana - tropical fruit and citrus highlight complex flavors on a balanced palate held in check by crisp acidity - enjoy with rich seafoods and poultry

Columbia Crest Chardonnay Columbia Valley - Pale gold - aroma of tropical fruit, pear - clean, crisp palate of apple and citrus - light finish of crisp citrus and vanilla

Continued on next page

Other Top-Rated Chardonnays

Covey Run Vintners Chardonnay Yakima Valley - Pale straw - toast, tropical fruit, pear on nose - lingering citrus finish - good with food

Covey Run Vintners Chardonnay Reserve Yakima Valley - Medium gold - toasty, apple nose - tropical fruit and vanilla on complex palate, long finish, crisp acidity - good for sipping or with rich sauces

Gordon Brothers Cellars Chardonnay Reserve - Gold - Pineapple, apple, butter and oak on nose - oaky, rich palate, complex, long finish - a very powerful Chardonnay, serve as an aperitif

Henry Estate Chardonnay Barrel Fermented Umpqua Valley - Medium gold - toasty wood and apple/pear nose with hints of mineral - tart palate with complex woody flavors - serve with smoked meats

The Hogue Cellars Chardonnay Reserve - Pale gold - Intriguing aroma of tropical fruit with apple and citrus notes - apple fruit with light oak on palate - an excellent wine for rich Northwest seafood dishes

Lange Winery Chardonnay Willamette Valley - Brassy gold - apple/oak nose, toasty notes - complex palate and long finish - great sipper

Latah Creek Wine Cellars Chardonnay - Medium straw - butterscotch and pear aromas - vanilla and apple palate with crisp acid finish

Marquam Hill Vineyards Chardonnay Willamette Valley - Medium straw - toasty aroma with vanilla and spice - long finish of fruit and toast - serves well with Asian dishes and light meats

McCrea Cellars Chardonnay Columbia Valley - Gold - citrus, tropical fruit and flowery nose with oaky butterscotch - balanced palate and finish - a nice sipper or serve with rich aperitifs

Ponzi Vineyards Chardonnay Willamette Valley - Medium straw - rich oak nose, buttery - soft palate offers tobacco, butterscotch flavors

SilverLake Chardonnay Reserve Columbia Valley - Gold - vanilla/anise nose, some vegetal-balanced acid on palate - simple, but nice

Sokol Blosser Chardonnay Redland Yamhill County - Straw - floral, anise, lily, tropical fruit on nose - lingering finish - intriguing sipper

Staton Hills Winery Chardonnay Reserve - Light gold - toasty, vanilla nose - light apple and oak on palate but sweetness balances

Van Duzer Chardonnay Reserve - Medium straw - apple and oak aroma with hints of spice - flavors follow, light buttery oak dominates on palate - serve with seafood in honey-based sauces

Waterbrook Chardonnay - Pale gold - aromas of pear, pineapple and oaky vanilla - palate of citrus and toast - good food wine

Willamette Valley Vineyards Chardonnay - Medium straw - tropical fruit and apple on nose - crisp citrus palate with light vanilla notes on finish - nice lighter style for sipping or light meals

Worden Winery Chardonnay - Gold - toast, pear and tropical fruit on nose - balanced palate, short finish - nice sipper

Chardonnays judged: 85   Chardonnays chosen for review: 27

Food and Wine Pairing with Chardonnay

Many Chardonnays don't go well with food. That said, let's see what wine types might prove this statement untrue. Toasty/oaky/powerhouses are certainly not the answer to the food with wine question. While blow-you-away tropical fruit and vanilla are great conversation starters (and, reputedly, aphrodesiacs), they don't have a complement in the food world. Enjoy these wines with a friend and marvel at the power.

Back off the scale a bit and retain a little barrel-fermented character with tropical fruit notes in the nose and add back in a crisp backbone of acidity. Now THIS wine will accompany herbed sauces with poultry and rich seafood. Tarragon with its licorice-like flavors works well in the herb mix.

Truly lean Chardonnays with hints of tropical fruit or apples in the nose and lighter palates, again with crisp acidity, are a great complement to cheeses, lighter poultry and seafoods. Herbs help make the marriage work while attempts to link fruit-based chutneys and sauces fail.

SAUVIGNON (FUMÉ) BLANC

The abundance of fresh seafood in the Northwest contributes mightily to the reputation of Sauvignon Blanc wines produced here. Serving more as a background and palate cleanser than an integral part of the food/wine match, these wines lend just the right touch. The panel noticed this tactile quality in a negative sense. Tasted blind, and without food, Sauvignon Blancs come off being austere, light and overly tart. Served with food after the judging, many of the wines came alive to show the wonderful herbal/citrus/toasty qualities that are the basis of the successful food/wine match.

The Very Best Sauvignon (Fumé) Blancs

Chateau Ste. Michelle Fumé Blanc Columbia Valley - Straw with green tinge - complex nose of lemon, mineral and grass - excellent balance of fruit and acid, mild flavors - lingering finish of oak and citrus - a perfect complement to NW seafood - 1990 tasted, widely available

Other Top-Rated Sauvignon (Fumé) Blancs

Arbor Crest Sauvignon Blanc Columbia Valley - Gold with green edge - "classic Columbia Valley aroma" of lemon, flowers, herbs - citrus palate with lightly vegetative finish - another classic seafood wine

Barnard Griffin Fumé Blanc - Medium straw - toasty oak and herbs dominate aroma - rich palate of citrus, fig and melon leads to long, complex finish - richer-than-normal food wine of Sauvignon Blanc

Chateau Ste. Michelle Sauvignon Blanc Columbia Valley - Straw color - "good fruit to herb balance" on aroma - refreshing citrus and melon palate with crisp finish

Chinook Wines Sauvignon Blanc Yakima Valley - Pale straw color - light aroma of lemon and grapefruit - steely palate with crisp citrus notes and toasty oak finish - a delightful contrast to rich sauces

 Continued on next page

Other Top-Rated Sauvignon Blancs, cont'd.

Columbia Crest Sauvignon Blanc Columbia Valley - Pale straw - vegetative aroma with hints of citrus - well-balanced palate offers flavors of figs and mild fruit - long, complex finish - great food wine

Covey Run Vintners Fumé Blanc - Medium yellow - light aroma of lemon and grass - melon and barrel toast on palate - very crisp finish, needs food - an excellent aperitif with rich hors d'oeuvres

The Hogue Cellars Fumé Blanc - Straw color - complex aroma of grapefruit and pear - mild palate with excellent balance of fruit to acid - light, but pleasant, finish

Livingstone Wine Cellars 1990 Sauvignon Blanc Columbia Valley Very pale straw - soft aromas of peach and lemon - light-bodied palate reveals slight vanilla notes - great sipper

Paul Thomas Winery 1990 Sauvignon Blanc Washington State Pale straw - clean aroma of lemon and herbs - light vegetative flavors on palate - refreshing, clean finish - a great wine to serve with seafood

Snoqualmie Winery 1990 Fumé Blanc Columbia Valley Pale straw - fresh aroma of citrus and hay - slight toasty oak notes on palate - medium body and crisp finish

Ste. Chapelle 1989 Fumé Blanc Idaho Pale straw - intriguing aromas of lemon, melon and grass - flat palate though clean - short finish

Valley View Vineyards 1991 Sauvignon Blanc Rogue Valley Pale straw - clean aromas of pineapple, melon, citrus - refreshing, crisp palate - "very food friendly"

Sauvignon Blancs judged: 25   Chosen for review: 13

Food and Wine Pairing with Sauvignon Blanc

As stated above, Sauvignon Blanc is a superb wine to accompany a wide range of foods. Its affinity for seafood is eclipsed only by its ability to complement herbed sauces and preparations. The very nature of the flavors found in Sauvignon Blanc (grassy, citrusy, vegetative) lead it into harmony with dozens of herb combinations.

Smoked salmon mousse with dill is a superb appetizer that balances crisp Northwest Sauvignon or Fumé perfectly. Grilled fresh halibut with lemon-oregano butter picks up both the herb and citrus hints of the wine.

Northwest vintners have brought Sauvignon Blanc farther than any other varietal in developing a regional style.   Affinity for local fresh ingredients is the key to this fact. Feel comfortable in preparing a menu around Sauvignon or Fumé Blanc to impress your next out-of-town visitors.

PINOT GRIS

Pinot Gris is a fascinating grape and an amazing wine to study. A relative newcomer to the popular wine scene, it is still seeking a stylistic norm among the 15 or 16 wineries producing it. The Pinot Gris judging panel agreed that the best versions highlighted the mineral aspect of the wine's personality. Crisp flinty-citrusy aromas accompanied by a palate light in flavor but tingling with pleasant acidity characterizes this attractive food wine at its best.

The Very Best Pinot Gris

Tyee Wine Cellars Pinot Gris - Very pale pink - elegant nose with interesting tropical fruit and mineral - mineral and earth flavors, crisp, balanced palate - superb character-defining Pinot Gris - 1991 tasted, limited availbility in Northwest states

Other Top-Rated Pinot Gris

Bridgeview Vineyards Pinot Gris - Pale salmon orange/pink - interesting aroma of spice and tropical fruit - balanced palate yields flavors of bananas and pears - clean finish - fruit salsas on meats pair well

Cooper Mountain Vineyards Pinot Gris Willamette Valley - Very pale straw - earthy/mineral nose, light citrus - mild clean palate, well-balanced with lengthy complex finish - light style, good value

Evesham Wood Pinot Gris - Pale gold - toasty nose with light pear undertones - rich palate of toasty oak, vanilla, sweet pear

Forgeron Vineyard Pinot Gris - Pale gold - tangy tropical fruit aromas of banana, pineapple, mango - rich tropical flavors follow on palate, slightly sweet finish

Kramer Vineyards Pinot Gris - Pale gold - intensely controversial herbal aroma of earth and hay - slight bell pepper on palate, crisp and well-balanced - herbal finish - matches well with many seafoods

Oak Knoll Winery Pinot Gris Willamette Valley - Pale gold - intriguing one-dimensional banana aroma - banana palate with crisp balance on finish - "an interesting wine!"

Yamhill Valley Vineyards Pinot Gris - Pale bronze - yeasty/mineral aroma "almost Grenache Blanc" - light, viscous palate lacks acidity - clean pleasant finish - a definite style of Pinot Gris

Pinot Gris judged: 14   Pinot Gris chosen for review: 8

Food and Wine Pairing with Pinot Gris

Pinot Gris offers many of the advantages of Sauvignon Blanc when it comes to menu planning. Crisp acidity and affinity for some herbal components are augmented by the mineral aspect of the wine. A natural for accompanying seafoods of wide array. Easily overwhelmed by sauces, Pinot Gris should be served with simple preparations that highlight fresh and flavorful ingredients.

SEMILLON

The raising of Sémillon to a premium varietal – that is, a cut above Chenin Blanc and some others – took place first in the Northwest and then in California. The Bordeaulais have long held Sémillon in high esteem but it was famous mostly as a botrytised dessert varietal. The Sémillon panel was aware, at the time of the tasting, of the high marks awarded these wines at recent prestigious competition. They concurred that Northwest Sémillon has achieved a plateau of quality.

The Very Best Sémillons

Barnard Griffin Sémillon - Pale straw - apple, pear and hints of vanilla on the nose - melon and toasty oak flavors on palate, rich and concentrated with lingering finish - a great food wine that can be appreciated as an aperitif - 1990 tasted, available in NW

Chinook Wines Sémillon Yakima Valley - Pale straw - toasty smoke on nose with apple/pear aromas, slight licorice note - flavorful palate of melon and grapefruit with excellent balance - crisp finish - needs food to show its finest character - 1990 tasted, limited NW availability

Other Top-Rated Sémillons

Arbor Crest Sémillon Columbia Valley - Dionysus Vineyard - Pale straw - slight tropical fruit aromas with toasty nuances - intense palate with ample acidity - good food wine

Chateau Ste. Michelle Sémillon Columbia Valley - Pale straw - grapefruit and melon aromas - flavors of vanilla and hints of apple on palate - crisp finish - nice seafood wine

The Hogue Cellars Sémillon - Light straw - aromas of apple, earth, and toast - flavors of pear and vanilla with crisp finish - good sipper

L' Ecole No 41 Sémillon Barrel Fermented - Pale gold - toasty, herbal aromas - apple fruit on palate with spicy finish - crisp acidity

Snoqualmie Winery Sémillon Columbia Valley - Pale greenish straw - apple and melon aromas, light lychee notes in background - clean fruity palate with apple and vanilla flavors on finish

Sémillons judged: 12 Sémillons chosen for review: 7

Food and Wine Pairing with Sémillon

Sémillon is a wine that provides a great service to fine cuisine by providing a stage – or background – on which the food can best show its strengths. Fine qualitya Sémillon is capable of providing character of its own but pairs best with dishes stronger in character than itselt. Try herbed seafoods and fowl or even fruit-based salsas or chutneys of light weight. The best of Sémillons are not expensive – try them!

GEWÜRZTRAMINER

The "spicy traminer" of Germany finds its way to the Northwest as an elusive varietal that frustrates those who know its potential and seek to match the world's best examples. The panel found most Northwest Gewürztraminers to be light in aroma and flavor – a severe problem in a wine that lives or dies by its distinctive lychee aroma and spicy palate.

The Very Best Gewürztraminers

Sokol Blosser Gewürztraminer Yamhill County - Pale straw - definitive aroma of lychee, spice and apple - medium sweet palate with strong flavors of lychee - clean lingering finish - great aperitif - 1991 tasted

Tyee Wine Cellars Gewürztraminer - Straw - lychee and toast on nose - medium body, dry palate with slightly bitter finish - good food wine - 1991 tasted, limited availability (NW only)

Other Top-Rated Gewürztraminers

Columbia Winery Gewürztraminer Yakima Valley - Light straw - light pear and lychee on nose - sweeter-than-offdry palate with resiny/lychee flavors - good with Asian dishes

Bridgeview Vineyards Gewürztraminer Vintage Select - Pale straw - light aroma of lychee and pear - light off-dry palate - good sipper

Chateau Ste. Michelle Gewürztraminer Columbia Valley - Very pale straw - light aroma of lychee and bitter almond - grapefruit and pear flavors on palate - goof food wine for spicy dishes

Columbia Crest Gewürztraminer Columbia Valley - Medium straw - light pear aroma, simple and clean - off-dry palate yields a good sipping wine but atypical Gewurztraminer

Elk Cove Vineyards Gewürztraminer Willamette Valley - Medium. straw - peppery/spicy aroma (controversial) - mild palate with light spice and herbal flavors - intriguing sipper or with appetizers

Kramer Vineyards Dry Gewürztraminer Oregon Willamette Valley Pale straw with amber edges - aromas of lychee and woodruff - herbal palate - odd woody flavors on finish - good food wine

Snoqualmie Winery Gewürztraminer Columbia Valley - Light straw - light aromas of pear and lychee, some odd alcoholic smells - mild, flavorful palate with pear and spice - needs food

Tualatin Gewürztraminer - Willamette Valley - Light straw - aromas of pear and spice - pear flavors dominate palate with slightly hot finish

Gewürztraminers judged: 26   Gewürztraminers reviewed: 10

Food and Wine Pairing with Gewürztraminer

A well-made Gewürztraminer (as are those listed above) is a wonderful thing. An unbeatable companion to Asian cuisine and a perfect complement to smoked fish and meats. Find a nice Gewürztraminer and give it a chance where any white wine would be used. (Gewürztraminer is a frequent blending grape.)

DRY RIESLING

This centuries-old Germanic varietal was among the first wine grapes to take hold in the wine countries of the Northwest. A prolific bearer and able to withstand cold winters, Riesling produces huge quantities of wine in the Northwest that for many years has been sold at bargain-basement prices. The emergence of the Dry Riesling style in the early 90s is a good sign that this noble varietal will again take its place on the tables of sophisticated wine drinkers. The panel found these to be excellent examples:

The Very Best Dry Rieslings

Knudsen Erath Dry Riesling Willamette Valley - Pale straw - fresh apple and spice aromas - light flavors frame a full-bodied palate with a slight bitter finish - great with oysters, great for sipping - 1991 tasted, widely available - look for current vintage

Hogue Cellars Dry Riesling Yakima Valley - Pale green/straw - hints of spice and herbs frame a central aroma of apple and pear - flavors lean toward the citrus and herbal - excellent with food - 1991 tasted, widely available

Ponzi Vineyards Dry Riesling Willamette Valley - Pale straw - complex aroma of peach, apple and toast - complex palate with herbal flavors and refreshing crisp apple and peach - great match with smoked foods - 1991 tasted, more limited availability than above

Other Top-Rated Dry Rieslings

Barnard Griffin Dry Riesling Columbia Valley - Pale gold - ripe aromas of pear and tropical fruit lead to a drier-than-expected palate with crisp and refreshing flavors of apple and vanilla

Kiona Vineyards Winery Dry Riesling Yakima Valley - Pale straw - peachy/apple aroma with hints of orange blossom - simple apple palate with light, crisp finish

Livingstone Dry Riesling Columbia Valley - Pale straw - aroma of grapefruit and apple - crisp palate challenges taster and shows need for food accompaniment

Snoqualmie Dry Riesling Columbia Valley - Pale straw - apple, pear and vanilla aromas - balanced palate offers clean apple flavor and refreshing crisp finish - nice sipper

Ste. Chapelle Dry Riesling Idaho - Vineyard Select - Pale silvery green - ripe apple and apricot aromas with herbal notes - rich palate with slightly bitter finish - needs food

Van Duzer Dry Riesling - Pale straw - ripe apple aromas with hints of smoky toast - vanilla and apple flavors on palate - long finish

Dry Rieslings judged: 27   Dry Rieslings chosen for review: 9

WHITE RIESLING

While Dry Riesling has taken the lead among informed wine consumers as the favorite version of the Riesling varietal, more off-dry bottlings are still produced to quench the thirsts of those seeking a refreshing, and inexpensive, quaff. Don't be confused if you encounter labels reading Riesling, Johannisberg Riesling or White Riesling – it's the same grape. Do be aware, however, that late harvest bottlings are often labeled White Riesling.

Top-Rated White Rieslings (Johannisberg Rieslings)

Chateau Ste. Michelle Johannisberg Riesling Columbia Valley
 Pale straw - floral aroma with spicy notes - flavors of fresh apples, crisp finish - good sipper or accompaniment to lighter fare

Columbia Winery Johannisberg Riesling Columbia Valley Cellarmasters Reserve - Pale green/straw - apple and peach aroma, classic Riesling - sweet, rich palate with lingering, clean flavors

Covey Run Vintners Johannisberg Riesling Yakima Valley - Pale silvery green - aromas of honey and apricot - balanced, off-dry palate with flavors of apple and crisp finish

Elk Cove Vineyards Riesling Willamette Valley - Pale straw - peach and honey aromas - intense fruity palate, sweet but balanced

Kiona Vineyards Winery White Riesling Columbia Valley - Medium straw - aromas of pear and vanilla - rich apple flavors on palate - long finish - excellent with light cheeses and fruit

Paul Thomas Winery Johannisberg Riesling - Very pale straw - apricot and peach on nose - balanced palate with flavors of apple and pear - crisp finish - nice style to sip or savor with light meats

Valley View Vineyards Riesling - Silvery straw - mixed fruit aromas - fresh, crisp palate with flavors of apple and apricot

Willamette Valley Vineyards White Riesling - Pale straw - rose and spice aromas - palate of apple and pear with crisp acid finish

Off-Dry Rieslings judged: 38   Off-Dry Rieslings reviewed: 8

Food and Wine Pairing with Dry and Off-Dry Riesling

Recent eno-culinary activities have singled out Dry Riesling as a comer that truly deserves attention as a food wine. Crisp acidity – while retaining exceptional fruity character – makes the wine a perfect complement to seafood. Complex notes in the aroma and palate help bring life to simple preparations. Off-Dry Riesling, labeled usually as Johannisberg or plain Riesling, offers a broader acceptance for beginning wine drinkers. Often available at deeply discounted prices, this style is popular for large gatherings such as wedding receptions and company picnics. The Riesling varietal is making a grand comeback and you should experiment with any of your favorite lighter foods. Use the drier style to match with richer dishes and the off-dry version to add body to simple preparations.

CHENIN BLANC

As the varietal behind the popular Vouvray of France, Chenin Blanc has similarly found favor in the Northwest While serious devotees of the varietal have diligently looked for its proper style and market niche, others blend it away in volume for dry white wine. Many of the dry-style Chenins that have emerged seem to lose the "pear drop" fruitiness and smooth vanilla character that make off-dry versions so appealing. The panel enjoyed the slightly sweet (and a few dry) Chenin Blancs reviewed below.

Top-Rated Chenin Blancs

Bethel Heights Vineyard Chenin Blanc Willamette Valley - Pale green/gold - clean pear and apple aroma with hints of herbs - fresh palate with apple and melon flavors with citrus notes - clean finish

Covey Run Vintners Chenin Blanc Yakima Valley - Pale green - floral aromas highlighted by notes of pear and apple - slightly sweet palate with a refreshing crisp finish - a nice sipping wine

The Hogue Cellars Chenin Blanc - Pale straw - apple and vanilla aroma with slight grapefruit notes - pleasant apple and pear flavors on palate with medium body and crisp finish - good with food

Kiona Vineyards Winery Chenin Blanc Yakima Valley - Pale straw - light aromas of pear and apple - crisp palate with green apple flavors and tart finish - good dry style - a great food wine

Latah Creek Wine Cellars Chenin Blanc - Pale straw - apple and pear aromas with distinct marshmellow notes - smooth palate of vanilla and apple - lingering finish of vanilla

Snoqualmie Dry Chenin Blanc Columbia Valley - Pale straw - Citrus and apple aroma with hint of vanilla - crisp palate with green apple flavor - good food wine, especially with crab

Worden Winery Chenin Blanc - Pale greenish straw - pear and flinty mineral aromas - fresh fruit palate with light body - good sipper

Chenin Blancs judged: 13   Chenin Blancs chosen for review: 7

MÜLLER THURGAU

A Germanic varietal that is planted throughout the famous Riesling regions, Müller Thurgau is most often found in German wines carrying no varietal identity. Northwest wineries have embraced Müller Thurgau for its ease of growing and winter hardinesswith wine styles ranging from slightly sweet and mildly fruity to dry and herbaceous. The best are those listed here.

Top-Rated Müller Thurgaus

Airlie Winery Müller Thurgau Willamette Valley - Pale straw - aromas of melon and green apple - refreshingly crisp palate with simple apple/ pear flavors - good sipper

Bainbridge Island Winery Müller Thurgau - Dry - Pale silvery green - light aromas of fresh grapes and apples - slightly off-dry palate holds fruitiness nicely - refreshing with lighter fare

Serendipity Cellars Müller-Thurgau Willamette Valley - Pale straw - light herb notes frame fresh apple and pear aroma - off-dry palate offers hints of peach - serve with cheeses or light appetizers

Willamette Valley Vineyards Müller Thurgau - Pale green/straw - light aromas of citrus and peach - pleasant off-dry palate with hints of melon and apricot - refreshing acidity makes a great food wine

Veritas Vineyard Müller Thurgau Yamhill County - Pale straw - light apple aroma with hints of herbs - clean palate highlighted by pear and apple flavors - sip or serve with lighter fare

Müller Thurgaus judged: 9   Müller Thurgaus reviewed: 5

DESSERT WINES

Several panels participated in evaluating three categories of dessert wines. Non-Riesling wines were presented in two sections, white and red. The late harvest Chenins, Sauvignons, Muscats and others were judged separately from the Ports and Black Muscats. Late harvest Rieslings were judged in regular and super-sweet (auslese) flights.

The Very Best Non-Riesling Dessert Wines

Kiona Vineyards Winery Chenin Blanc Ice Wine Yakima Valley - Bright gold - pear and raspberry (!) aromas with tropical fruit notes - strong, sweet palate of pear, honey and botrytis - superb example of NW late harvest

Yakima River Winery John's Port Yakima Valley - Medium ruby, brick edge - smoky, burnt orange aroma, berry notes - smooth palate with "wood port" complexity - nice finish

Other Top-Rated Non-Riesling Dessert Wines

Columbia Crest Late Harvest Sauvignon Blanc Columbia Valley - Gold color - aroma of pipe tobacco and toasty botrytis - dusty palate of citrus and earth - long, peculiar finish - an interesting wine

Horizon's Edge Winery Muscat Nouveau Riche Yakima Valley - Pale gold - Muscat aroma, delicate and floral - flavors of Catawba grape and orange - short finish

Preston Wine Cellars Tenrebac Port Washington - Medium ruby - "nice melange of vanilla and red grape" - oaky palate with good structure - sweet and flavorful finish

Staton Hills Winery Late Harvest Semillon Washington - "Amber color like lager beer" - meaty aroma reminiscent of honey-lemon dressing - lemon and honey notes on palate

Continued on next page

Other Top-Rated Non-Riesling Dessert Wines

Columbia Crest Late Harvest Sauvignon Blanc Columbia Valley - Gold color - aroma of pipe tobacco and toasty botrytis - dusty palate of citrus and earth - long, peculiar finish - an interesting wine

Horizon's Edge Winery Muscat Nouveau Riche Yakima Valley - Pale gold - Muscat aroma, delicate and floral - flavors of Catawba grape and orange - short finish

Preston Wine Cellars Tenrebac Port Washington - Medium ruby - "nice melange of vanilla and red grape" - oaky palate with good structure - sweet and flavorful finish

Staton Hills Winery Late Harvest Semillon Washington - "Amber color like lager beer" - meaty aroma reminiscent of honey-lemon dressing - lemon and honey notes on palate

Thurston Wolfe Port Washington - Deep ruby - sweet raisin character on nose, "scent of Scotch" - lighter palate with hints of oak - pleasant finish

Thurston Wolfe Black Muscat Washington - Pale ruby/purple - peppery, spicy boysenberry aroma - intense palate with hot finish - berry character carries through to end

RIESLING DESSERT WINES

The quality of Northwest late harvest Rieslings and ultra-late harvest Rieslings (ice wines) is superb. Not only are the wines among the best in the world – rivalling even Germany's finest – but they are excellent bargains. Our panels thoroughly enjoyed reveling in the interesting nuances of the Northwest's best.

Arbor Crest Late Harvest Riesling - Pale gold - aroma of pineapple, apricot with nuances of butterscotch - balanced light palate with honey and herbs - light finish

Chateau Ste. Michelle White Riesling Sweet Select - Medium straw - aroma of fresh, sweet apple; light honey and spice. Palate offers apple, pear and tropical fruit nuances with finish of dried apple.

Henry Estate Select Cluster White Riesling - Umpqua Valley Oregon Gold color - aroma of honey and tropical fruit - palate reveals complex flavors of apricot, lychee and mango - long complex finish with botrytis edge

Hyatt Vineyards White Riesling Ice Wine - Yakima Valley - Deep gold - piney, buttery nose with medicinal notes, herbaceous hints of botrytis - well-balanced palate with good acidity - pleasant tropical fruit finish

Silver Lake Winery Ice Wine - Medium gold - Aroma of honey and apricots with hints of pear and coconut. Rich palate offers apple, apricot, tropical fruit with long unctuous finish with botrytis and honey.

Stewart Vineyards White Riesling Late Harvest - Pale gold - Classic aroma of peach, apricot and honey. Medium rich palate offers complex flavors of peach and honey. Great accompaniment to hazelnut cookies!

FRUIT WINES (NON-GRAPE)

Many Northwest wineries got their start by winning medals at the local fair for their fruit and berry wines. The pure flavors and aromas of wines made from the region's delicious raspberries, loganberries, pears and other fruits are remarkable. If you've never enjoyed NW raspberry wine with chocolate, you haven't lived.

The Very Best Fruit Wines

Paul Thomas Winery Raspberry - bright garnet - fresh raspberry aroma literally explodes from the glass - clean, true flavor of raspberry on palate

Kramer Vineyards Raspberry Wine - Bright garnet with ruby edges - distinct raspberry aroma - palate of sweet raspberry with slightly bitter finish - good as a refreshing tipple or as a flavor enhancer in recipes

Paul Thomas Winery Crimson Rhubarb - Pale salmon - light aromas of pear, rhubarb and herbs - flavor character is definitely rhubarb - crisp finish, good food wine

Other Top-Rated Fruit Wines

Hoodsport Winery Raspberry Wine - Garnet - medium raspberry aroma - clean raspberry flavors on palate with slightly bitter finish - sweet

Paul Thomas Winery Bartlett Pear Wine - Pale green/gold - distinct pear aroma with hints of vanilla - forward flavor of pear with crisp finish - nice sipper or serve with turkey or chicken

Whidbeys Loganberry Wine - Bright ruby - aroma of fresh loganberries - palate flavors echo aroma, mouthfeel is sweet to almost cloying - use as flavor enhancer in desserts or light tipple

Fruit Wines judged: 9   Fruit Wines chosen for review: 6

Food and Wine Pairing with Dessert Wines

A crushing question for many home chefs is what to serve with a treasured bottle of late harvest Riesling or icewine. Should the wine stand alone to be sipped and lingered-over as the subtle aromas develop in the glass? Should the chef prepare a flaming extravagance of peaches and berries and chocolate, all served with a sculpted marzipan Bachanallian orgy? Somewhere between the two, I think. While it is nice to linger over aromas, it is also nice to have something edible to help your palate deal with the tongue-coating, viscous, late-harvest nectar. Apricot or peach strudel is nice. Tropical fruit strudel (papaya, mango) are daring but also work well. Light almond cookies are an easy alternative that serve well.

As dessert wines become redder and offer more berry-like nuances, chocolate comes to mind and may come to the table. Full-bodied sweet reds like port are best paired with savory accompaniments like the traditional Stilton cheese and walnuts. Commercially available Huntsman (Stilton layered with double Gloucester) is also a cheesey favorite with port.

SPARKLING WINES

Northwest sparkling wine is searching for a style. While most producers use the traditional methode champenoise to create complex bottlings from cuvées of Pinot Noir and Chardonnay, others make fresh, affordable bubblies from Riesling and Chenin Blanc. For special celebrations seek a complex vintage version from those listed below. For just adding fun to a party, several Charmat process wines are affordable and simply delicious.

The Very Best Sparkling Wines

Mission Mountain Winery Pale Ruby Champagne Montana - Pale salmon orange/pink - very fine bead - toasty nose, earthy - rich mouthfeel and crisp finish. 1988 tasted, verylimited availability.

Staton Hills Winery Brut Washington - Gold, steady bead - rich creamy-yeasty nose - creamy/yeasty palate with rich mouth feel - light fruit finish. 1986 tasted, available at the winery only.

Other Top-Rated Sparkling Wines

Argyle Vintage Brut Oregon - Pale straw, fine bead - pear and spice aromas - mellow palate with flavors of Gewurztraminer and citrus - crisp finish

Argyle Vintage Rose Brut Oregon - Pale rose pink, fine bead - light yeast and cherry aroma - off-dry palate with low-acid finish - a pleasant sparkler for beginners

Mountain Dome Winery Vintage Sparkling Brut Columbia Valley - Light yeast and grapefruit nose with hint of pear. Toasty palate, long clean finish

Staton Hills Winery NV Brut Rose Washington - Pale salmon pink, fine bead - flinty nose with pear and melon - bright flavors on palate echo aroma, rich texture - crisp, flavorful finish

Ste. Chapelle NV Sparkling Johannisberg Riesling Special Harvest Demi-Sec - Pale straw, fine bead - distinctive aroma of apple-pear nectar - sweet, grapey palate - sweet finish

Ste. Chapelle NV Brut - Very pale straw, medium bead - spicy Riesling/ Gewurz. nose - Muscat-like flavors on palate - appley/Riesling finish

Whittlesey Mark Vintage Oregon Brut - Pale gold, fine bead - yeasty/ toasty nose of smoke and earth (controversial) - toasty smoky palate and lingering finish

Food and Wine Pairing with Sparkling Wines

While bubbly wines are traditionally served as toasts at weddings and on festive holidays like birthdays and New Years Eve, there is good cause to buy them more often and try them with some of your favorite foods. Bone-dry spraklers (often referred to as 'Brut') pair nicely with seafoods and especially well with preparations adding earthy or smokey nuances to the dish. Crisp acidity cuts through sauces featuring cheese or other rich ingredients.

Washington Wine Touring

Seattle Area Wine Touring

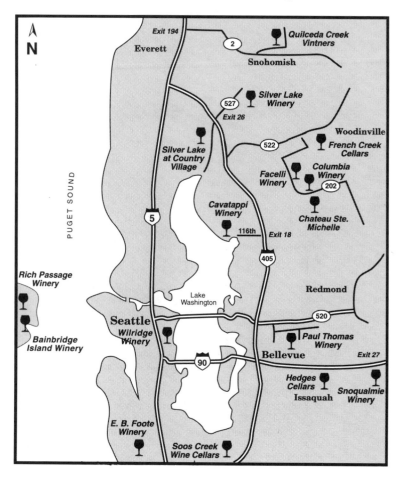

Seattle Area Wine Touring

Within an hour's drive of downtown Seattle are some of Washington's best known and largest wineries as well as some small, family operations and several wineries in between. The Seattle area listings include all wineries within a one hour driving radius and it may take several days to see them all.

Bainbridge Island

The temptation to hop a ferry and visit this independent community just across Puget Sound is irresistable. You can walk on if you plan to limit your visit to Bainbridge Island Winery and downtown Winslow. Add an appointment to visit Rich Passage Winery and you'll need your car. This trip is a great way to spend a summer Saturday or to serve as a springboard to further adventures on the Olympic Peninsula. Don't miss Thomas Kemper brewery in Poulsbo!

West Side of Lake Washington

On the west side of the lake only one winery is open with regular hours for public touring. Down in the industrial area of south Seattle, E. B. Foote Winery continues under the new ownership of Sherril Miller and Rich Higginbotham, they invite you to stop by on Saturdays or selected weekday evenings. Several operations have tried to make a go of a tasting room in or near the Pike Place Market but all have found the seasonal aspect of the business unprofitable. Andrew Will Cellars operates their winery on Elliott Ave. West but have no facilities for visitors. You may call the owners to arrange an appointment to view the operation. Wilridge Winery in the Madrona Bistro is open for tours by appointment, but you can buy a bottle of Paul Beveridge's Cabernet Sauvignon to accompany your dinner anytime.

Eastside Wineries – Woodinville, Bellevue, and Points North and East

The Woodinville area is now home to four wineries open to the public and several more facilities under construction. The grand Chateau Ste. Michelle is bigger and better than ever and Columbia's broad veranda encourages visitors to cross the road and stay awhile. Facelli Winery is just north on Highway 202 in a business park. Expect a warm and friendly welcome from Lou and Sandy Facelli and their daughter Lisa. French Creek Cellars is closer to downtown Woodinville on the banks of Little Bear Creek. A great fair-weather picnic site.

North of Woodinville you can visit Silver Lake Winery either at the winery in Mill Creek or at the tasting room at Country Village shopping center in Bothell. Near Snohomish, Quilceda Creek Vintners continue to make great Cabernet and they are open by appointment for tasting and sales.

Traveling east on Interstate 90, Hedges Cellars is open in Issaquah, and Snoqualmie Winery welcomes visitors daily to their facility overlooking the Snoqualmie Valley and the Cascade Foothills.

Cafe Juanita, just a block north of Juanita Beach Park, is home to Cavatappi Winery. The winery is not open to the public but the restaurant serves some of the Seattle area's finest Italian cuisine. Cavatappi wines are on the list, of course. Paul Thomas Winery is located near Bellevue, just off Highway 520 but is not open except by prior appointment.

Washington State
Andrew Will Winery

Mailing address:
8624 SW Soper Rd.
Vashon, WA 98070
(206) 282-4086
(206) 463-3290
Winemaker:
  Chris Camarda
First Year: 1989
Winery Capacity:
  600 Gallons

Winery History
Andrew Will is a small Seattle winery producing limited quantities of Cabernet Sauvignon and Merlot. Owners Chris and Annie Camarda named the winery after their son Will and their nephew Andrew when beginning the operation in 1989. As winemaker, Chris brings experience gained in the culinary arts working at Il Bistro restaurant in the Pike Place Market for many years. His gentle sense of humor reveals that he "finally found some use for the chemistry classes I was forced to take in high school." Andrew Will wines are in limited distribution in the Seattle area and visits to the winemaking facility in Seattle are offered by appointment only.

The Wines
Both the Cabernet Sauvignon and Merlot produced by Andrew Will Winery are intense oak-aged versions that require further bottle age to realize their full potential as premium, powerful wines.

Bainbridge Island Winery

682 State Hwy. 305
Bainbr. Is., WA 98110
(206) 842-9463
Owner: Gerard and
  JoAnn Bentrynn
First Year: 1982
Winery Capacity:
  7,000 Gallons
1991 Production:
  5,050 Gallons

Winery History
The first vines were planted at Bainbridge Island Winery in 1978 with the purpose of producing low alcohol, German-style wines from grape types suited to the climate of the Puget Sound region. A decade later, the winery declared independence from Eastern Washington grape growers by making wine only from grapes grown at their two Bainbridge Island vineyards.

A visit to Bainbridge Island Winery
The handsome winery building and immaculate vineyards stand ready to welcome visitors with tastings and tours. The wine museum in the tasting room reflects the life-long hobby of JoAnn Bentryn, collecting antique wine glasses – and most of the pieces are for sale. Out in the vineyard, a self-guided tour explains the grape-growing process to visitors.

B.I.W. hosts a wonderful Oktoberfest Celebration fundraiser for the Kitsap Humane Society each October. Beer and bratwurst augment the Bainbridge Island wines and the polka music wafts down almost to the ferry terminal. Call for details.

Many fruit wine lovers are attracted by the annual release of Bainbridge Island's Strawberry Wine. This wonderful, fruity wine has a broad reputation but a small production and is released during the holidays.

Harvest time at Bainbridge Island Winery

Tasting Room Hours:
Wednesday to Sunday,
Noon to 5 PM
Vineyard tours and
viticulture classes are
available. Call winery
for more information.

Cavatappi
Winery

9702 NE 120th Place
Kirkland, WA 98034
206-823-6533
Owner/Winemaker:
Peter Dow
First Year: 1984
Winery Capacity:
1,500 Gallons
1991 Production:
1,500 Gallons

The Wines

Preferring Bainbridge Island's cool climate, Gerard Bentryn grows several early ripening varieties including Müller Thurgau and Siegerrebe. This cross between Madeleine Angevine and Gewürztraminer yields a deliciously spicy, rich dessert wine. Bainbridge Island's fine Müller Thurgau is reviewed in our **Best of the Northwest** section on page 33.

Winery History

Peter Dow's Cavatappi Winery is located in a cellar adjacent to his locally famous Cafe Juanita restaurant. The Italian focus of the restaurant is echoed in the wines of Cavatappi. Washington's first Nebbiolo was crafted by Dow using traditional techniques (natural yeast fermentation among them). Grapes for Cavatappi's *Maddalena* (Nebbiolo) come from Red Willow vineyard near Yakima. The most enjoyable way to discover Peter Dow's wines are to have dinner at Cafe Juanita. Additional distribution is limited to a few Seattle-area retail outlets and to selected restaurants in San Francisco and New York. Winery visits by appointment only.

The Wines

The above-mentioned Maddalena is Peter Dow's pride and joy. The wine features the distinct varietal character of Nebbiolo presented in a medium to lighter style. Highly fragrant and enjoyable at a young age. Other wines of recent release include Bayless Blanc (after the late Washington wine pioneer Alec Bayless) and Molly's Muscat after Dow's other daughter (Maddalena is his oldest).

41

Washington State
Chateau Ste. Michelle

One Stimson Lane
Box 1976
Woodinville, WA
98072
(206) 488-1133

Owner: Stimson Lane
  Wine & Spirits
Winemaker:
  Mike Januik
First Year: 1967
Winery Capacity:
  1,000,000 Gallons +

Winery History

The Chateau Ste. Michelle winery dates back to the 1930's when Washington's bountiful harvest of fruits, berries and grapes were vinified to produce some of the Northwest's first wines. The winery's Grandview facility (see Yakima Valley touring) is a reminder of those days but is currently used solely for the production of the Chateau's red wines and may soon be only a storage facility.

The beautiful Woodinville Chateau was constructed in 1976 as a showplace winery and tourist attraction within a half-hour's drive metropolitan Seattle. The 87 acres of park-like grounds were originally designed and landscaped by the Olmstead brothers (designers of New York City's Central Park) in 1912 as part of lumber magnate Fred Stimson's Hollywood Farms.

A Visit to Chateau Ste. Michelle

The combination of grand architecture, lush landscaping and perfect picnicking make Chateau Ste. Michelle a stop not-to-be-missed on any Seattle-area wine tour.

Exploring the grounds you'll find a large pond and picnic area adjacent to the demonstration vineyard. Tucked under the trees next to the amphitheater are the original trout rearing ponds of Fred Stimson. These concrete tanks are often stocked with hungry trout who splash about and nip at the ducks who drop in for a swim. Winding paths through the gardens lead you to many enjoyable surprises of horticultural and architectural note.

In the winery, tours of the cellar accurately describe every aspect of winemaking and include a complimentary tasting Chateau Ste. Michelle wines. The well-stocked gift shop offers a broad selection of wine, picnic fare and wine-related gifts.

Special Events

Special events at Chateau Ste. Michelle are too numerous to mention individually, but you can call the winery to request a monthly calendar of happenings. The outdoor amphitheater and now offers symphonic concerts, the ballet and plays throughout the summer. Culinary events have been added under the direction of Executive Chef John Sarich.

The Wines

Winemaking at Chateau Ste. Michelle is now in the capable hands of Mike Januik. A native Northwesterner, Januik gained experience making wine for several other wineries before joining Chateau Ste. Michelle. His insightful handling of the winery's

The Chateau Ste. Michelle winery in Woodinville, WA.

Chateau Ste. Michelle

Domaine Ste. Michelle

One Stimson Lane
Box 1976
Woodinville, WA
98072
(206) 488-1133

Owner: Stimson Lane
Wine & Spirits
Winemaker:
Allan Pangborn
First Year: 1988

many varietals and vineyard sources are testament to his innate ability as a winemaker. Among the best of his efforts are Chardonnay and Sauvignon Blanc, while Cabernet and Merlot are favorite reds. Watch for special reserve bottlings and blends of varietals in Meritage type assemblings. See reviews of several CSM wines in our **Best of the Northwest** section.

Winery History

Although Chateau Ste. Michelle produced small amounts of methode champenoise sparkling wines since 1975, only in 1988 was a firm commitment made to increased production and a complete line of champagne-style sparklers. Winemaker Allan Pangborn was brought on board in 1989, fresh from experience in California's sparkling wine industry. His efforts continued the quality standards established by winemaker Cheryl Barber, who crafted the first DSM wines in 1988. In 1990, a breakthrough in pricing was reached with Champagne Brut, a methode champenoise sparkling wine available for under $10.

The Wines

The original wines released from Domaine Ste. Michelle were Blanc de Noir and Brut. The Blanc de Noir offers a creamy, yeasty nose, fine bead (tiny bubbles) and an austere, yet flavorful palate. The Brut brings a fresh aroma of apples and citrus with a similar crisp palate. Newer to the line is the Blanc de Blanc, a cuvee of Chardonnay, and Champagne Brut, blended from several grape types to achieve a delicate flavor with a universally appealing palate.

43

Washington State
Columbia Winery

1445-120th NE
Bellevue, WA 98005
(206) 453-1977

President: Dan Baty
V. P. and Winemaker:
  David Lake, M.W.,
V. P. Operations:
  Max Zellweger
**Quality Control
Enologist:**
  Bruce Watson
First Year: 1962
Winery Capacity:
  250,000 Gallons
1992 Production:
  150,000 Gallons

Tasting RoomHours:
Open Daily, 10 AM to
5 PM, Complete
winery tours - tour
groups by appointment.
Call the winery for
information on special
events held throughout
the year.

Winery History

Columbia Winery is the descendent of Associated Vintners (AV), a group of amateur winemakers that bonded a winery in 1962. Led by Dr. Lloyd Woodburne, a professor at the University of Washington, this group is credited with producing the first premium varietal wines made in the State.

The winery moved from Woodburne's Laurelhurst garage to more spacious quarters in Kirkland when it became clear that larger volumes of wine were needed to meet rising demand. In 1979, Master of Wine David Lake was hired to assume winemaker duties, producing a wide range of varietals both red and white.

The wines produced by David Lake at Columbia have long been recognized as fine quality wines which set an example for Northwest style and elegance. Recent reserve vintages of Cabernet, Chardonnay and other varietals have won rave reviews and many awards at festivals and fairs.

A Visit to Columbia Winery

Columbia Winery is located directly across the road from Chateau Ste. Michelle in a magnificent Victorian winery building. Tours of the winemaking facility and tastings of the winery's current releases are conducted by a well-informed staff of local wine aficionados. The tasting room offers a complete selection of wine-related gifts, including may unique shirts and other apparel designed to tickle the wine lover's fancy.

The Wines

Both David Lake and Max Zellweger are skilled craftsmen when it comes to creating fine wines. A division of the work load finds David more often at the vineyard and directing the winemaking activity and Max handling the day to day winery operations. The broad selection of varietals includes five signature reserves, single vineyard bottlings designed to highlight the best bottlings from each vintage and a complete line of regular releases.

Specialties include single vineyard offerings of Cabernet Sauvignon, a special Merlot: Milestone, an annual bottling of Syrah from Red Willow Vineyard and a varietal Cabernet Franc. The Cellarmaster Reserve Riesling is always a good example of Northwest style and the Pinot Noir made from grapes harvested in Southwest Washington has been a consistent award winner. Our **Best of the Northwest** panels found many Columbia wines attractive. Cabernet, Merlot, Gewurztraminer and Riesling are reviewed beginning on page 14.

Gordie Rawson, cellarman, David Lake, M.W., and Bruce Watson, quality control enologist of Columbia Winery.

Delille Cellars/ Chaleur Estate

P.O. Box 2233
Woodinville, WA
98072 • (206) 489-0544
Owners: Partnership
Winemaker:
Chris Upchurch

An exciting startup winery in the Woodinville area, DeLille Cellars is a project of longtime amatuer winemakers Chris Upchurch and Jay Soloff with wine lovers Charles Lill and his son Greg. Plans are to create a signature wine of new-oak-aged Cabernet and Merlot. No wines or appointments available at press time, but the winery has broken ground on Woodinville's east hill and selected a name for their first release: Chaleur Estate.

E. B. Foote Winery

9354 - 4th Ave. South
Seattle, WA 98108
(206) 763-9928

Owners/Winemakers:
Sherrill Miller and
Rich Higginbotham
First Year: 1978
Winery Capacity:
5,000 Gallons
1991 Production:
300 Gallons

Winery History
E. B. Foote Winery was founded in 1978 by Eugene Foote and is the seventh oldest winery in the state. Gene Foote recently retired and the current owners took over with Gene as their consultant. Grapes from the Yakima Valley are trucked to the South Seattle industrial location where the crush and winemaking take place.

A visit to E. B. Foote Winery
Free tasting and tours are offered on two weekday evenings and on Saturdays. Tasting is offered in the winery with the owners your most frequent hosts. The keen enthusiasm of these new wine entrepreneurs is to be admired.

The Wines
Dry White Riesling, Chardonnay, Gewürztraminer and Late Harvest Riesling are currently available along with some Cabernet from over a decade ago. Time has not rendered the older wines undrinkable but I'm sure the new owners will create more smiles with their own vinifications of more recent era.

Washington State

Facelli Winery

16120 Woodinville-
Redmond Road N.E. #1
Woodinville, WA
98072
(206) 488-1020

Owner: Facelli Family
Winemaker:
  Louis Facelli
First Year: 1988
Winery Capacity:
  10,000 Gallons
1992 Production:
  7,000 Gallons

Tasting Room Hours:
Noon to 4 PM,
weekends or by appt.

Winery History
The history of the Facelli Winery is the history of its owner. After relocating from California to Idaho in the early 1970s, Lou Facelli began making homemade wine from fruit grown in the area around his new home of Caldwell. His newfound passion for winemaking led to the bonding of his own winery but through an unfortunate turn of events he was soon left winery-less but much wiser about the ways of the wine business. Things are now on an upswing and headed in the right direction as this talented winemaker stakes his future on his ability to coax quality and magic out of a load of grapes. His efforts with recent harvests include Fumé Blanc, Sémillon, Merlot, Chardonnay and a small amount of Riesling. Special bottlings of Cabernet and Pinot Noir are sold only at the winery.

A visit to Louis Facelli Winery
Although the winery is not a grand chateau, there are plenty of reasons to visit the Facelli Winery. Family members offer an insightful tour and tasting in the cozy location, explaining the traditional winemaking methods used and offering samples of current releases.

The Wines
Lou Facelli crafts his wines as each vintage tells him to. The grapes and wine "speak to him." Our **Best of the Northwest** panel reviews his fine Merlot on page 20.

French Creek Cellars

17721-132nd Ave. NE
Woodinville, WA
98072
(206) 486-1900

Owners:
  Corporate partnership
Winemaker:
  Richard Winter
First Year: 1983
Winery Capacity:
  15,000 Gallons
1991 Production:
  10,500 Gallons

Tasting Room Hours:
Daily, Noon to 5 PM,

Winery History
French Creek Cellars traces its roots to a group of friends who began to make home wine in 1973. Ten years later, with some of the original partners changed but the dedication to producing fine wine still intact, commercial production was begun. Originally tucked away in the corner of a Redmond business park, the winery now enjoys larger and more elegant quarters adjacent to downtown Woodinville on the banks of Little Bear Creek.

Day to day winemaking operations at the new Woodinville facility are carried out by former vineyardist Richard Winter and his crush and bottling crews. Knowledgeable staff members work the tasting room pouring wine for visitors and telling the French Creek story.

A visit to French Creek Cellars
The new winery and tasting room just northwest of downtown Woodinville offers the winelover an enjoyable wine tasting experience and a tour of

the winery, if requested. A shaded picnic area alongside Bear Creek beckons weary travelers to enjoy their lunch to the sounds of gently rushing water while harvest time visitors can also marvel at the sight of salmon spawning in the stream. The winery offers many special events during the year and interested wine lovers should ask to be put on their mailing list to receive advance notice.

The Wines

Red wines produced at French Creek include Cabernet Sauvignon, Merlot and Lemberger. These are crafted in a big style with oak and tannin evident in most bottlings. (See **Best of the Northwest** Cabernet review on page 15.) White varietals include delicious versions of Dry Gewürztraminer and Dry Riesling as well as Chardonnay.

Hedges Cellars

1105 12th Ave. N.W.,
Suite A4
Issaquah, WA 98027
Mailing address:
1420 NW Gilman Blvd.
#2573
Issaquah, WA 98027
(206) 391-6056

Owners:
  Tom & Anne-Marie
  Hedges, Mats Hanzon
First Year: 1990
Winery Capacity:
  50,000 Gallons
1991 Production:
  45,000 Gallons

Tasting Room Hours:
Thursday thru Saturday,
Noon to 6 PM

Winery History

With a background in international management and a love for fine wine, it's no wonder that Tom Hedges' first transaction in the wine business was providing an affordable red wine blend to a European client. With this initial success, Hedges Cellars has built its reputation on producing principally this one red wine, a blend of Cabernet Sauvignon and Merlot. The 1989 Hedges, the first vintage to be released in the U.S., won a gold medal at the Seattle Enological Society tasting. Subsequent bottlings have been lauded by The Wine Spectator as "best buys." Hedges Cellars is constructing a new winery next to their vineyard site on Red Mountain at the east end of the Yakima Valley.

A visit to Hedges Cellars

Hedges current Issaquah location houses the winery tasting room, offices and aging room for the Hedges Red Mountain Reserve. Don't be fooled by the humble location, once inside visitors are surprised by the warm decor, including an impressive mural done by a local artist.

The Wines

Hedges Cellars' Cabernet Merlot is an excellent example of blended red wine in the Columbia Valley style. Barrel-aged for a short time, the wine is approachable on purchase but will gain complexity for one to two years. This bottling is reviewed in the **Best of the Northwest** section on page 22. Red Mountain Reserve is a very limited bottling of the best lots featuring additional barrel-aged character and requiring two to three years additional bottle age to bring out the distinctive flavor and aroma.

Washington State
Paul Thomas Wines

1717-136th Pl. NE
Bellevue, WA 98005
(206) 747-1008

Owner: Associated
Vendors, Inc., parent of
Columbia Winery
Winemaker:
 Mark Cave
First Year: 1979
Winery Capacity:
 36,000 Gal.
1991 Production:
 45,000 Gallons

Tasting Room Hours:
By appointment only

Winery History
Paul Thomas Winery in Bellevue continues to undergo changes as a new owner has taken over and directed the winery's increased production. Varietal grape wines continue to wine awards, while the fruit wines that launched the winery to regional fame have taken a back seat. "Crimson" (the winery's rhubarb wine) and "Dry Bartlett" (a light sipping wine made from Bartlett pears) are still a major part of the production but the finely-crafted Cabernet, Merlot, Fume Blanc and Chardonnay appear more often on store shelves and wine lists. In 1993 the owners of Columbia Winery purchased Paul Thomas Winery but will operate it separately.

A visit to Paul Thomas Winery
The Paul Thomas Winery in Bellevue is a production facility dedicated to making wine. Winemaker Mark Cave and his wife Colleen often represent the winery at festivals and fairs throughout the Northwest. Stop by their booth to visit and enjoy samples of current-release wines.

The Wines
The fruit wines that put the winery on the map are still produced. Crimson rhubarb wine and Dry Bartlett pear wine are delightfully true to origin but the Washington Raspberry wine has achieved deserved fame for its intense fruit character. The blended Cabernet-Merlot is a wonderfully versatile red wine with bright fruit flavors and lingering pleasant finish. (See our **Best of the Northwest** review on page 21.)

Quilceda Creek Vintners

5226 Old Machias Rd.
Snohomish, WA 98290
(206) 568-2389

Owner/Winemaker:
 Alex Golitzin, Paul
 Golitzin
Consulting Enologist:
 Andre Tchelistcheff
First Year: 1978
Winery Capacity:
 2,600 Gallons
1991 Production:
 2,400 Gallons

Winery History
Some of Washington's best Cabernet Sauvignon is also the hardest to get. Alex Golitzin produces just 1,000 cases of this varietal each year and it always sells out before the next vintage is released.

The nephew of Andre Tchelistcheff, Alex has had constant encouragement in his winemaking endeavors since receiving his degree in chemical engineering from U.C. Berkeley. (A winemaking curriculum is almost identical to that of chemical engineers.) Now an engineer at Scott paper in Everett, he divides his time between his work there and his love of fine Cabernet. Alex and Jeanette's son Paul has studied winemaking science and is now assistant winemaker for Quilceda Creek.

A visit to Quilceda Creek Vintners
A telephone call to the winery (at the Golitzin's home just north of Snohomish) will allow you to

Paul Golitzin and his father Alex now share winemaking responsibilities at Quilceda Creek Vintners near Snohomish, WA.

make an appointment to taste and buy some of this excellent wine and to chat with Alex and Paul about matters enological. Their Cabernet is also poured at several wine events throughout the year.

The Wines

Alex Golitzin's appreciation for fine wine in the style of famous French chateaux was amplified when his own 1983 Cabernet placed second in a tasting that included some of Bordeaux's finest wines. Quilceda's rich and fruity Cabernet Sauvignon is reviewed by our **Best of the Northwest** panel on page 16.

Washington State
Rich Passage Winery

7869 NE Day Road W.
Bainbridge Island, WA
98110 •(206) 842-1199
Owners:
 Linda & Jeff Owen
Winemaker:
 Jeff Owen
First Year: 1989
Winery Capacity:
 1,500 Gallons
1991 Production:
 1,200 Gallons

Winery History
Rich Passage is a small, family operation annually producing about 500 cases of Pinot Noir, Chardonnay and Fumé Blanc. All the wines are barrel fermented and aged in small French oak barrels. Owners Linda and Jeff Owen took their home winemaking hobby commercial in 1989 and now occupy the same space where Will Kemper and Andy Thomas began Thomas Kemper brewery! (Building A at the address listed)

A visit to Rich Passage Winery
When you visit Rich Passage Winery on Bainbridge Island, chances are you'll catch winemaker Jeff Owen testing wine, labeling bottles or tinkering with equipment. Wine tastings and tours can be arranged by calling the winery for an appointment.

The Wines
Small quantities of Chardonnay, Fumé Blanc and Pinot Noir are produced at Rich Passage Winery. Production is sold mostly at the winery.

Silver Lake Winery

17616 15th Ave. SE
Suite 106B
Bothell, WA 98012
(206) 485-2437

Owner: Washington
Wine & Beverage Co.
Winemaker:
 Cheryl Barber Jones
First Year: 1989
Winery Capacity:
 30,000 Gallons
1991 Production:
 15,000 Gallons

Tasting Room Hours:
Noon -5 PM Mon - Fri.
Country Village daily,
Noon - 6 PM, Saturday
10 AM - 6PM, and
Sunday Noon -5PM

Winery History
Silver Lake Winery began life as the producer of Spire Mountain Ciders. Apple, pear and other hard cider products which continue to have a strong following of loyal fans. With all the equipment and licenses necessary for winemaking, the owners and winemaker decided to produce some wines from the 1989 vintage. A good crop, a talented winemaker, and the rest was history. Strong marketing efforts and continued high-quality wines are keeping Silver Lake in the limelight.

A visit to Silver Lake Winery
Your choices for visiting Silver Lake are to stop by the winery near Mill Creek during the week or to visit their satellite tasting room at the Country Village Mall in Bothell any day of the week or weekend. Country Village is a complex of shops and unique boutiques offering a variety of gifts and goodies. A nice visit and wine tasting, too! If you are more serious about the making of the wine and have technical questions that would best be answered by winery personnel, then visit the winery. The winery offers a Thanksgiving weekend open house and a spring barrel tasting. Call for details.

The Wines

Silver Lake offers a wide selection of varietals including Chardonnay (regular and reserve), Merlot, Cabernet Sauvignon, Sauvignon Blanc, Dry Riesling, Off-Dry Riesling and Riesling Ice Wine. The Merlot is a real crowd pleaser along with the rich, buttery Reserve Chardonnay. Our **Best of the Northwest** panels review Silver Lake Chardonnay and Late Harvest Riesling on pages 24 and 34.

Snoqualmie Winery

1000 Winery Road
Snoqualmie, WA
98065 • (206) 888-4000
Owner: Stimson Lane
    Wine & Spirits
Winemaker:
    Joy Andersen
First Year: 1983
Winery Capacity:
    120,000 Gallons

Tasting Room Hours:
Daily, 10 AM to
4:30 PM

Winery History

Begun in 1984 as a partnership between winemaker Joel Klein and vineyard owner David Wyckoff, Snoqualmie Winery has evolved away from those two men. A corporate partnership for several years, Mike Januik made the wines at Snoqualmie and their Mattawa facility that was originally F. W. Langguth. Purchased in 1990 by Stimson Lane, Snoqualmie has regained pride and direction. Winemaker Joy Andersen is crafting several varietals that have become Snoqualmie's flagship wines.

A visit to Snoqualmie Winery

Just two minutes off I-90, Snoqualmie Winery beckons the visitor with a modern visitor facility complete with picnic area and a panoramic view second to none. The facility staff are courteous and well-informed, pouring a wide selection of Snoqualmie's wines. The gift shop includes edibles for picnicking on the spacious lawn and amphitheater as well as a selection of wine-related gifts. Concerts and other arts events are held on the large amphitheater which features a grand view of Mount Si and the Cascade foothills.

The Wines

Snoqualmie offers a complete line of varietals including Cabernet, Reserve Chardonnay, Dry Chenin Blanc, Gewürztraminer, Muscat Canelli, Late Harvest Riesling and Sémillon. The Muscat Canelli is a favorite offering aromas and flavors of orange blossom and honey. The toasty/buttery Chardonnay and refreshing Sémillon are also nice. Five Snoqualmie varietals were favored by our judging panels for the **Best of the Northwest**. Look for reviews beginning on page 14 of this guide.

Washington State
Soos Creek Wine Cellars

14223 SE 180th Pl.
Renton, WA 98058
(206) 255-9901
Owner:
  David & Cecile Larsen
Winemaker:
  David Larsen
First Year: 1989
Winery Capacity:
  2,000 Gallons
1991 Production:
  450 Gallons

Winery History
David Larsen has pursued winemaking as a hobby and avocation for eight years. His admiration for several of Washington's boutique wineries specializing in Cabernet inspired him to try his hand at the big red. His first release was a 1989 Cabernet Sauvignon – rich and powerful – made in the winery at his home in Renton. His position in the finance department at Boeing is the stabilizing influence away from the excitement and romance of winemaking. David's wife Cecile and their children all help out in the winery operation.

The Wines
Soos Creek Wine Cellars intends to produce only Cabernet Sauvignon made in an intense style emphasizing oak aging. The current release is deep ruby with violet edges and offers aromas of toasty oak over layers of cherry and earth. The wine needs to age until at least 1994-95.

Vashon Winery

12629 SW Cemetery Rd.
Vashon, Washington
98070 • (206) 463-2990

Owners/Winemakers:
  Will Gerrior
  and Karen Peterson
First Year: 1990
Winery Capacity:
  2,300 Gallons

Tasting Room Hours:
Fri. and Sat. by appointment, 11 AM - 5 PM

Winery History
Will Gerrior and Karen Peterson, husband and wife, began the Vashon Winery inspired by their original contacts with Chalone Winery and Joseph Swan Winery in California. They have released three vintages of Cabernet Sauvignon from grapes grown at the Portteus Vineyard in Zillah. They plan to release their first Chardonnay and Semillon soon.

A visit to Vashon Winery
Take the short ferry ride from West Seattle to beautiful Vashon Island and you are transported to a relaxing country atmosphere. Will Gerrior and Karen Peterson graciously welcome you to taste and purchase their personally crafted wines by appointment on Fridays or Saturdays.

The Wines
All wines are handmade and purposely on a small scale. Currently the winery produces about a thousand cases a year. The hope is to remain small and personal.

Whittlesey Mark

5318 22nd Ave. NW
Seattle, WA 98117
(206) 789-6543

Owner: Oregon Methode
Champenoise, Inc.
Winemaker:
Mark Newton
First Year: 1984
Winery Capacity:
5,750 Gallons
1991 Production:
3,510 Gallons

Tasting Room Hours:
By appointment only

Winery History

Mark Newton makes no pretense about his mission in life: to make the finest champagne possible from Oregon grapes. This dream began in 1983 when Newton & Newton (the winery's original name) obtained their winery bond. Mark Newton was encouraged by his U.C. Davis trained brother, Jeff, to follow his desires and try his hand at production of fine sparkling wine.

Undaunted by the enormity of the task, Mark set out to obtain first hand knowledge of his chosen craft from some of the best in the business. His training at Maison Deutz included tutelage from Harold Osborne of Schramsburg Champagne Cellars and from Christian Roguenant of Deutz & Gelderman. Plans for grander facilities exist, but for now the winery occupies a small basement space in the Seattle suburb of Ballard.

The Wines

Two sparkling wines are currently available: Brut and Blanc de Noir. Both offer toasty, smoky notes from barrel fermentation and an austere, complex palate that makes them good with food.

Wilridge Winery

1416-34 Ave.
Seattle, WA 98122
(206) 328-2987

Owner: Paul Bevridge
Winemaker:
Paul Beveridge
First Year: 1993
Winery Capacity:
600 Gallons
1992 Production:
600 Gallons

Tasting Room Hours:
By appointment only

Winery History

Wilridge Winery is located in the cellar of the Madrona Bistro restaurant. This neighborhood gathering spot has been yearning to samle winemaker Paul Beveridge's Cabernet Sauvignon which he crafts in small lots from grapes purchased at Klipsun Vineyards on Red Mountain in the Yakima Valley. With all the jumping through hoops that is required when trying to bond a winery in an already licensed restaurant, the final approval came through in 1993, almost a year late.

A visit to Wilridge Winery

Bring an appetite and stop by the Madrona Bistro for delightful regional fare. Wilridge Cabernet is on the list and winemaker Paul Beveridge might be around to answer questions. If you have a strong desire to visit with the winemaker, call ahead for an appointment.

Seattle Area Accommodations

The greater Seattle area is worthy of a visit even without the prospect of visiting Washington's largest and smallest wineries and a half-dozen in-between. Such a welcoming Northwest city is not lacking in choices of accommodations. Included here is a brief selection of lodgings that are among the finest available – but still a good value. Other less expensive offerings may be found near the eastside wine country (Marriott Residence Inn, Wyndham Garden) and the local B & B Association (784-0539) offers homey suggestions.

Sheraton Seattle Hotel & Towers – 1400 Sixth Ave., (206) 621-9000

The reputation of Fuller's restaurant alone should be enough to coax a weary traveller into this delightful hotel (see restaurant listings). The hotel staff makes a similar effort to cater to the needs of each and every guest. Reserve a Tower room for added amenities and a great view.

The Salish – P.O. Box 1109, Snoqualmie, 98065 (206) 888-4230

The Salishan Resort folks took over the former Snoqualmie Falls Lodge and added a 91 room 'country inn' that looks remarkably like a fancy hotel. All the rooms have fireplaces, whirlpool tubs, refrigerators and custom furnishings. Great winemaker dinners and other culinary extravaganzas take place in the restaurant. Rates are $150 to $235.

The Hotel Vintage Park – 1100 5th Avenue, (206) 624-8000

The idea of a wine-themed hotel was long overdue and Kimco Hotels have thoughtfully provided one in Seattle and one in Portland. Each room is individually decorated and named for a Washington winery or vineyard. Tulio Ristorante serves delectable Italian specialties on premises.

Seattle's Great Dining Discoveries

Fuller's – The Sheraton Hotel, 1400 Sixth Ave. (206) 621-9000

Chef de Cuisine Monique Barbeau provides the creative culinary flair for one of Seattle's most elegant restaurants. The preparations include selections of Northwest specialties innovatively served with delicious accompaniments. The bright, elegant, decor features a wide assortment of Northwest art on display. Ask for a peek into the Pilchuck Room if it is not being used. Expensive.

The Metropolitan Grill - 820 - 2nd Avenue (206) 624-3287

Voted one of America's top ten Steak houses, The Met Grill offers the red wine lover a place to indulge the fantasy of thick, juicy cuts of the finest aged beef and other carnivore's delights. Attentive service and wine presentation by sommelier Rich Horton add to the enjoyment.

Labuznik - 1924-1st Avenue (206) 682-1624

A meat-eater's paradise created by Peter Cipra in 1979 features fantastic roast pork, chateaubriand and other specialties. Suitable red wines can be selected from the modest wine list featuring some extremely good values. Expensive. Dinner only, Tues. - Sat.

Ray's Boathouse - 6049 Seaview NW, 789-3770

Since its grand re-opening in early 1988, Ray's has regained its place in the upscale, yuppie-dining, Hall of Fame. Enjoy the seafood creations of chefs Wayne Ludvigsen and Charles Ramseyer while watching the views of Shilshole Bay or checking out the other diners. Jeff Prather's wine selections favor Northwest producers but offer quality above all. Great winemaker dinners. Moderate to expensive.

Seattle's Great Dining Discoveries

Anthony's HomePorts – Multiple view locations: Shilshole Bay 783-0780, Kirkland 822-0225,Edmonds 771-4400, Everett, Des Moines.

Anthony's motto is fresh fish daily and they back up the claim with their own government inspected wholesale seafood operation. Specialties include halibut, salmon, Dungeness crab, fresh oysters and other offerings. Great selection of NW wines. Moderate.

Cafe Juanita - 9702 NE 120th Pl., Kirkland 823-1505

The home of Cavatappi Winery, Café Juanita specializes in Northern Italian cooking. Pastas, delicious sauced fishes and tempting desserts. Moderate to expensive. Dinner only.

The Painted Table - 92 Madison, in the Alexis Hotel, 624-3646

When it comes to creating foods for pairing with wines, Chef Emily Moore is the Northwest's best. Period. Don't miss a chance to dine at TPT.

Kaspar's – 2701 1st Ave., 441-4805

Kaspar and Nancy Donier are the proprietor's of one of Seattle's most elegant view dining spots. The innovative cuisine created by Kaspar features seasonal local ingredients in delicious adaptations of traditional continental style. Nancy keeps the front of the house in order with help from Seattle's most courteous and helpful staff. Good NW wine selection. Moderate. Dinner only Mon. - Sat.

Spirit of Washington Dinner Train - P.O. Box 835, Renton, WA 98055 1-800-876-7245, (206) 227-7245

A great outing for visitors and curious locals, the Spirit of Washington Dinner Train travels the rails between Renton and Chateau Ste. Michelle in Woodinville offering views of Lake Washington, the Seattle skyline and other eastside points of interest. Delicious meals prepared by Gretchen's Of Course Catering.

Seattle Area Wine & Specialty Shops

Downtown

Champion Wine Cellars

108 Denny Way, 284-8306 Stephanie Ninaud hosts this cozy bottle shop featuring a great selection of wines from around the world at the foot of Queen Anne Hill.

McCarthy & Schiering

Queen Anne Ave. N., 282-8500, also in the Northend at 6500 Ravenna Ave. NE 524-9500 Dan McCarthy and Jay Schiering have a loyal following owing to their sound wine advice. Tastings. Vintage Select discount club. M-F, 10:30-7, Sa 'til 6.

Pike & Western Wine Merchants

Pike Pl. at Virginia St. (206) 441-1307 Michael Teer and his helpful staff share their expertise at this popular Pike Place wine shop. Extensive NW section. Frequent dinners and tastings. M-F, 9:30-6:30, Sa 9-6.

North End

Brie & Bordeaux

2108 N. 55th (206) 633-3538 Alison Leber now operates this charming fromagerie in Wallingford to the cheers of every cheese lover in Seattle! Cheese, wine & catering.

The Cellar

14411 Greenwood N. 365-7660 Friendly north Seattle shop with a good selection of beers as well as the area's most extensive selection of wine and beer making supplies. M-F 10-7, Sa 10-6, Su 12-4.

Eastside - Bellevue, etc.

The Grape Choice

436 Central Way - Kirkland, 827-7551 Larry Springer and Penny Sweet offer fine wines, beers and foods in their deli-wine shop near Moss Bay. Open daily.

For Parents Only

For those with young children in tow, read on to find enjoyable activities for all members of the family. Many attractions are located near wineries or can be made into a fun excursion for adults also.

Seattle Area

Seattle Parks - Located in the city itself their are dozens of parks and playgrounds. Some of the better ones are: Greenlake (Northeast corner children's play area), Volunteer Park on Capitol Hill (plant lovers can also enjoy the conservatory here), Gasworks Park (north shore of Lake Union, bring your kite!), Golden Gardens beach and park on Shilshole Bay and Discovery Park in Magnolia with a dandy play area and nature trails.

Woodland Park Zoo - NE 50th St. at Phinney - This is one of our country's most lauded zoos with natural habitats for hundreds of species of animals and birds. Recent completion of the Thai logging camp elephant exhibit and the Alaska Tiaga exhibit are the frosting on the cake to the long-respected Mountain Gorilla, African Savanna and Northwest Marsh areas. There is a Seattle City park just north of the zoo with swings, slides, jungle gym and picnic areas.

The Seattle Waterfront - Get your hands on a starfish at the Seattle Aquarium or have some fish and chips and a huge waffle ice cream cone. Lots to do and see for young and old. Don't miss a ride on the waterfront trolley or horse-drawn carriage and shopping for trinkets at all the import stores.

The Seattle Aquarium - Pier 59 - Another of Seattle's widely acclaimed public displays bent on instilling conservation and respect for nature values in kids and adults alike. Exhibits of Hawaiian reef fishes, sea otters, seals and much more await those with a little free time.

The Space Needle at the Seattle Center - Kids are thrilled by the ride to the top and both adults and kids love the view.

The Eastside

Marymoor Park at the end of Highway 520 is a huge place with areas set aside for everyone. Bring the kids, the dog, the frisbee, the bat & ball, etc.

Farrel-McWhirter Park - Avondale Road - Redmond - Although this huge natural park is out-of-the-way, it's worth the drive to allow the kids to appreciate the farm animals and nature trails set amidst the Eastside's largest forested preserve.

Sammamish River Bike Trail - A greenbelt has been established along the Sammamish Slough so you can ride your bike from Woodinville to Redmond. One access point is just east of Ch. Ste. Michelle off Hwy. 202.

Country Village - Bothell - Silver Lake Winery has opened a satellite tasting room in this quaint collection of shops just down the Bothell-Everett Highway from the winery.

Gilman Village - Issaquah - Just around the corner from Hedges Cellars is a fun shopping center of recycled vintage houses offering a wide variety of wares.

Snoqualmie Steam Train - Located right in downtown Snoqualmie (5 minutes from the winery of the same name) you can ride a restored steam train and peruse the railroad museum and gift shop.

Bellevue Square Mall - Downtown Bellevue - Bring your teenagers for a totally awesome mall experience. Not a bad place for mom and dad to shop in a classy environment, either.

McDonalds - Locations near every winery. 140th NE in Woodinville, inside Bellevue Square mall, Issaquah, Totem Lake area west of I-405, Seattle Ferry Terminal. Take the kids out for a burger BEFORE touring to prevent a case of the dreaded "crankies."

Northwest Winemaking

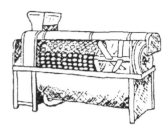

As in other winegrowing regions, most Northwest wines are made from the grape species vitis vinifera – wine grapes. The grapes arrive at the winery from the vineyard in large bins or boxes and our story begins . . .

Grape clusters are dumped into the mechanical crusher/stemmer where rollers break the grape skins releasing juice and pulp for fermentation. Stems are removed by fast-ratating impellers that throw the berries off the stems and then deposit the stems into a collector where they are later hauled to the vineyars for use as compost.

White grapes (and red grapes destined to be white wine, blanc de noir) are pressed after minimal skin contact. The Willmes bladder press gently extracts the juice by inflating a neoprene balloon inside the mass of skins and pulp. The pulp is pressed against a stainless steel wire cage and the juice trickles into a trough from where it is pumped into tanks.

Fermentation is carried out in stainless steel tanks, large wooden tanks, open-top plastic bins or oak barrels. White and blush wines are chilled in special refrigerated tanks for a cool fermentation.

Red wine fermentation is carried out on the skins and pulp during which color is extracted to give the wine its deep ruby hue. The fermenting wine is "punched down" or "pumped over" to maintain contact between wine and skins.

Aging in tanks or barrels is followed by filtration or other clarification methods.

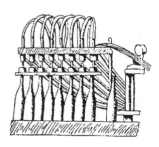

Modern, self-contained bottling lines are used at many wineries. The bottles are sterilized, then filled, corked and labeled. The capsule spun onto the top of the bottle is more decorative than functional and is nowadays most often made from aluminum alloy or plastic. Lead capsules have been banned from use.

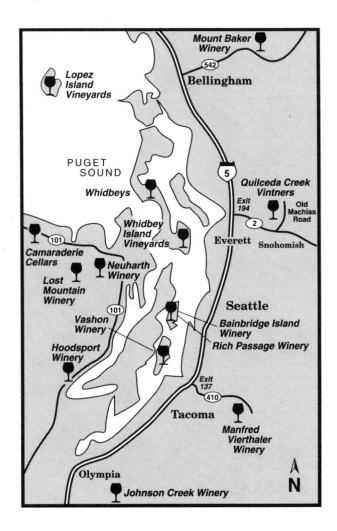

Olympic Peninsula & Greater Puget Sound Wine Touring

As you leave the greater Seattle metropolitan area of Western Washington, the wineries become fewer in number and much further apart. It's time to commit a weekend and visit some of Washington's most scenic areas and include stops at some very nice winery facilities.

Olympic Peninsula Tour

Leaving Seattle via the Winslow Ferry you can start your tour by visiting Bainbridge Island Winery just before lunch (see Seattle area listings) or plan a picnic beside their vineyard. Continue north on Highway 305 to cross the Hood Canal Bridge to the Olympic Peninsula. Along your way, you can stop to stretch

Olympic Peninsula & Greater Puget Sound Wine Touring

your legs at any of several county parks right on the water. Continue north on Highways 104 and 101 to enter Sequim, home of Neuharth Winery. Just east of "downtown" Sequim take the southward turn to head up into the mountains to visit Lost Mountain Winery. Prior arrangements are necessary unless you plan your trip during their annual month-long "open winery" each June. Port Angeles is home to Camaraderie Cellars, open by appointment only.

Your next day you have plenty of time to follow Highway 101 south along Hood Canal to Hoodsport Winery. After this pleasant stop follow the hook of Hood Canal back to Bremerton via Highways 106 and 3 or return through Gig Harbor and across the Tacoma Narrows Bridge to join I-5.

North Puget Sound

Enjoy the island life, Washington style, by taking the ferry from Mukilteo to Whidbey Island for visits to Whidbey Island Vineyards and Whidbey's Greenbank Farm. Be sure to allow time to visit Langley, Penn Cove and Coupeville as you drive north. Continuing your drive along Whidbey Island you cross Deception Pass and can then return to Interstate 5 to make tracks to Bellingham in time for a visit to Mount Baker Vineyards in the Nooksack Valley. An alternate plan would be to time your visits to make the Anacortes Ferry to Lopez Island to visit the winery of the same name.

Olympia Wine Touring

Near Olympia and in the scenic Skookumchuck Valley further south, you can visit McCrea Cellars (opened in Fall of '93) and Johnson Creek Winery near Tenino. Johnson Creek is located on the same plot as Alice's Restaurant, a local dinnerhouse famed for delicious country cooking.

Camaraderie Cellars

165 Benson Road
Port Angeles, WA
98362 • (206) 452-4964

Winery History

Camaraderie Cellars is located on the scenic Olympic Peninsula in the shadow of the majestic Olympic Mountain ridges. The winery's first commercial vintage was in 1992 with an emphasis on limited production of premium Cabernet Sauvignon. The small winery building with a view of the mountains is located just west of Port Angeles, 1/4 mile off Highway 101.

The Wines

Grapes for the Cabernet Sauvignon of Camaraderie Cellars come from many prestigious vineyards in Eastern Washington. A small operation, but one to watch in the future for intense, rich Cabernets.

A visit to Camaraderie Cellars

An appointment is necessary to visit this small, out-of-the-way operation. The proximity to other northern Peninsula wineries makes it an attractie addition to a weekend tour itinerary.

Washington State

Hoodsport Winery

N 23501 Highway 101
P.O. Box 597
Hoodsport, WA 98548
(206) 877-9894

Owners: Hoodsport
  Winery, Inc.,
  Peggy Patterson, CEO
Winemaker:
  Edwin R. Patterson
First Year: 1980
Winery Capacity:
  45,000 Gallons
1991 Production:
  40,000 Gallons

Tasting Room Hours:
Daily, 10 AM to 6 PM

Winery History

The first vintages produced at Hoodsport Winery were fruit wines vinted by the Patterson family on a small scale. These flavorful wines were sold at the highway-side winery to local residents and interested passers-by. Something happened to propel the winery into large scale production and that something was Hoodsport's Raspberry Wine. A fruity, aromatic and delightfully sweet dessert wine that wins gold medals every year! This instant fame and winery recognition spurred the Patterson family into action - employing all family members - to expand production into varietal grape wines while continuing to make the popular fruit wines.

In addition, a special wine – Island Belle, is made each October. The winery hosts the annual grape picking party on Stretch Island where their vineyard of "Island Belle" grapes is harvested with friends and fellow winelovers. This grape variety is a vinifera (winegrape) cross with a labrusca (concord) variety that was created on Stretch Island by early grapegrowers around the turn of the century. Some of the vines harvested today are upwards of 70 years old.

A visit to Hoodsport Winery

The highwayside location of the Hoodsport Winery makes it a popular stop for vacationers who would like a look at a winery and a taste of wine. Hood Canal is a popular spot for scuba divers and water skiers as well as those seeking the famous shrimp and oysters that do so well in the area. Also offered for sale at the winery are Chocolate Truffles filled with Hoodsport's Raspberry Wine.

The Wines

Hoodsport's fruit wines are hard to find except at the winery as is the Island Belle wine. Take the opportunity to sample these specialties. Hoodsport has also become well known for their Lemberger, Gewürztraminer and other grape varietals. The special Raspberry dessert wine was a favorite with our Best of the Northwest panel. See page 35.

Johnson Creek Winery

19248 Johnson Creek
Rd. S.E., Tenino, WA
98589 • (206) 264-2100
Owner & Winemaker:
  Vincent de Bellis, Sr.
First Year: 1984

Winery History

As proprietor of Alice's Restaurant in Tenino, (with his wife Ann), Vincent de Bellis had an interest in providing a unique wine experience to accompany the meals at their fine country dinner house. A small vineyard is planted next to the restaurant and winery, but most grapes are purchased from Eastern Washington vineyards.

A visit to Johnson Creek Winery

The best way to visit Johnson Creek Winery is to call and make dinner reservations at Alice's Restaurant. The featured country fare includes such items as baked ham, country spare ribs, chicken, rabbit, pheasant, quail and other game. The five course meal is reasonably priced and includes a tour of the winery and a free wine tasting of Johnson Creek wine before dinner. Other visits to the winery may be arranged by contacting the owners for an appointment.

The Wines

Vincent de Bellis' wines are available only at the restaurant or by special arrangement with the owner. Cabernet Sauvignon and Lemberger take their place alongside several white varieties including Blush Riesling, Chenin Blanc and Chardonnay.

Lopez Island Vineyards

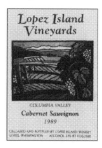

Rt. 2, Box 3096
Fishermans Bay Road
Lopez Island, WA
98261 • (206) 468-3644

Owners:
Brent Charnley,
Maggie Nilan
First Year: 1991
Winery Capacity:
2,000 Gallons

Tasting Room Hours:
Summer: Wednesday
through Sunday, Noon
to 5 PM, Winter:
weekends only
Closed Christmas
through March 15th.

Winery History

Lopez Island Vineyards is a small family-run winery, growing grapes and making wine in the San Juan archipeligo. The vineyard consists of unique, high quality varieties (certified organically grown), selected for growing in the rain shadow of the Olympic Mountains. Also produced are wines from well-known vinifera grape varieties grown in Eastern Washington.

A visit to Lopez Island Vineyards

The owners invite you to come by the small stone and timber winery for a tasting and a visit. Take the ferry from Anacortes (or east from Victoria, B.C.) and follow the road southwest to Fisherman Bay Road.

The Wines

Brent Charnley, as winemaker for Mount Baker Vineyard in the mid-1980s, learned the making of Madeleine Angevine and other cool-weather varietals. His lineup at Lopez Island Vineyards inclues Cabernet Sauvignon and Chardonnay made from grapes grown in Eastern Washington.

Washington State

Lost Mountain Winery

3174 Lost Mtn. Road
Sequim, WA 98382
(206) 683-5229

Owner & Winemaker:
Romeo J. Conca
First Year: 1981
Winery Capacity:
1,500 Gallons
1991 Production:
1,300 Gallons

Tasting Room Hours:
By arrangement or by
chance
Annual Open Winery:
Last week of June and
first week of July

Winery History

Romeo Conca remembers fondly the wines he made with his father (a famous chef) during his boyhood in Connecticut. These were red wines of Italian style, strong in flavor and rich in body and texture. Those are the wines that Romeo Conca strives to produce today at Lost Mountain Winery.

Trained as a research chemist, Romeo combines the technical and mystical aspects of fermentation science as he cajolls every last bit of character out of a load of grapes. After his retirement, he found his Shangri-la in the mountains above Sequim and began making wine as a leisure pastime. As production increased, the winery went commercial and now serves a clientele of locals and visitors.

A visit to Lost Mountain Winery

Set well back in the forested foothills of the Olympic Mountains, the winery occupies the basement of Romeo's comfortable home. It is here that wine is made from grapes purchased in California and Eastern Washington. If you're keen on birdwatching, then bring your binoculars to Romeo's neighborhood to check out some of the local fauna. Hummingbird feeders attract the common local species during the spring and summer.

Just after crossing the Dungeness River (westbound on Hwy. 101) turn left on Taylor Cutoff Road. Head toward the hills turning right just before you descend to the fish hatchery. Watch for Lost Mountain Road as you ascend from the valley and watch for the address on the driveway signpost.

The Wines

Romeo Conca makes his wines from the heart. Whether you revel in his Cabernet or Merlot or enjoy a glass of Lost Mountain Red ("Here's a red wine your Grandmother will like!"), you'll know your gaining more than just a refreshing tipple.

McCrea Cellars

12707 - 18th St. S.E.
Lake Stevens, WA
98258 • (206) 334-5248

Owner & Winemaker:
Douglas McCrea
First Year: 1988
Winery Capacity:
2,000 Gallons
1991 Production:
1,100 Gallons

Winery History

Barrel-fermented Chardonnay and red wines produced from Rhone varietals Grenache and Syrah are the emphasis at this micro-winery. Doug McCrea strives to achieve elegance, balance and richness in his wines by carefully nurturing the essence of each vineyard's unique fruit flavors. In 1993 the winery will relocate southeast of Olympia where both home and production facility will be contructed at a lovely rural site with a stunning view of Mt. Rainier. A delightful after-noon's journey to this often un-

explored area of Puget Sound awaits the wine enthusiast. Tours and tastings available by appointment. McCrea Cellars new winery address (effective fall of 1993) is 13443 - 118th Ave. S.E., Rainier, WA 98576. Please call "information" for Yelm, WA after August 1st for the new phone number.

The Wines

Doug McCrea crafts his unique varietals by traditional, labor-intensive methods. Production is small and distribution is limited but his wines are worth seeking out. Both his Grenache-blend "Mariah" and his Chardonnay received high praise from our **Best of the Northwest** panels. See reviews on pages 22 and 24.

Mount Baker Winery

4298 Mt. Baker Hwy.
Everson, WA 98247
(206) 592-2300

Owners: Randy Finley,
Dr. Albert Stratton
Winemaker:
Stan Petelinz
First Release: 1982
Winery Capacity:
30,000 Gallons
1991 Production:
10,000 Gallons

Tasting Room Hours:
Wednesday through
Sunday, 11 AM to 5 PM

Winery History

The long, mild growing season of Washington's Nooksack Valley provides a perfect microclimate for the growing of Mount Baker Vineyards favored varietals. Experimentation by viticulturalist Albert Stratton with over 100 varietals led to the planting of Chardonnay, Gewürztraminer, Madeline Angevine, Müller-Thurgau, Pinot Noir, Sauvignon Blanc and others.

A new infusion of interest and capital has come from retired movie theater owner Randy Finley. Finley has brought new life to the winery by creating culinary events that feature Mount Baker wines. Call the winery for details of upcoming opportunities to visit and participate in these special dinners.

A visit to Mount Baker Vineyards

The drive to Mount Baker from Interstate 5 serves to soothe the soul as one passes from freeway construction and growing clusters of condominiums to rural residences and finally to the quiet of farm and field disturbed only by the sound of birds and the rush of the Nooksack River. Bring your picnic lunch to enjoy on the deck or under the spreading cedar trees nearby. Visitors can gain valuable insights into the region, climate and winery-specific varietals poured for tasting.

The Wines

The cool-climate varietals grown at Mount Baker Vineyards include Madeleine Angevine, Siegerrebe, and others. Some grapes are purchased from Eastern Washington to make Cabernet Sauvignon.

Washington State

Neuharth Winery

148 Still Road
Sequim, WA 98382
(206) 683-9652

Owners: Mr. and Mrs.
Eugene Neuharth
Winemaker:
Dan Caudill
First Year: 1979
Winery Capacity:
4,400 Gallons
1991 Production:
3,500 Gallons

Tasting Room Hours:
Summer (5/15 to 10/1):
Daily, 9:30 AM to 5:30
PM, Winter: Wed. thru
Sun., 12 - 5 PM
Tours and large groups
by appointment only.

Winery History

Gene Neuharth came north from California to retire from the grape growing business only to find himself making homemade wine and then opening a winery. His first wines were made from Washington and California grapes. Current production is limited to Washington-grown grapes exclusively.

A visit to Neuharth Winery

The winery is located only a half-mile from downtown Sequim with views of pastoral farmland and the Olympic Mountain foothills. Inside you'll find a comfortable tasting room with windows looking out into the winery and bottling room. The selection of wines for tasting echoes the winery's slogan of producing "fine dinner wines", dry or almost dry wines to complement seafood or meats as an enhancement of life.

The winery building dates to the 1930's when it began life as a barn for a dairy farm. The huge wooden structure is constructed of massive cedar logs in a post-and-beam method yielding a cavernous interior space visible from the tasting room windows.

The Wines

Neuharth's proprietary "Dungeness" table wines are among the best values in Washington wine providing full flavor and a balanced palate to accompany any meal. The Dungeness white is flavorful and crisp and is perfect with crab. The Dungeness Red is a Beaujolais-style wine that can be drunk with a meal or used for sipping with cheese and crackers.

Manfred Vierthaler Winery

17136 Hwy. 410 East
Sumner, WA 98390
(206) 863-1633

Owner/Winemaker:
Manfred J. Vierthaler
First Year: 1976
Winery Capacity:
40,000 Gallons

Tasting Room Hours:
Daily, Noon to 6 PM

Winery History

The Manfred J. Vierthaler Winery stands as a local landmark above the Puyallup Valley, a monument to strong will and almost two decades of hard work to make a business succeed. The winery's owner and winemaker has forged a place in the local community by offering a wide variety of wines to travelers heading to Chinook Pass from Tacoma and Seattle.

The Swiss-style chalet is home not only to the Vierthaler Winery but to the Roofgarden Restaurant owned and operated by the Vierthalers. The restaurant fare is also of widely varying origin – everything from traditional German dishes to hippopotamus and wild boar. The tables are neatly arranged to make the most of the view of the Puyallup Valley below.

A visit to Manfred Vierthaler Winery

The unique winery tasting room offers a chance to sample the wines and hear about their making.

The Wines

Manfred Vierthaler's wines follow a non-Northwest tradition of being named for internationally famous wine regions as well as varietal grapes. Chablis, Cream Sherry, Burgundy and Rhine are presented alongside Riesling and Chardonnay.

Whidbey Island Vineyard

5237 So. Langley Rd.
Langley, WA 98260
(206) 221-2040

Owners: Gregory & Elizabeth Osenbach
First Year: 1991
Winery Capacity: 1,200 Gallons

Tasting Room Hours:
Friday, 2 to 6 PM
Sat./Sun., 12 to 5 PM

Winery History

Scenic Whidbey Island offers many things to visitors and residents alike. The natural beauty of this jewel of Puget Sound is undeniable and the historical and cultural aspects of the small island communities are unique and interesting. Langley, with its artists, booksellers and small cafes, offers an intellectual side to island life and it is here that Whidbey Island Winery follows the example of other Puget Sound area wineries in growing locally suitable grapes for estate-bottled wines.

A visit to Whidbey Island Vineyard

The distinctive red barn of Whidbey Island Winery is unmistakable along Langley Road. A picnic area adjacent to the winery building offers a tranquil view of the vineyard and a decades-old apple orchard.

The Wines

A proprietary "Island White" of Madeleine Angevine, Madeleine Sylvaner and Müller Thurgau is a refreshing sipping wine – well balanced and characterful. A pleasant version of Siegerrebe is available as well as Rhubarb wine and a Lemberger made from grapes grown in Eastern Washington.

Washington State

The Whidbeys facility in Greenbank on Whidbey Island

Whidbeys

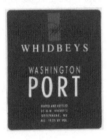

Wonn Road off High-
way 525
Greenbank, WA 98253
(206) 678-7700

Owners: Stimson Lane
Wine and Spirits
First Year: 1985
Winery Capacity:
134,000 Gallons

Tasting Room Hours:
Daily, 10 AM - 4:30 PM

Winery History

Located on Whidbey Island, this wonderful
loganberry farm-turned-winery was opened to public visits in 1985 by Stimson Lane Wine & Spirits.
The historic buildings date back to the turn of the
century when school was held for local youngsters
in the farm's barn. The first loganberry vines were
planted in the 1940s with total plantings now at 125
acres. The crop is harvested each year by more than
75 island residents who have come to enjoy the
traditional summer employment as more than a job.

A visit to Whidbeys

A scenic ferry ride from Mukilteo to Clinton
and a short drive up the island leads to the visitor
center at Whidbeys – arranged so that tourists can
guide themselves through an exhibit detailing the
farm's operation and the making of the loganberry
liqueur. Antiques and decor echo Whidbey Island's
nautical flavor. Outside there are picnic tables for
casual snacking and manicured lawns for strolling
about. The tasting room offers tasting and sales of
Chateau Ste. Michelle wines (Whidbeys' sister winery) as well as gift items and picnic supplies.
Whidbeys Liqueur, being a proof spirit in the eyes of
the State Liquor Board, is not available for sampling
but may be purchased.

The Wines

Whidbeys Liqueur, produced from the farm's
loganberries, is a popular cordial and is also used as
a flavor base or as a fruity accent for desserts, entrees
and beverages. Alcohol content is 22%.

A Port-style wine of Cabernet Sauvignon is
available under the Whidbey's label and a fruity
loganberry wine has also been released.

Olympic Peninsula & Puget Sound Accommodations & Dining

The Olympic Peninsula and the shore-side communities of Puget Sound offer many choices for accommodations and dining. The further reaches of the region are unspoiled nature at its best and provide for great family outings. The brief listings here are but a sampling of many available.

Poulsbo

Manor Farm Inn - 26069 Big Valley Road off Hwy. 3, Pouslbo, WA 98370 (206) 779-4628 Country charm with city amenities and livestock to boot! Robin and Jill Hughes offer guest rooms with private baths, cottages for more privacy and conference facilities. In addition the restaurant on the premises is one of the finest on the Peninsula. Strolling the working farm, relaxing in the hot tub and enjoying a leisurely breakfast (served at 9:00 AM) are but a few of the temptations.

Port Townsend

The James House B & B – 1238 Washington St., Port Townsend, 98368, (206)385-1238 A collection of 12 rooms beautifully furnished in Victorian style, some with private bath, some with a terrific view of Puget Sound, some with both. Continental breakfast. Children over 12 only, no pets.

Fort Worden State Park – (206) 385-4730 For the budget conscious or those with a large family, this is the place to stay. Accommodations range from restored multi-bedroom homes (officers quarters) to youth hostel dormitories to campsites and trailer/RV hookups. Bring the kids and the dog.

Chuckanut Drive (Bow)

Oyster Creek Inn, 190 Chuckanut Drive, Bow, WA 98232, (206) 766-6179 Doug Charles keeps the seafood fresh and the preparations original at the Oyster Creek Inn. Renowned for their selection of Northwest wines, the restaurant hosts special retrospective tastings of Cabernet every year or two. Lunch and dinner daily.

Whidbey Island

The Inn at Langley - 400 - 1st St., (P.O. Box 835), Langley, WA 98260 (206) 221-3033 Exploring the quaint shops in Langley, visiting nearby wineries or simply relaxing and enjoying the view of Saratoga Passage, The Inn at Langley can be your convenient base of operations. Muted Northwest decor accents 24 guest rooms featuring fine views and fireplaces. Dinner is offered in the Inn's dining room on weekends.

Sequim/Dungeness

Groveland Cottage B & B - 1673 Sequim-Dungeness Way, Dungeness, WA 98382 - (206) 683-3565 On the road that eventually leads to the Three Crabs restaurant, Groveland Cottage is close by to the activities of the area, but removed from the hustle and bustle of Highway 101. An expanded beach house circa 1900, the charm of the place has survived despite modernizing of facilities. Owner Simone Nichols is keeps the guests coming back with delicious food and service that is efficient but not hovering.

The 3 Crabs, 101 Three Crabs Rd., Dungeness (206) 683-4264 The friendly, homey atmosphere is hard to beat but the marine view would be better with larger windows. Good seafood, even better service! Waitresses who like kids, too! Fresh fish market next door for take-out.

Port Angeles

C'est si Bon, 2300 Highway 101 E. (206) 452-8888 If you want a wonderful French meal on this side of the Hood Canal then you'll have to visit C'est si Bon. White linens, good wine list. Dinner only. Tu- Sun.

Olympic Peninsula and Puget Sound
Activities for Young and Old

Olympic Peninsula

Fort Worden State Park -
Port Townsend
Let the kids run wild on the sand dunes and play in the old gun emplacements while mom and dad surf-fish or bask in the sun. Lots of clean restrooms in this state park and a little grocery store and an aquarium and camping . . .

Port Townsend Shopping -
Dozens of shops are eager to take your money for antiques, trinkets, cards, shirts, wine, everything under the sun. When you're shopped out, grab a sandwich or a snack at one of the delis and restaurants that line Water Street.

Olympic Game Farm - Dungeness Zebras and Tigers and Bears, oh MY! Check out these and other wild animals at close range and enjoy the performing bears and the kids petting farm.

Dungeness Spit Wildlife Area -
If you enjoy birdwatching and your kids enjoy beachwalking then bring your binoculars and tennis shoes for this fantastic natural seabird habitat. No dogs allowed.

Olympic Rain Forest -
With more than 140 inches of rain a year, the forest is thick and mossy. A natural wonder not to be missed. Sol Duc Hot Springs is one interesting side trip that takes in this attraction.

Hurricane Ridge - south of Port Angeles exit is clearly marked from Hwy. 101. This drive up into the Olympic Mountains offers spectacular panoramic views and wild flowers in summer months and white views with cross country skiing and slippery roads in the winter. Check your anti-freeze level in either season because the elevation gain can cause boil-overs.

Puget Sound

San Juan Islands
Lopez Island
Starting with the smallest of the three important islands served by Washington State Ferry, Lopez Island is also the only one with a working, full-time winery. See listing on preceding pages. If you are the active type, you'll arrive on the ferry with your bicycle, backpack and sense of adventure. Lopez is mostly flat so the cycling is easy and the rural, sleepy atmosphere doesn't at all interfere with having a relaxing ride. Odlin County Park and Spencer Spit State Park offer camping and several quaint restaurants are wine-friendly in tiny Lopez Village.

San Juan Island
Famed for its many attractions and historic significance, San Juan Island has recently become the whale-watching capitol of Puget Sound, if not the entire west coast. The main population center is Friday Harbor where the University of Washington Oceanographic Center gives tours in summer and The Whale Museum is open daily. Roche Harbor on the northern tip of the island was developed by lime magnate John McMillin and features many historic sites, a variety of accommodations and a large "boatel" for wandering sailors. Don't miss the spooky mausoleum in the woods, eek!

Orcas Island
The most developed of the major islands featuring many small villages on the several bays that finger into the southern coastline of the island. Rosario Resort, Moran State Park (visit Mount Constitution for the view), and Deer Harbor are spots not to be missed. Plenty of funky shopping, dining and accommodations in true island style.

Late Harvest Wines and Their Terminology

As the harvest season comes and goes, most of the grapes are crushed and fermented into wine to begin their journey to your table, picnic or favorite restaurant. Certain varieties, however, have proven over the years to yield remarkable dessert-style wines if allowed to "hang" unpicked on the vine for a few extra days or weeks. These "late harvest" wines are a tradition in Europe as Sauternes (France) or Auslese (Germany, Austria, Switzerland) and are among the most prized wines available anywhere in the world.

An interesting phenomenon sometimes takes place as the grapes over-ripen in the vineyard. The noble rot, botrytis cinerea, attacks the grape clusters, thinning the skin of each grape so that moisture from within can evaporate. The resulting concentration of sugar and flavor – along with the special honey-like flavor of the botrytis – is the secret to these delectable sweet wines.

Late harvest wines in the Northwest are most often made from Riesling and Gewürztraminer. Occasional use of Chenin Blanc, Sauvignon Blanc and Semillon has provided interesting examples for evaluation but few standouts. Some wineries have access to specific vineyard sites where climatic conditions make possible flavorful late harvest wines each year. If you find a producer with a tasty late harvest, check back each year and you'll probably find another!

In 1971 the German wine industry established uniform standards defining the minimum requirements for making late harvest wines. Based on the sugar content of the grapes at harvest, each category is slightly sweeter and often provides wines of greater flavor concentration and character. A similar system is in use on an informal basis in the Northwest with the following categories:

No Designation

Dry style wines. Minimum sugar content of grapes is 17° to 24° brix (percent sugar by weight) with residual sugar at bottling less than 4%.

Late Harvest

White wine grapes picked in an overripe condition with some incidence of botrytis cinerea mold. Minimum sugar is 24° brix with residual sugar at bottling of at least 4% but not more than 10%.

Select Cluster or Select Late Harvest

Picked only from grapes infected with botrytis, and having a minimum sugar level at harvest of 27.5° brix. Residual sugar of the resulting wine is less than 15% by weight.

Individual Bunch Selected

Picked clusters must be completely infected by botrytis with minimum sugar content of 32° brix. Residual sugar from 15% to 19.9%.

Dry Berry Selection or Individual Dry Berry Selection

Picked berries are partially or completely raisined and have been infected by botrytis. Minimum sugar of 38° brix. Residual sugar greater than 20%.

Ice Wine

Grapes must be hard frozen on the vines at the time of harvest. Sugar at harvest a minimum of 35° briz and residual in wine of 18% or more.

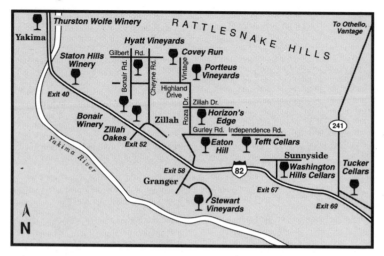

Yakima Valley Touring – West End

The West Yakima Valley offers a broad range of wineries more spread out along Interstate 82 than the cluster of vintners assembled at Prosser. We'll begin just east of Yakima.

Exit 40 from the freeway takes you up Gangl Road to visit Staton Hills Winery - a beautiful place with warm weather picnicing on the patio and cool weather warming by their large stone fireplace in the tasting room.

Exit 52 at Zillah leads you first to the Zillah Oakes facility (part of the Covey Run operation) near the freeway. By following Cheyne Road to Highland Drive you can then turn left to visit Bonair Winery where Gail and Shirley Puryear offer a warm welcome. Continue north on Cheyne Road to Gilbert Road and turn left to find Hyatt Vineyards winery. The large Hyatt vineyard surrounds the winery with its picturesque windmill and picnic area. Returning to Highland Drive, follow signs eastbound to Vintage Lane and Covey Run. The Covey Run winery is a larger operation and features expansive decks and patios for picnicking with views of the vineyards. Follow Highland Drive further east (it turns into Houghton Road) and watch for a left turn to Portteus Vineyards winery. Paul Portteus has been growing excellent Cabernet, Merlot and other varietals for over 10 years but opened his own winery in 1990. Tom and Hema Campbell welcome you to their Horizon's Edge Winery on East Zillah Drive featuring a wonderful valley view from the tasting loft window. The historic Rinehold Cannery Homestead is home to Eaton Hill Winery on Gurley Road. Continue east to Independence Road to visit Pam and Joel Tefft at Tefft Cellars.

Crossing under Interstate 82 at Granger just south of Eaton Hill, you'll enjoy a short drive through cherry orchards along Cherry Hill Road to Stewart Vineyards winery. Taste wine above the cherry tree-tops on the deck with a view of the valley!

Return to I-82 and travel ten miles to exit 67 where a left turn north leads to Lincoln Ave. and Washington Hills Cellars. A courtyard for picnicking adjoins the tasting room and gift shop. A couple of miles further east on I-82, take exit 69 to pickup Highway 12 for a visit to Tucker Cellars winery and produce market. Garden fresh vegetables and fruits from Tucker Farms accompany a pleasant wine tasting stop.

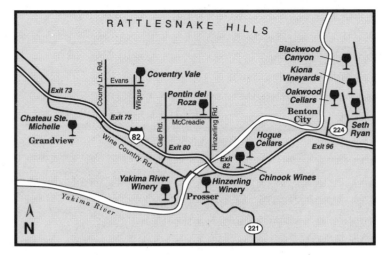

Yakima Valley Touring – East End

Note: if you're still on day one and have completed the west end tour, you should strongly consider dinner and a good nights sleep before continuing!

The east end tour begins in Grandview where Chateau Ste. Michelle operates a red wine production facility. This winery has been in operation continuously since 1937. A new facility at Canoe Ridge along the Columbia River may take over much of the production now occurring at Grandview.

Just east in Prosser no fewer than five wineries await your inspection. On the west side, Yakima River Winery is but a short drive out North River Road. John and Louise Rauner offer their wines in the barrel filled tasting room. A few miles north of I-82 on Hinzerling Road, members of the Pontin family welcome visitors to Pontin del Roza winery.

Closest to downtown Prosser is Hinzerling Vineyards winery where the owners host the tasting room and offer tours of the winery that began much of the current wine enthusiasm by planting grapes in the early 1970s.

Just east of town Clay Mackey and Kay Simon welcome visitors to Chinook Wines tasting room on Wine Country Road. A small but exceedingly friendly operation hosted by two of Washington's most knowledgeable wine/grape scientists. Further east on Wine Country Road is The Hogue Cellars winery. You can sample Hogue's wines and also try some of the prepared fruits or vegetables from Hogue Ranches. A dandy gift shop here includes something for almost everyone.

Travel east on I-82 from Prosser about 15 miles to the Benton City exit where you follow signs to Highway 224 to Richland. Oakwood Cellars awaits you on Demoss Road where Bob and Evelyn Skelton offer tasting and tours of their operation. Up the highway, a short drive down Sunset Road leads to Seth Ryan winery, Kiona Vineyards and Blackwood Canyon winery. This group of wineries share the microclimate of Red Mountain, an area well-known for the production of intense and flavorful Cabernet, Merlot and other wines.

Kiona offers the most complete visitor facilities in the area with a spacious, air-conditioned tasting room and a large expanse of lawn that beckons kite flyers, picnickers and general leg-stretching recreation. The other Red Mountain wineries offer pleasant tasting experiences, often with the owners or winemaker.

Washington State

Blackwood Canyon

Rt. 2, Box 2169H
Sunset Road
Benton City, WA
99320 • (509) 588-6249

Owner & Winemaker:
M. Taylor Moore
First Year: 1983
Winery Capacity:
70,000 Gallons
1991 Production:
35,000 Gallons

Tasting Room Hours:
Weekends, 10 AM to
6 PM or by chance.

Winery History
Mike Moore of Blackwood Canyon continues on the road back from the disastrous fire of 1985 that destroyed his winery building and thousands of gallons of wine. A new building and tasting room welcome visitors for informative tasting sessions with the winemaker.

A visit to Blackwood Canyon Winery
Out Sunset Road past the entrance to Kiona Vineyards, Blackwood Canyon Winery is perched on the edge of the ridge above the Yakima River. A fabulous view of the Yakima Valley extends west as far as the eye can see. Winemaker/owner Mike Moore is often on hand to pour wine from current releases and to explain his philosophies about wine-making and grape growing.

The Wines
Recent vintages have provided opportunities for Mike Moore to explore the complexities of vinting late harvest wines from record-setting sweet must. Besides the enticing late harvest Riesling and Gewürztraminer, Mike creates some very intense barrel-fermented Chardonnay and Sémillon. Prolonged lees contact and use of toasty French oak have resulted in very characterful versions of these varietals. Cabernet Sauvignon, Merlot and Pinot Noir are the reds crafted at Blackwood Canyon.

Bonair Winery

500 S. Bonair Rd.
Zillah, WA 98953
(509) 829-6027

Manager:
Shirley Puryear
Winemaker:
Mr. Gail Puryear
First Year: 1985
Winery Capacity:
12,000 Gallons
1991 Production:
7,500 Gallons

Winery History
After a number of years in California, Gail and Shirley Puryear returned to their native Yakima Valley to grow grapes and make wine. The dream that began on the outskirts of Zillah in 1979 is now a full-blown reality with several wines winning awards and the tasting room brimming with interested visitors.

A home winemaker for more than a decade, Gail traded in his carboys for stainless steel tanks and French oak barrels to begin making commerical quantities of Chardonnay, Johannisberg Riesling and Cabernet Sauvignon from the 1985 crush. The addition of a new building in 1988 doubled the floor space of the winery and provided a larger tasting room and office facilities.

A visit to Bonair Winery
One of the most friendly welcomes you'll ever receive at a winery comes from Shirley Puryear at Bonair. Her enthusiasm for the wines and winery operation are high and her friendly interest in every

Tasting Room Hours:
Daily, 10 AM to 5 PM
Midwinter: weekends
only or call for an ap-
pointment

visitor to the tasting room makes everyone feel at home. If you're a visitor from a far-flung locale, Shirley will even put a pin in their world map to make a permanent record of your visit!

The new tasting room has made a big difference with room for more visitors to taste and roam about the displays of gift items and wine. Outside, a shady gazebo and picnic area entices an alfresco meal with a view of Mount Adams. The friendly winery dog Filter Pad (Paddy for short) has been joined by winery cat Pussy Galore.

The Wines

Bonair Winery enjoys a reputation for rich and flavorful Chardonnay and Cabernet with several vineyard-designated bottlings often available. Cabernet Sauvignon is in short supply and is sold mostly at the winery. Barrel-fermented Dry Riesling has become a favorite in recent years complementing the Johannisberg off-dry bottling. Sunset blush wine and Nouveau Rouge red are popular picnic wines with winery visitors.

Chateau Ste. Michelle

205 W. 5th
Grandview, WA 98930
(509) 882-3928

Owners: Stimson Lane
Wine and Spirits
Winemakers: Mike
Januik, Charlie
Hoppes, Gordie Hill
First Year: 1937
Winery Capacity:
240,000 Gallons

Tasting Room Hours:
Daily, 10 AM to
4:30 PM

Winery History

The smallest of Stimson Lane Wine and Spirits Northwest wine operations, Grandview has the historical significance of being the oldest operating winery in Washington State. The building was bonded as a winery in 1937 and now produces much of Chateau Ste. Michelle's red wines. A new red wine facility is being constructed at Canoe Ridge near the Columbia Crest winery. This state-of-the-art winery will probably mean the retirement of the Grandview winery - stay tuned.

A visit to Chateau Ste. Michelle - Grandview

A visit to this winery is most informative in late September or early October when the red wines are fermenting. Huge epoxy-lined, concrete tanks hold the grape skins and juice creating the deep ruby-colored wine. Tours of the operation have been scaled back, but if you visit during harvest (early to mid-October) you can probably sneak a peek at the rush to crush that takes place at the winery.

The tasting room here is rather plain but is well-stocked with wine, gifts and gourmet edibles. Please note that this is Chateau Ste. Michelle's least touristed facility and you won't encounter the crowds found in Woodinville on a summer weekend. Take advantage of this opportunity to talk with your host and sample the wines produced here at Grandview

Continued on next page

Washington State

and at the other Chateau Ste. Michelle facilities.

During the harvest season, many Yakima Valley wineries enter teams in the "Grandview Grape Stomp." This traditional celebration of the successful harvest features grapes being crushed by foot in a fastest is bestest competition. Held on the 3rd Saturday in September each year.

The Wines

For the time being, all red wines labeled Chateau Ste. Michelle are crushed and fermented in the Grandview winery. Many of these wines are transferred to the Woodinville winery for finishing and bottling, but their life begins here in the wine country. A luxury afforded the winemakers at Chateau Ste. Michelle is the ability to hold red wines for release later (by a year, or often two) than other, smaller wineries. Chateau Ste. Michelle Cabernet Sauvignon and Merlot are thus more ready for at-time-of-purchase consumption and offer rich, complex aromas and flavors. Seek out some of the vineyard-designated red wines sold at the winery for the most exciting tasting experiences.

Chinook Wines

P.O. Box 387
Wine Country Road at
Wittkopf Road
Prosser, WA 99350
(509) 786-2725

Owners/Winemakers:
Kay Simon and
Clay Mackey
First Year: 1983
Winery Capacity:
5,000 Gallons
1987 Production:
4,500 Gallons

Tasting Room Hours:
Friday, Saturday and
Sunday, Noon to 5 PM
or by appointment.
Closed Christmas until
President's holiday.

Winery History

Chinook Wines was born of the union between an enologist and a viticulturist. The winemaker, Kay Simon, is one of the most experienced in the Northwest with over a dozen successful harvests to her credit while her equally talented husband, Clay Mackey, tends to the farming side of the business, nurturing the grapevines so important to the production of quality wine. Kay and Clay were married in August of 1984 on a date that celebrated the release of the first Chinook wine.

The winery and tasting room occupy several buildings that were once part of a small farm. Remodelling of all components is now complete and the winery capacity is just perfect for hands-on operation by the owners.

A visit to Chinook Winery

This visit is a must for serious winelovers. The two owners are not only charming and friendly but hold a wealth of knowledge about all aspects of wine - both art and science. The picnic area under a spreading oak tree offers the visitor a chance to relax on the lawn after a taste of Chinook's wines in the quaint tasting room.

Clay Mackey and Kay Simon of Chinook.

The Wines

Kay Simon and Clay Mackey creatively craft Chardonnay, Sauvignon Blanc and Semillon in a dry style that is a wonderful complement to food. The Merlot, released each year on Memorial Day with a wonderful accompanying barbecue, is deliciously fruity and full when released but can benefit from a year or two of further bottle age in your cellar. All Chinook wines were highly rated by the tasting panels for the **Best of the Northwest**.

Coventry Vale Winery

Wilgus & Evans Roads
P. O. Box 249
Grandview, WA 98930
(509) 882-4100

President:
Reed McKinley
Winemakers:
Tom Sans Souci
First Year: 1983
Winery Capacity:
1,000,000 Gallons

Visits by appointment only.

Winery History

Originally known in the Northwest wine industry as a "custom crush" facility, Coventry Vale produced wine for many Yakima Valley and Columbia Valley wineries who did not have the tank space for their own winemaking efforts.

Vineyard owner David Wyckoff was the original driving force behind Coventry Vale with a background in agriculture and extensive holdings in the Yakima Valley. Processing equipment for his vineyards was a logical next step. His investment in thousands of gallons of cooperage (mostly stainless steel tanks) and modern crushers and presses led others to his winery to process their grapes.

Although Coventry Vale is a fascinating, busy winery crammed with the best of modern winemaking equipment, no tours or visits are offered. Appointments can be made to look through the facility.

Washington State
Covey Run Wines

1500 Vintage Road
Zillah, WA 98953
(509) 829-6235

Owners:
General Partnership
**Winemaker &
General Manager:**
David Crippen
First Year: 1982
Winery Capacity:
90,000 Gallons
1991 Production:
90,000 Gallons

Tasting Room Hours:
Monday thru Saturday,
10 AM to 5 PM
Sunday, Noon to 5 PM

Winery History

The Quail Run Vintners winery began in 1980 as a partnership of fruit growers diversifying into winegrapes. Two vineyard sites were planted in the Yakima Valley, one near Prosser and the other at the present winery site near Zillah. Stan Clarke was hired to oversee the vineyard operation, Wayne Marcil was hired from Monterey Peninsula Winery to become the winemaker. The grapes flourished and the rest would have been history save a minor disruption by Quail Ridge winery of California who squawked about name similarity and forced the change of Quail Run's label to Covey Run. But the wine behind the label didn't suffer and today Covey Run offers a broad range of quality varietals.

U.C. Davis-trained David Crippen came on board as winemaker in 1988 and now handles the operation of Covey Run as General Manager.

A visit to Covey Run

Visiting the Covey Run Winery outside of Zillah is a treat. The expansive decks and patios overlook the vineyards and provide an excellent opportunity to picnic. Inside the spacious tasting room, large windows look down to the winery operation below.

The Wines

A wide range of quality varietals is offered by Covey Run and our **Best of the Northwest** tasting panels found many of them worthy of review. See tasting notes on Merlot, Chardonnay, Fumé Blanc, Riesling and Chenin Blanc beginning on page 20.

Cuvée Montagne

9900 Bittner Road
Yakima, WA 98901
(509) 575-3747

Owner/Winemaker:
Rob Stuart
First Year: 1984

Winery History

Rob and Maria Stuart hand craft their sparkling wine from 100% Oregon Pinot Noir. Barrel fermentation and extended sur lees aging add depth and complexity to their special limited bottling of just 200 to 500 cases each year. The grapes are harvested mostly in southern Oregon and are partially processed there with the remainder of the work done at Staton Hills winery in the Yakima Valley where Rob is winemaker.

A visit to Cuvée Montagne

There is no facility for this brand but you can purchase the wine at many Seattle and Portland wine shops as well as at several restaurants in major Northwest cities. Rob and Maria sometimes enter the wine in festivals where you can sample a glass and chat with the owners/winemaker.

Eaton Hill Winery

Route 1, Box 1117
Gurley Road
Granger, WA 98932
(509) 854-2508

Owners:
Edwin & JoAnn Stear
Winemaker:
Edwin Stear
First Year: 1988

Tasting Room Hours:
Daily (except Thursday)
10 AM to 5 PM

Winery History

Scientist Edwin Stear has extensive background and experience in the business of technology and its application to the real world. Currently serving in several capacities at the University of Washington, he finds time for rest and relaxation in the Yakima Valley by restoring an 80-year-old homestead.

The "home" part of the Rinehold Cannery Homestead has been in operation as a bed and breakfast since 1985, offering rooms to business travellers and tourists staying in the Valley.

The "cannery" part of the homestead is beginning life as the Eaton Hill Winery producing 1,500 gallons of Riesling with the 1988 harvest. The restoration of the 12,000 square foot winery building has been more involved than Dr. Stear anticipated. The winemaking experience Dr. Stear gained as a large production "home" winemaker contributes the necessary skill to operate the winery. The tasting room for the fledgling winery is in the corner of the winery building.

A visit to Eaton Hill Winery

Not far from I-82 exit 58, around Punkin Corner on Gurley Road, is Rinehold Cannery Homestead and Eaton Hill Winery.

The Wines

Expansion of winemaking is underway but currently all that is available is the winery's Johannisberg Riesling

Hinzerling Vineyards

1520 Sheridan
Prosser, WA 99350
(509) 786-2163

Owner:
The Wallace Family
Winemaker:
Mike Wallace
First Year: 1976
Winery Capacity:
15,000 Gallons
1991 Production:
2,600 gallons

Tasting Room Hours:
Monday thru Saturday,
10 AM to 5 PM,
Sunday, Noon to 4 PM

Winery History

More than two decades of winemaking and grape growing sets Hinzerling Vineyards apart from almost every other winery in the state. The winery was begun by Mike Wallace, a pioneer in grape-growing and winemaking in the new era of Washington viticulture.

Upon leaving the Air Force in the late 1960's, Mike studied biology and chemistry at Western Washington State College and then worked at the University of Washington as a research technician. After some enlightening conversations with Dr. Walter Clore, Mike departed for U. C. Davis to do graduate work in viticulture and enology.

Returning to Washington in 1971, a 25 acre vineyard was planted north of Prosser with the purpose of eventual production of fine table wines. In 1976 the wine was made and the die was cast. Hinzerling Vineyards (the name taken from Prosser-area pioneers and the road where the vineyard is

Continued next page

Washington State

planted) has been a consistent producer of quality wine and Mike Wallace is one of Washington wine's strongest advocates. The winery changed hands for a short period during 1988 and 1989 but the Wallace family is back in control with Mike once again at the winemaking helm.

A visit to Hinzerling Vineyards

Visits to the winery present an opportunity to purchase some of the sought after Hinzerling 'library' Cabernet Sauvignon and other wines from vintages past. Tasting and brief tours of the small winery are offered. Come to the winery during harvest and participate in their fall festival "Life Among the Grapes." Write or call the winery for their current newsletter detailing upcoming events.

The Wines

While the Hinzerling reputation was made on Cabernet Sauvignon, several other varietals have become popular recently. Merlot, Dry Gewürztraminer and several Port-style wines are available.

The Hogue Cellars

P.O. Box 31 • Lee Rd.
at Wine Country Rd.
Prosser, WA 99350
(509) 786-4557

Owner: Mike Hogue
Winemaker:
  David Forsyth
**Vineyard Manager and
  General Manager:**
  Wade Wolfe
First Year: 1982
Winery Capacity:
  420,000 Gallons
1991 Production:
  375,000 Gallons

Tasting Room Hours:
Daily, 10 AM to 5 PM

Winery History

Already well-known for many quality agricultural products, The Hogue Cellars burst onto the NW wine scene in the early 1980s with several award-winning wines and since have expanded their repetoire to include many more.

The source for many of the grapes that go into The Hogue Cellars wines are the Hogue Ranches – a 1,200 acre farm that has been producing for the Hogue family since the 1950s. Grape acreage planted in the 1970s totals 300 acres of premium varietals. Winemaker Rob Griffin guided Hogue's operation until 1990 when he left to pursue his Barnard Griffin label and Wade Wolfe came on board to handle winery and vineyard operations. Talented David Forsyth is the creative force behind the current releases of The Hogue Cellars wines. A new winery production building was added in 1990-91 to increase the capacity of the Hogue operation.

A visit to Hogue Cellars

The current winery and tasting room just northeast of Prosser are a must for wine tourists in the area. An attractive tasting bar and gift shop complement a tour of the facility handled by experienced and friendly personnel. The Hogue Ranches prepared fruits and vegetables are also available for sale in the The Hogue Cellars' tasting room.

The Hogue Cellars facility in Prosser, WA.

The Wines

A complete line of quality Hogue Cellars varietals is offered at very reasonable prices. Reserve bottlings, while more pricey, offer added depth, complexity and ageability for avid enophiles. Our **Best of the Northwest** panels found wines by The Hogue Cellars rating highly in many categories. See reviews on pages 15 to 35.

Horizon's Edge Winery

4530 East Zillah Drive
Zillah, WA 98953
(509) 829-6401

Owners: Tom and
 Hema Campbell
Winemaker:
 Tom Campbell
First Year: 1984
Winery Capacity:
 5,000+ Gallons
1991 Production:
 5,250 Gallons

Tasting Room Hours:
Daily, 10 AM to 5 PM

Winery History

Tom Campbell set his sights on winemaking and never looked back. After finishing his studies at U.C. Davis in 1979, Tom worked for Jekel Vineyards in California before relocating to the Yakima Valley. No fewer than four local wineries benefited from his services between 1981 and 1985 when Tom struck out on his own and bonded Horizon's Edge Winery just east of Zillah.

A visit to Horizon's Edge

The winery building stands out behind Tom and Hema Campbell's house. From the second floor tasting loft in the winery you enjoy samples of Horizon's Edge wines as you admire the view across the top of an apple orchard to Mount Rainier and Mount Adams. A new gazebo was added during 1988 to make for improved picnicking around the winery and vineyard.

Continued on next page.

Washington State

The Wines

Tom Campbell has been a winemaker in the Northwest for a long time and he is very talented at working with locally grown fruit. His efforts with Chardonnay and Cabernet Sauvignon have found many followers and the Horizon's Edge sparkling wine has also been well-received. One of the few remaining producers of quality Muscat Canelli, Horizon's Edge offers a dry version and a sweet dessert style, both intensely aromatic and enjoyable. A Dry Riesling and Pinot Noir are also made.

Hyatt Vineyards Winery

2020 Gilbert Road
Zillah, WA 98953
(509) 829-6333

Owners: Leland & Lynda Hyatt
Winemaker: Joel Tefft
First Year: 1987
Winery Capacity: 45,000 Gallons
1991 Production: 16,000 Gallons

Tasting Room Hours: Daily, 11 AM to 5 PM, closed during January

Winery History

Leland and Lynda Hyatt began their adventure with grape growing in the Yakima Valley in the early 1970s growing concord grapes for the local juice plant. The challenge of wine grape growing seemed interesting so they purchased land and planted a vineyard site near Zillah that had been pointed out to them by Dr. Walter Clore. The site proved to be an excellent spot and their high-quality grapes have been sold to many area wineries to produce excellent (and frequently award-winning) wines.

The beautiful view from the vineyard first inspired the Hyatts to build a home there, but they changed their minds and decided to create a winery to utilize some of the production of their 73 acres of wine grapes. Respected vineyardist Wade Wolfe handled the first vintages as both winemaker and vineyard supervisor. Stan Clarke took over both functions for a few years and today Joel Tefft handles the winemaking duties.

A visit to Hyatt Vineyards Winery

The short drive north of Bonair Winery (take either Bonair or Cheyne Road) leads to the Hyatt winery on Gilbert Road. The panoramic view across the valley is enhanced by the broad vineyard and distant views of Mount Adams and Mount Rainier. Wine tasting in the well-appointed tasting room is often presided over by winery owner Lynda Hyatt. A beautifully manicured picnic area provides a welcome place to rest and enjoy your lunch.

The Wines

Hyatt Vineyards' wines have continued the award-winning ways of wines made by other wineries using Hyatt grapes. Look for the Hyatt Merlot and late harvest wines of Riesling and Black Muscat.

Jim Holmes, John Williams and Ann Williams of Kiona Vineyards.

Kiona Vineyards Winery

Route 2, Box 2169E
Sunset Road
Benton City, WA
99320 • (509) 588-6716

Owners:
Jim & Pat Holmes
John & Ann Williams
Winemaker:
Jim Holmes
General Manager:
Scott Williams
Cellarmaster:
Peter Silverberg
Winery Capacity:
30,000 Gallons
1991 Production:
28,000 Gallons

Tasting Room Hours:
Daily, Noon to 5 PM

Winery History

John Williams and Jim Holmes have let their hobby run wild. These two metallurgical engineers from Westinghouse Hanford produce wine in Jim's garage-turned-winery in Richland and then age and bottle it in the basement of John's home-turned-winery in the Kiona (pronounced Ki´ o nah) hills near Benton City.

Kiona's vineyards are out behind John's home on the lower slopes of Red Mountain. A wide variety of grapes are grown there: Chardonnay, Chenin Blanc, White Riesling, Cabernet Sauvignon, Lemberger and Merlot. Before the winery began, these grapes were sold to other wineries and moade many award-winning wines. Most of the grapes now go into wines sold under the Kiona label.

Scott Williams, the son of John and Ann, is a tireless general manager for the winery. Hands-on experience has provided him with keen insights into the realities of winemaking and grape growing.

A visit to Kiona Vineyards Winery

Kiona Vineyards is a great place to visit. The broad expanse of lawn that fronts the vineyard is a perfect place for a casual picnic or a game of frisbee. The tasting room staff is helpful and informative.

The Wines

Jim Holmes has a special fondness for the Lemberger grape which he makes into a rich and supple wine that is aged in oak to mellow out its rough edges and add some complexity. Our tasting panels found Kiona's Lemberger a deserving candidate for **Best of the Northwest** and also other Kiona bottlings: Cabernet Sauvignon, Dry and White Riesling, Chenin Blanc and Chenin Blanc Ice Wine. Reviews begin on page 15.

Washington State

Oakwood Cellars

Route 2, Box 2321
Demoss Road
Benton City, WA
99320 • (509) 588-5332

Owners: Bob and
Evelyn Skelton
Winemaker:
Bob Skelton
First Year: 1986
Winery Capacity:
6,000 Gallons

Tasting Room Hours:
Weekends, 12 to 6 PM
Summers, Wed.-Fri.,
6 to 8 PM

Winery History

Bob and Evelyn Skelton pursue the French family-style winery tradition. The two winery owners spent June of 1988 in Europe studying winemaking techniques at wineries in France and Germany. Insights gained in Chablis shed some new light on Chardonnay production while discussions with German producers of Lemberger offered interesting comparisons of red wine style.

A visit to Oakwood Cellars

Bob and Evelyn are friendly folks who love to talk about their wines. Whether out in the winery working on the wines or in the tasting room sharing the fruits of their labors, the two winery owners have lots of information for wine lovers. Exit 96 from I-82 leads you on to Highway 224 where a left turn onto Demoss Road leads to Oakwood Cellars.

The Wines

Bob Skelton's Riesling and Late Harvest Riesling appeal to those wanting a slightly sweeter wine while his Chardonnay and Semillon are drier wines to accompany food. Merlot and Cabernet are released early and offer a fair amount of tannin for further aging or accompanying robust foods.

Pontin del Roza

Rt. 4, Box 4735
Prosser, WA 99350
(509) 786-4449

Owner: Pontin Family
Winemaker:
Scott Pontin
First Year: 1984
Winery Capacity:
15,000 Gallons

Tasting Room Hours:
Daily, 10 AM to 5 PM

Winery History

Nesto Pontin has farmed along the Roza Canal for over 25 years and his father before him arrived in the Yakima Valley in the 1920's. Now a third generation of Pontins (pronounced pon teen´) has entered the picture with Nesto's son Scott becoming the winemaker for the family winery which was begun in 1984. Scott received training at Columbia Basin College and also at U.C. Davis before undertaking his current role at Pontin del Roza.

A visit to Pontin del Roza

The winery is located north of Prosser on Hinzerling Road just a short 10 minute drive from I-82 (take exit 80, Gap Road). A large shade tree cools a grassy picnic area where winelovers can relax with a bottle of their favorite Pontin del Roza wine. Gifts, snacks and, of course, wines are all available in the tasting room hosted by Scott's sister Diane Pontin-Miller.

The Wines

In addition to a complete line of traditional Washington varietals, Pontin del Roza is the first Washington winery to produce Pinot Gris.

Portteus Winery

P.O. Box 1444
5201 Highland Drive
Zillah, WA 98953
(509) 829-6970

Owner:
 Paul Portteus III & Jr.
Winemaker:
 Paul Portteus III
First Year: 1987
Winery Capacity:
 10,000 Gallons
1991 Production:
 3,500 Gallons

Tasting Room Hours:
Daily, 11 AM to 5 PM,
Sunday, Noon to 5 PM

Winery History

Paul Portteus, Jr. was given a birthday present on his 21st birthday that would change his life. A box of 21 different wines from around the world began his appreciation of fine wine. His familiarity with the fermentation sciences was already well established through his hobby of home brewing beer. Purchase of vineyard land near Zillah in 1980 moved this interest along even further.

Now firmly established in the Zillah community, Paul and his wife Marilyn appreciate the farm-country life. Over a decade of grape-growing has Paul convinced that the land he farms is the finest vineyard land in the state. While some of the vineyard's harvest is sold to other wineries, a wide array of Portteus wines is produced from estate grapes.

A visit to Portteus Winery

At the east end of Highland Drive, an orchard-lined driveway heads north toward the Rattlesnake Mountains and leads to the Portteus vineyards and winery. The tasting bar is set up in the winery building affording a glimpse of production equipment and the tools of the winemaking trade. Paul and Marilyn host the tasting room.

The Wines

Portteus wines are hearty in style and richly structured for the long haul. Enjoy the powerful Cabernet, spicy Zinfandel (the first in Washington), ripe and fruity Merlot or toasty Chardonnay.

Seth Ryan Winery

Rt. 2, Box 2168-01
Sunset Road
Benton City, WA
99320 • (509) 588-6780
Owners/Winemakers:
 Brodzinski and
 Olsen Families
First Year: 1986
Winery Capacity:
 40,000 Gallons
1991 Production:
 800 Gallons

Tasting Room Hours:
Sat./Sun., 12 to 6 PM

Winery History

The proximity to the wine country is luring more and more Richland scientists into the wine-making avocation. Ron and Jo Brodzinski along with Khris Olsen and his father Robert are the owners of the small winery operation that began in the Brodzinski family garage but now occupies a new winery building on Sunset Road near Red Mountain. Ron and Khris are research scientists at Battelle Laboratories while Jo holds a position with the Richland School District. Robert Olsen is retired and lives on the East Coast providing financial and moral support.

A visit to Seth Ryan winery

The new winery facility on Sunset Road brings Seth Ryan wines to the public. Plans for the site include additional visitor amenities.

Continued on next page.

Washington State

The Wines

The winery goal at Seth Ryan is to consistently make quality wines specializing in German-style Gewurztraminer and Riesling, "unique" Chardonnay, Cabernet Sauvignon, Cabernet Franc and Merlot. Chardonnay is barrel fermented to produce a "gorgeous floral nose and superb balance." The Germanic wines offer slight residual sweetness while reds are still aging and awaiting release.

Staton Hills Winery

71 Gangl Road
Wapato, WA 98951
(509) 877-2112

Owners: Washington
  Corporation
Winemaker:
  Rob Stuart
First Year: 1984
Winery Capacity:
  160,000 Gallons
1991 Production:
  100,000 Gallons

Tasting Room Hours:
Tuesday - Sunday,
11 AM to 5 PM
(Summer to 5:30 PM)
(Open on Monday
holidays)
Tours available on
request.

Winery History

When David and Susanne Staton moved to the Yakima Valley 18 years ago there were just the beginnings of a Yakima Valley wine industry. They planted test blocks of vinifera grapes near their orchards and started laying out plans for a first class winery to make first class wines.

The dream became a reality in 1985 with the construction of a striking cedar and glass building just off I-82 east of Yakima. The 4,000 square foot visitor facility features a huge native-rock fireplace set across the room from the long tasting bar. Two story windows provide a spectacular view of the Yakima Valley with Mount Adams in the distance. The Staton's now own less than 10% of the winery but a well-organized corporate team is overseeing progress in both winemaking and sales of the popular Staton Hills wines.

A visit to Staton Hills Winery

The close proximity of Staton Hills to Yakima and particularly to I-82 insures that almost every wine-loving tourist will not get lost finding the place. The owners have provided a real first-class setup and the tasting room staff is friendly and informative. Afternoon visits on weekends can get crowded so plan your visit early in the day.

The Wines

Staton Hills' current production focuses on red wine. Seventy percent of all wine made here is red with the remainder being still white wine and sparkling wine. Cabernet Sauvignon, Pinot Noir, Merlot and Port are joined by Chardonnay and Fume Blanc. Champagne production is being reduced to one style only. Brut Rose is the likely candidate. Staton Hills Cabernet Sauvignon, Chardonnay Reserve and two sparkling wines are reviewed in the **Best of the Northwest** section beginning on page 14.

Stewart Vineyards

1711 Cherry Hill Road
Granger, WA 98932
Mailing Address:
1381 W. Riverside Ave.
Sunnyside, WA 98944
(509) 854-1882

Owners: George and
Martha Stewart
First Year: 1983
Winery Capacity:
23,000 Gallons
1991 Production:
11,000 Gallons

Tasting Room Hours:
Monday to Saturday,
10 AM to 5 PM
Sunday, Noon to 5 PM

Winery History

Since George and Martha Stewart came out to the Northwest in the 1950s, they have found the time for pioneering vineyard sites on the Wahluke Slope and in the Yakima Valley. After watching other wineries win top awards with wines made from their grapes, the Stewarts began the winery operation that bears their name. The choice of a first winemaker was, in hindsight, auspicious as Mike Januik's efforts under the original Stewart label reaped medal after medal. Mike's successor, Scott Benham, continued the winning traditions.

A visit to Stewart Vineyards

The Stewart Vineyard winery and tasting room is located near Granger atop a hill surrounded by cherry orchards that literally reach right out to the winery. The Cherry Blossom Festival is held the first weekend in April. A few weeks after the Blossom Festival, some of the ripe cherries find their way to the tasting room to accompany the wines, especially the namesake Cherry Hill Blush.

The Wines

Stewart Vineyards' makes a wide selection of varietals and proprietary wines. Serious enophiles most often seek out the outstanding late harvest Rieslings and the crisp and complex Chardonnay. The rich and fruity Cabernet Sauvignon joined these two favored varietals as a candidate for review in the **Best of the Northwest** section of this guide.

Tefft Cellars

1320 Independence Rd.
Outlook, WA 98938
(509) 837-7651

Owners:
Joel & Pam Tefft
Winemaker: Joel Tefft
First Year: 1990
Winery Capacity:
1,000 Gallons

Tasting Room Hours:
Sat./Sun., Noon - 5 PM

Winery History

Joel and Pam Tefft are in love with Yakima Valley winemaking. Leaving more lucrative fields to pursue the dream of owning their own winery, Joel gained experience as cellarmaster for Hyatt Vineyards and continues helping out there and operating his own venture simultaneously.

A visit to Tefft Cellars

On your way from the Zillah area to Sunnyside, you'll find Tefft Cellars on Independence Road in the community of Outlook. The Tefft vineyard is neatly laid out in front of the winery and home of Joel and Pam Tefft who are your enthusiastic hosts on weekend afternoons.

The Wines

Serious winelovers are often taken aback at the unusual wines offered by Tefft Cellars. Late harvest Chardonnay, Cabernet Champagne and Sweet Nebbiolo are not commonly found. These wines and other more traditional bottlings are, however, well made and have attracted a loyal following.

Washington State

Becky Yeaman and Wade Wolfe share a happy moment after Wade received the 1993 Alec Bayless Prize for his contributions to Washington viticulture.

Thurston Wolfe Winery

27 N. Front St.
Yakima, WA 98901
(509) 452-0335

Owner: Wade Wolfe
& Becky Yeaman
Winemaker:
Wade Wolfe
First Year: 1990
Winery Capacity:
1,600 Gallons
1991 Production:
1,600 Gallons

Tasting Room Hours:
Wed., Thurs., Fri., Sat.:
11 AM to 6 PM
Sunday, Noon to 5 PM

Winery History

Wade Wolfe is no stranger to the Washington wine industry. His 16 years experience as vineyard manager and consultant have been well spent learning the finer points of grape growing and winemaking. Now general manager at The Hogue Cellars, Wade continues his own personal label with the hallmark bottlings of personal varietal favorites that started the production in 1987.

A visit to Thurston Wolfe

Tucked into a storefront in the Yakima Historic Disrict (in the original space of Grant's Ale Pub), Wade and his wife, Becky Yeaman, meet and greet the public who come to enjoy their unique wines. You'll not find more informative or charming hosts in all of the wine country of the Northwest. (By the way, Grant's Ale Pub is now just across the street in the old Yakima train depot.)

The Wines

Wade Wolfe created a special niche for his personal wine brand when he released a sweet Black Muscat and Sauternes-style Sweet Rebecca in the late 1980s. The wines were well-received and have gained an enthusiastic following among the wine press as well as consumers. These two bottlings have been joined by a vintage Port, Lemberger table wine, and other table wines blended of white varieties. A Clarke (as in Stan Clarke) Champagne is also offered for sale at the tasting room.

Tucker Cellars

Ray Road and Hwy 12
Rt. 1, Box 1696
Sunnyside, WA 98944
(509) 837-8701

Owners:
Dean & Rose Tucker
Manager/ Winemaker:
Randy Tucker
First Year: 1981
Winery Capacity:
30,000 Gallons
1991 Production:
22,000 Gallons

Tasting Room Hours:
Daily, 9 AM to 6 PM
(summer)
Daily, 9 AM to
4:30 PM (winter)
Tours available, large
groups by appointment.

Winery History

The history of Tucker Cellars goes back almost 50 years when some of the first vinifera (winegrape) plantings in the Yakima Valley were made by William Bridgman. Dean Tucker's father had brought his family out from Nebraska during the depression and was exposed through Bridgman to vinifera grapes and winemaking. This early education planted a seed in the Tucker family that would bear fruit in the early 1980s when Tucker Cellars winery became a reality.

Already well-known for their fresh fruit and produce market on Highway 12 east of Sunnyside, the Tuckers expanded into the wine business making award-winning Riesling and Chenin Blanc wines from the 1981 crush. Randy Tucker is the winery manager and is responsible for day to day operation.

A visit to Tucker Cellars

Don't get the idea that the Tuckers are going out of the fruit and produce business! The carrots, asparagus and other crops that have long put food on the family table are right there for sale - fresh and in-season - next to the winery tasting room. A unique snack provided free for visiting wine tasters is the Tucker's White Cloud Gourmet Popcorn, a healthful and delicious treat. The Tucker's wines are also available at their tasting room in Yakima, just a block west of Front Street on Yakima Ave.

The Wines

Tucker Cellars produces some of the Valley's most consistent sipping varietals including a refreshing Johannisberg Riesling and a Chenin Blanc with a touch of sweetness. Red varietals and reserve Chardonnay are available at the winery only.

Washington Hills Cellars

111 East Lincoln Ave.
Sunnyside, WA 98944
(509) 839-9463

Owners: Harry
Alhadeff, Brian Carter
Winemaker:
Brian Carter
First Year: 1990
Winery Capacity:
30,000 Gallons
1991 Production:
30,000 Gallons

Winery History

The principals involved in Washington Hills Cellars are two of Washington's most well-known wine men. Brian Carter has consistently demonstrated the ability to make the finest wine possible from Northwest grapes and his partner, Harry Alhadeff, has a wide reputation as an innovative and competitive wine marketer. First utilizing custom crush facilities to create their initial bottlings, Washington Hills has now acquired the Sunnyside facility originally owned by Cascade Estates Winery (no longer in business). Two lines of varietals satisfy the premium and super-premium market tiers and both labels have been consistent winners of medals in local and national wine judgings.

Continued on next page.

Washington State

Tasting Room Hours:
Daily, 11:00 AM to
5:30 PM

A visit to Washington Hills Cellars

The old Carnation Dairy plant has never looked better with a bright tasting room and gift shop and a courtyard complete with umbrella'd picnic tables for an alfresco snack. The tasting room employees are both friendly and well-informed about the wines.

The Wines

The Apex brand of ultra-premium varietals includes a tempting Chardonnay (see **Best of the Northwest** wine reviews in the front of this book) along with Cabernet, Late Harvest Riesling, Sémillon and Merlot. Washington Hills wines include varietal offerings as well as blends of white varietals. Good values are found throughout the line.

Yakima River Winery

1657 North River Rd.
Prosser, WA 99350
(509) 786-2805

Owners: John &
Louise Rauner
Winemaker:
John Rauner
First Year: 1978
Winery Capacity:
25,000 Gallons
1991 Production:
22,500 Gallons

Tasting Room Hours:
Daily, 10 AM to 5 PM

Winery History

John and Louise Rauner came out to Washington in the mid-1970s with winemaking in mind. It didn't take long for John to catch on to the ins and outs of enology and he bonded Yakima River Winery in 1978. Many of Yakima River's first wines were whites that won many awards. Today, red wine production is 85% to 90% of the total.

A visit to Yakima River Winery

Find Yakima River Winery by heading west from Wine Country Road in Prosser (the turn is just past the Yakima River bridge) on North River Road. A couple of sharp turns along the way are well marked.

John and Louise Rauner are your hosts for enjoyable tastings of the winery's white and red wines.

John really puts his all into the special events held at the winery. During the yearly barrel tasting tour (April) he pours a vertical tasting of his Cabernet (the same variety but from different vintages). His Fourth of July new release weekend sees a special tasting of the same vintage and varietal but samples have been aged in barrels made of different types of oak. On Thanksgiving he offers a five-year vertical tasting of Merlot. For red wine lovers these educational tastings are not to be missed.

The Wines

As mentioned above, Yakima River Winery produces mostly red wines. Cabernet Sauvignon and Merlot are joined by a proprietary red wine, Rendezvous, which is 100% Lemberger. Several ultra-late harvest Rieslings and Gewürztraminers are for sale at the winery only. "Johns Port" is a popular dessert-style red that has received many awards and was a favorite of the **Best of the Northwest** panel judging dessert wines. (See page 33.)

Zillah Oakes Winery

Exit 52, I-82 at Zillah
c/o Covey Run Wines
P.O. Box 1729
Zillah, WA 98953
(509) 829-6235

General Manager and Winemaker:
David Crippen

Tasting Room Hours:
Monday - Saturday,
10 AM to 5 PM
Sunday, Noon to 5 PM

Winery History

"Shortly after the turn of the century, when both railroads and irrigation systems were first being established in the Yakima Valley, Mr. Walter Granger became entranced by the beauty of the daughter of the local railroad manager, a Mr. Oakes. Mr. Granger asked Mr. Oakes if he could name the township he was surveying at the time after his daughter, seventeen-year-old Zillah. Mr. Oakes gave his permission, and the town of Zillah was born."

With the coming of Zillah Oakes (the winery), Miss Zillah has now been honored with her own enological namesake, smack dab beside the freeway where all and sundry can appreciate the up and coming future of Yakima Valley wine!

A visit to Zillah Oakes

The freeway-side location of the Zillah Oakes facility is a natural draw for tourists not keen on venturing into the foothills for a taste of wine. The tasting room and gift shop make for a pleasant visit but no tours are available. Head up to the parent winery, Covey Run for a closer look at the actual production of grapes into wine.

The Wines

Many of Zillah Oakes wines are made with beginning consumers in mind - slightly off-dry and very easy to drink.

Yakima Valley Accommodations

Yakima

Rio Mirada Best Western, 1603 Terrace Heights Dr. 98901 (509) 457-4444 - Every room has a view of the river with balcony, queen beds, TV, telephone. Spa and heated pool are located riverside. Top quality and reliable. Just east of exit 33 off I-82.

Cavanaugh's at Yakima Center, 607 East Yakima Ave., Yakima, 98901 1-800-THE INNS Cavanaugh's quality accommodations are well known throughout Eastern Washington. Nicely appointed rooms, two outdoor pools, and local wines are featured at Libby's Restaurant, Adjacent to the Yakima Convention Center and just a couple of blocks from Grant's Ale Brewery Pub!

Birchfield Manor B & B, See listing under Dining.

Sunnyside

Sunnyside Inn B & B
800 East Edison, Sunnyside (509) 839-5557 All private baths, jacuzzi tubs, phones, TV. A great find in this mid-valley location!

Grandview

Apple Valley Motel, Highway 12, (509) 882-3003 Queen beds, swimming pool, cable TV. Some kitchens. Clean and comfortable. Bargain rates.

Prosser

Prosser Motel, 206-6th St., (509) 786-2555 Cable TV and air conditioning make this a popular choice.

Wine Country Inn - 104 - 6th St., Prosser, (509) 786-2855 Beautiful riverside setting. Comfortable rooms. Gourmet country breakfast.

Washington State
Yakima Valley Dining & Activities

Yakima

The Greystone Restaurant, 5 N. Front St. (509) 248-9801 One of Yakima's finest restaurants with fabulous specialties (duck and lamb are superb) and a broad selection of favorites. Wine list is extensive and reasonable!

Birchfield Manor Gourmet Restaurant and B & B, Birchfield Rd. off Hwy. 24, 2 miles east of Yakima (509) 452-1960 Will & Sandy Massett operates this elegant dinner house featuring multi-course dinners with wine in a pleasant country farmhouse east of town. Reservations req. Weekends only. The B & B is right upstairs!

Gasparetti's, 1013 North 1st, (509) 248-0628 Fine Northern Italian cuisine in a restaurant that can handle both families with kids and fancy food critics from the big city. Delicious specialties highlight local ingredients.

The Brewery Pub, 25 N. Front, (509) 575-1900 Visit the home of Grant's Ale and have a pint and a pasty! Friday nights are hectic, come early.

Deli de Pasta, 7 N. Front St., (509) 453-0571 Tasty Italian specialties are made on the premises. Great desserts and a nice selection of local wines. Dine in or carry out for picnics.

Zillah

El Ranchito Restaurant, Gift Shop and Tortilla Factory, 1319-1st Ave., (509) 829-5880 Even with continuous publicity El Ranchito remains humble and homey. The food is authentic Mexican, the gifts are authentic, everything is aimed at the local Latino population. The food is good but the experience is much more than eating!

Sunnyside

Taqueria La Fogata, 1300 Yakima Vly. Highway, (509) 839-9019 Enjoy Mexican food in its native style. All the regulars plus the specialties you won't find at your local taco stand.

Grandview

Dykstra House, 114 Birch Ave. (509) 882-2082 A restored home in Grandview's quiet residential area is the setting for tasty lunches (M-F) and dinners (Fri., Sat.) featuring fresh local ingredients and wines to accompany the delicious fresh-made fare.

Prosser

The Blue Goose, 306-7th St., (509) 786-1774 A wine-knowledgeable staff, ample portions and a varied menu keep locals and visitors coming back to The Blue Goose. Outside patio seating.

For Parents Only

Picnicking and Camping - Your best bet may be the campground along the Yakima River on Highway 821 between Yakima and Ellensburg (camping), the Riverfront Park in Prosser and the Prosser city park (picnicking). In Yakima, the State Park and KOA are just across the river from town.

A note about picnicking - most area wineries offer picnic tables and encourage visitors to enjoy their lunch or snacks on their grounds. Staton Hills, Covey Run and Kiona Vineyards are among the best. Kay and Clay at Chinook offer a shady picnic area under the oak tree out back.

Indian Cultural Center, Highway 97 - Toppenish - Devoted to the history of the Yakima Indian Nation, the Indian Cultural Center features extensive exhibits illustrating the history of the area and the culture of the native inhabitants.

Sunnyside Museum, 704 S. 4th - A nice collection of pioneer artifacts documenting the settlement of the Yakima Valley. (Park nearby at W. Edison St.)

Benton County Historical Museum, Prosser City Park, Prosser 7th St. at Paterson Drive - Museum, shady play area, picnic tables.

Oak Barrels – Their Construction and Use

The use of oak barrels for aging and storing wine is a centuries-old practice that is just now being scientifically researched and understood. Two types of barrels are used by Northwest wineries, American oak and French oak.

It is generally agreed that French oak provides a subtle, "toasty" quality to the wine and American oak provides a more "woody" flavor. Both types of barrels mellow the wine by permiting slow oxidation through the pores in the wood. Flavors introduced into the wine by oak aging gradually marry with the fruity qualities of the wine over time.

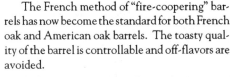

The French method of "fire-coopering" barrels has now become the standard for both French oak and American oak barrels. The toasty quality of the barrel is controllable and off-flavors are avoided.

Barrel making in France begins in one of the several oak forests from which wood is harvested each year. Different forests produce slightly different oak flavors in wines but more important to final selection is the cooperage firm making the barrels.

Trunk sections from oak trees are split – not sawn – to provide the barrel side pieces or "staves." These pieces are then stacked and aged for several years to dry and season. When ready, the staves are shaped to provide a tight fit in the assembled barrel.

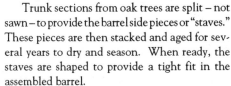

Since staves do not naturally conform to the rounded shape of a barrel, they are warped with steam and heat. Wetted staves are partially assembled into the barrel shape then heated over a fire of oak trimmings. The heat from the fire makes the staves more pliable and they are then drawn tight with a wire loop to complete the final barrel shape. The final step is to assemble the "heads" or ends of the barrels.

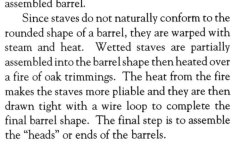

The inside of the barrel is scraped of char from the fire, but a certain amount of the smoky flavor remains. The toasty character is controlled by length of exposure to the fire and other factors. The resulting barrels are then classified as being of light, medium or heavy "toast."

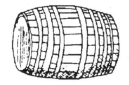

A barrel imparts a strong oak character to wine only during the first few years of use. After that time, it is considered "neutral" and is used for longer-term storage of wine.

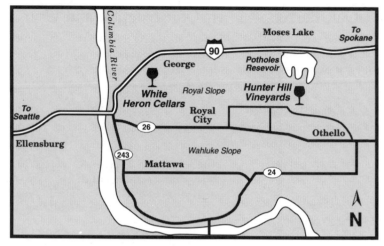

Columbia Valley Touring – North

Most of the North Columbia Valley is off the major path of tourism in Washington State. Travelers zip by on I-90 on their way to Spokane or roar north past Wenatchee to take in the Lake Chelan and Sun Lakes resorts. The attraction of wine touring the desolate miles of sage brush punctuated by an occasional winery or small town is minimal. Perhaps the demise of several North Columbia Valley wine operations will thus not surprise you.

Making a success of a small winery requires that you sell wine either through regional distribution or to local folks out of your tasting room. The hundreds of brands flooding the wine market in Seattle and Portland make distribution very difficult for startup winery operations. Combine that with an out-of-the-way location (read: no tasting room traffic) and you're facing the kiss of death for your small winery.

Some very delightful people have had to close their wineries in the past two years. Cascade Mountain Cellars in Ellensburg and Wenatchee Valley Vintners in East Wenatchee both succumbed to lack of wine sales to keep their businesses going. Champs de Brionne – a larger and better financed operation – couldn't decide if the concerts in the gorge were good for business or if the business was good for the concerts. Both have sputtered with the winery suffering more.

Grape growing on the Wahluke and Royal Slopes is still an ongoing and successful venture. Several large vineyards supply wine grapes to Yakima Valley wineries and to wineries in Spokane and the Tri-Cities. Two wineries are still open for business in this area.

Cameron and Phyllis Fries are just off I-90 in the town of George where they are visited by cross-state travelers (many are regular customers!) who enjoy the wines of Cameron's making. A nice stop on the long drive to Spokane.

Near the Potholes Recreation Area, hunters and fishermen have kept things lively for Art Byron's Hunter Hill Vineyards. New roads and RV parking at the winery have increased the attraction for this detour from the sporting business at hand.

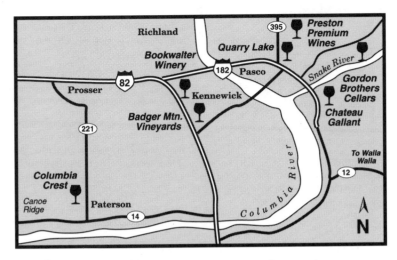

Columbia Valley Touring – Tri-Cities Area

The South Columbia Valley has a larger population to support local wineries and offers more amenities to tourists who are passing through or are coming for an escape from damp weather. Most of the wine operations are clustered around the Tri-Cities of Richland, Pasco and Kennewick.

North to south, you'll first find Preston Premium Wines just north of Pasco on Highway 395. The large park at the winery is a great picnic stop and the Preston family offers a nice, self-guided tour of the winery facility. Open daily.

A little closer to town, but also near Highway 395 is Quarry Lake winery located just south of the Jack Diddley Truck Stop on Commercial Ave. The winery is open by appointment for tasting and sales.

A scenic drive up the Kahlotus Highway follows the Snake River past Ice Harbor Dam to Levey Road where the Gordon Brothers Winery is open weekends during the summer. Nearby Levey Park gives the kids a chance to play by the river while mom and dad sip some wine with their picnic. Summer weekends are the best time to find someone handy to pour you a sample.

South on I-182 and up Highway 124, you'll find Chateau Gallant within duck-calling distance of McNary Wildlife Refuge. Enjoy a view of migrating waterfowl with your Chardonnay or Merlot.

In Kennewick, Rob Griffin is helping out at Badger Mountain Vineyards making organically-grown varietals for the Powers label and also his own Barnard Griffin wines. Call for an appointment.

Interstate 82 runs from Kennewick to the Columbia River making a quicker drive through the wheat fields to visit the Northwest's largest winery, Columbia Crest Winery near Paterson. Columbia Crest is a magnificent facility. The winery tour is awe-inspiring and tourist amenities are first rate.

Mercer Ranch winery, miles west of Paterson and up a long gravel road to boot, succumbed to lack of winery traffic as described on the preceding page. Grapes from the vineyard at the site are still finding their way into many wonderful Northwest reds.

Washington State

Badger Mountain Vineyard

110 Jurupa
Kennewick, WA
99336 • (509) 627-4986

Owners: Bill Powers,
Tim DeCook
Winemaker:
Greg Powers
First Year: 1987
Winery Capacity:
85,000 Gallons
1991 Production:
80,000 Gallons

Tasting Room Hours:
By appointment only

Winery History

Badger Mountain Vineyard staked its claim to fame on organically grown grapes and is proud to be one of the first Northwest wineries to produce organically-grown wines. Owners Bill Powers and Tim DeCook have moved their wine into foreign markets and offer a wide selection of varietals - all organically grown.

A visit to Badger Mountain Vineyard

This operation is tucked away in the hills near the back side of Kennewick. Exit from Highway 82 and follow a winding set of turns (get instructions when you phone for an appointment) to reach the winery. The owners are busy folks and your visit is not unwelcome but may need to be arranged around their schedules.

The Wines

Talented winemaker Rob Griffin is helping out with winemaking at Badger Mountain. Chardonnay, Gewürztraminer, White Riesling, Chenin Blanc, Cabernet Franc and a blend named Seve are produced from 80 acres of vineyard. A new label named after owner Bill Powers is now available.

Barnard Griffin

1707 West 8th Place
Kennewick, WA 99336
(509) 582-3272

Owners:
Deborah Barnard
and Rob Griffin
Winemaker:
Rob Griffin
First Year: 1983
Tasting Room Hours
None. Write for a
appointment

Winery History

So why would a winemaker take up winemaking as a hobby? That question might have occurred to Rob Griffin and Deborah Barnard sometime during Rob's tenure as general manager for The Hogue Cellars. He worked hard creating a popular style for Hogue and separately crafted his own brand where he alone controlled the stylistic appeal. Barnard Griffin winery was never intended as a hobby and now Rob has left Hogue to pursue the success of his well-established brand. Rob and Deborah sometimes pour their wines at enological festivals and fairs as production levels permit.

The Wines

The wines made for Barnard Griffin represent the 'high end of the market,' being costly to produce and thus costing more to consumers. The **Best of the Northwest** reviews beginning on page 14 of this guide show Barnard Griffin wines well represented as favorites of our panels. Merlot, Sauvignon Blanc and Sémillon scored the highest marks. Cabernet Sauvignon and Chardonnay are also made.

Bookwalter Winery's new facility is just off the freeway in Richland, WA.

Bookwalter Winery

710 S. Windmill Road
Richland, WA 99352
(509) 627-5000

Owners: Jerrold &
Jean Bookwalter
Winemaker:
Jerry Bookwalter
First Year: 1984
Winery Capacity:
10,000 Gallons

Tasting Room Hours:
Daily, 10 AM to 5 PM
Tours Available

Winery History

After graduating from U. C. Davis in 1963, Jerry Bookwalter began his agricultural career by managing orchards and vineyards in California. In 1976, his experience led to a move north to Washington where he was general manager of Bacchus and Dionysus Vineyards for Sagemoor Farms until 1983.

A belief in the quality of Washington wines and the dedication to produce only small lots of quality wines led to the bonding of Bookwalter Winery in 1984. Careful selection of grapes and consultation with other Northwest winemakers have proved to be a successful combination. Bookwalter wines do well in competitions but more importantly for Jerry, they are well liked by consumers. New winery quarters just off Highway 182 in Richland were completed in 1993.

A visit to Bookwalter Winery

The new Bookwalter location at the corner of Windmill Rd. and Columbia Dr. offers easy access to wine lovers traveling between Yakima and the Tri-Cities. The cozy tasting room and small vineyard being planted on the site make for an interesting and educational stop.

The Wines

Clean and crisp whites and rich, fruity reds are the Columbia Valley style of Bookwalter Winery. Cabernet, Merlot, Chardonnay, Chenin Blanc and Riesling are frequent medal winners, as are Bookwalter's Cabernet Sauvignon and Red Table Wine.

Washington State

Chateau Gallant

S. 1355 Gallant Rd.
Pasco, WA 99301
(509) 545-9570

Owners: David &
Theresa Gallant
Winemaker:
Mike Wallace
First Year: 1987
Winery Capacity:
10,000 Gallons
1991 Production:
16,000 Gallons

Tasting Room Hours:
Daily, 2 to 5 PM

Winery History

The first Gallant vineyard was planted in 1972 followed by additional plantings in later years for a current total of 25 acres. The vineyard, winery and tasting room are located on the edge of the McNary Wildlife Refuge providing a year round display of waterfowl using the slough for rest stops on their annual migrations.

A visit to Chateau Gallant

The Gallant Winery is located a short drive up Highway 124 from its junction with I-182 and then down Gallant Road. Come to enjoy the wines and the view of the adjacent wildlife.

The Wines

Chateau Gallant produces wines from estate grapes of several varietals. Included are Sauvignon Blanc, Chardonnay, Gewürztraminer, White Riesling, Merlot and Cabernet Sauvignon.

Columbia Crest Winery

P.O. Box 231
Paterson, WA 99345
(509) 875-2061
(Located on Highway
221 from Prosser)

Owners: Stimson Lane
Wine and Spirits
Winemaker:
Doug Gore
First Year: 1985
Winery Capacity:
1,000,000 Gallons+

Tasting Room Hours:
Daily, 10:30 AM - 5 PM

Winery History

Columbia Crest began life as Chateau Ste. Michelle's River Ridge winery, created to handle most of the thousands of tons of grapes processed by Washington's largest winery each year. It soon became clear that the winery could use it's own identity and in 1985 Columbia Crest, the wine and winery were born. An individual winemaking style and unique market niche have propelled Columbia Crest into the 1990s limelight for value and quality.

A visit to Columbia Crest

Columbia Crest is without question the most impressive winery in the Northwest. The huge complex houses more than a million gallons of wine plus first-rate tourist facilities. The landscaping around the winery includes acres of manicured lawn for impromptu picnics and a delightful duck pond. A courtyard by the entrance is furnished with café tables for more formal snacking. The lobby of the winery is resplendent with tapestries, antique furnishings (now used as display cases for winemaking

Columbia Crest Winery near Paterson, Washington is the Northwest's largest.

Columbia Crest

and grapegrowing exhibits) and immaculate decor at every turn. No detail has been missed in creating this masterpiece.

The tour guides at Columbia Crest are very well informed and do an excellent job of explaining the facility to visitors. An appropriately well-appointed tasting room caps the tour and guests are invited to browse a well-stocked wine and gift shop after sampling some recent bottlings of Columbia Crest wines. The half hour drive from Prosser is time well spent to see the Northwest's largest wine facility.

The Wines

Columbia Crest winemaker Doug Gore does a tremendous job putting value in every Columbia Crest bottle. The wines are true to varietal type and are enjoyable accompaniments to food. There is no better bargain in Northwest varietal wine. Recently, the winery has released some of its first Barrel Select designation wines. These bottlings feature greater depth of flavor and complexity while retaining fresh fruit character and a less-than-reserve-level price tag. Great values.

See reviews of Columbia Crest Merlot, Chardonnay and Sauvignon Blanc in the **Best of the Northwest** section beginning on page 14.

Washington State
Gordon Brothers Cellars

531 Levey Road
Pasco, WA 99301
(509) 547-6224

Owners:
Jeff & Bill Gordon
Winemaker:
Jeff Gordon
First Year: 1983
Winery Capacity:
6,000 Gallons
1991 Production:
6,000 Gallons

Tasting Room Hours:
Weekends, 11 AM
to 5 PM
(summer months only)

Winery History

Ten miles east of Pasco along the Snake River Jeff and Bill Gordon have been growing grapes since 1980. This is the tame part of the river where broad, fertile banks have been formed and flooding is controlled by several dams. With the coming of dams also came irrigation for potatoes and other row crops - an important part of the Gordon Brothers farming efforts.

Some of the winegrapes grown by Jeff and Bill are sold to other wineries. Spokane, Walla Walla and Tri-Cities area vintners have been steady customers for the grapes produced on the 80 acre vineyard which came into bearing in 1982. Roughly 20% of the harvest is vinified for the Gordon Brothers label.

A visit to Gordon Brothers Cellars

The scenic area along the Snake River offers recreational possiblities for tourists of all ages. Boating, fishing and sightseeing are popular with travelers as well as a visit to the remarkable Ice Harbor Dam. The winery offers tasting on summer weekends. The small tasting room at the winery is an air-conditioned haven on hot Eastern Washington afternoons and the tasting room help is friendly and informative. Great view of the valley!

The Wines

The power of Chardonnay has moved Gordon Brothers' reserve bottling into the top echelon at many wine competitions - rich and buttery, with a long finish of vanilla and apple. Jeff Gordon's Merlot has also been a gold-medal-regular, brimming with ripe berry fruit and toasty nuances of American oak. A very impressive Cabernet Sauvignon is also produced.

Gordon Brothers Reserve Chardonnay is reviewed on page 24 as part of the **Best of the Northwest** selection.

Hunter Hill Vineyards

2752 W.
McMannaman Rd.
Othello, WA 98344
(509) 346-2736

Owner/Winemaker:
Art Byron
First Year: 1984
Winery Capacity:
10,000 Gallons
1991 Production:
10,500 Gallons

Tasting Room Hours:
Daily, 11 AM to 5 PM

Winery History

Hunter Hill Vineyards is one of the original pioneers of the Royal Slope. This promising viticultural area northeast of the now-famous Wahluke Slope is just beginning to attract attention of major grapegrowers. Back in 1978, Western Airlines pilot Art Byron was looking for investment property and this area was brought to his attention. As a serious amateur winemaker Art saw more potential in the land than just a tax deduction. Twenty-eight acres of vineyard were planted in 1981 and 1982 and the first commercial harvest came in 1984.

A visit to Hunter Hill Vineyards

Art Byron doesn't worry about attracting wine tasters to his new winery since the area just north of the Royal Slope is a recreational heaven for fishermen, hunters, wildlife enthusiasts and boaters, all of whom Art hopes will take the short side trip to visit Hunter Hill Vineyards. A picnic area and RV parking are adjacent to the winery to further encourage wine-loving visitors to stay awhile.

The Wines

Hunter Hill currently produces a Muscat Canelli, Select White Riesling (4% residual sugar), Chenin Blanc, Chardonnay and Merlot.

Preston Premium Wines

502 E. Vineyard Dr.
Pasco, WA 99301
(509) 545-1990

Owners:
Preston Family
Winemaker:
Brent Preston
First Year: 1976
Winery Capacity:
180,000 Gallons

Tasting Room Hours:
Daily, 10 AM-5:30 PM
Closed on major
holidays.

Winery History

Preston Wine Cellars (now Preston Premium Wines) is a Columbia Valley institution that began in the earliest days of Washington's modern wine history. In 1972 Bill Preston planted 50 acres of winegrapes along Highway 395 and later hired Rob Griffin to make his first wines. The widely acclaimed first releases from Preston began a tradition that continues to this day, and helped create a positive image of Washington's fledgling wine industry. Several members of the Preston family now handle the various aspects of operating the state's largest family-owned winery.

A visit to Preston

A short drive north of Pasco, the Preston vineyard and winery are a dramatic sight on the east side of Highway 395. The park-like picnic area invites visitors to relax and "stay awhile" and the unique, second-story tasting room offers views of the vineyard along with wine tasting and a chance to admire the Northwest's largest collection of corkscrews. The addition of a large gazebo overlooking the koi pond has added even more enticement to linger. Call the winery for a schedule of special events.

The Wines

Preston winery has long offered a broad range of varietals from refreshing, off-dry whites to crisp Fume Blanc and Chardonnay to hearty oak-aged reds. The Preston reserve Cabernet Sauvignon was judged by our panel to be one of the Northwest's finest (see reviews, beginning on page 14).

Quarry Lake Vintners

2520 Commercial Ave.
Pasco, WA 99301
(509) 547-7307

Owner:
Balcom & Moe, Inc.
Winemaker:
Maury Balcom
First Year: 1985
Winery Capacity:
59,000 Gallons

Tasting Room Hours:
by appointment only

Winery History

From grapegrower to winemaker was a popular transition in the Columbia Valley during the 1980s. Maury Balcom of Quarry Lake waited 15 years since the planting winegrapes at Balcom and Moe Farms to ferment some of his harvest instead of selling all of it to other wineries. The Quarry Lake name comes from a scenic area along the Columbia River north of Pasco. The current business park location houses wine aging in oak barrels and a reception area for visitors.

A visit to Quarry Lake

The small industrial park just down the road from Jack Diddley's truck stop is still the home for Quarry Lake's barrel-aging activity and a limited amount blending. A call for an appointment is necessary to visit the winery, but Quarry Lake wines may be sampled at many NW regional wine events.

The Wines

Quarry Lake's Cabernet Sauvignon and Merlot have received the most attention from fans of Northwest wine. Indeed, our panel found QL Merlot to be one of the best (see reviews, beginning on page 14).

Saddle Mountain - Langguth Winery

2340 Winery Road
Mattawa, WA 99344

Winery History

An investment in American winegrowing by a large German winery spawned this monolithic facility on the Wahluke Slope. While there is still a winery on the site, there is little or no activity here. The current owners, Stimson Lane Wine & Spirits, are relocating winemaking activity for Saddle Mountain to other facilities. Stay tuned . . .

Tagaris

P.O. Box 5433
Kennewick, WA 99336
Retail Store:
1625 'A' St., Unit E
Pasco, WA 99301
(509) 547-3590

Owner:
Michael Taggares
First Year: 1987

Winery History

Michael Taggares is the proprietor of Taggares Vineyards located northeast of Othello near 'Radar Hill.' A very successful farming family, Taggares is also a familiar name as you drive through the Yakima Valley. Many acres of Concord grapes have been producing for this enterprise for decades.

The spelling of the winery's name is the original Greek spelling of Michael Taggares name. His grandfather Peter, like many immigrants with a limited command of English, had his name spelled incorrectly at Ellis Island upon his arrival in 1911.

Continued on next page.

Washington State

A visit to Tagaris Winery

The Tagaris Winery sales office in Pasco is open from 8 AM to 5 PM, Monday through Friday.

The Wines

The 1987 harvest from his 120-acre wine grape vineyard provided the fruit for the first Tagaris Winery wines. These included Chenin Blanc, Johannisberg Riesling and Sauvignon Blanc. In addition to the above varietals, Chardonnay, Pinot Noir and Cabernet Sauvignon are now made along with Late Harvest Riesling and sparkling wine.

White Heron Cellars

101 Washington Way N., George, WA 98824
(509) 785-5521

Owners: Phyllis & Cameron Fries
Winemaker: Cameron Fries
First Year: 1990
Winery Capacity: 3,500 Gallons
1991 Production: 3,400 Gallons

Tasting Room Hours: Wed.-Sun., 12 - 5 PM

Winery History

Both Washington natives and graduates of Pacific Lutheran University in Tacoma, Phyllis and Cameron Fries relocated to Switzerland for five years so that Cameron could study winemaking. Upon their return to Washington, Cameron served as winemaker for two Washington wineries prior to establishing his own operation in 1990.

A visit to White Heron

Located just off Interstate 90 in George, White Heron's facility is a converted gas station on a quiet back street. Phyllis and Cameron have spruced up the place and enjoy pouring their wines for interested visitors. Dispensing humor along with fine wine, they makes fast friends with all who stop by. White Heron makes a great mid-point rest on the long drive to Spokane, or an interesting side-visit if you're heading to a concert at the Gorge.

The Wines

The winery's vineyard near Trinidad (above the Columbia Gorge near Crescent Bar) produces some of the grapes for White Heron wines. Additional fruit is purchased from Yakima Valley vineyards. Pinot Noir, Dry Riesling and a Bordeaux-style red blend named Chantepierre are the wines produced.

Columbia Valley Accommodations & Dining

Waterlogged winelovers seeking a sunny vacation can escape to the sundrenched Columbia Valley to bake away their cares and troubles. Special events, water sports and a dozen wineries are an extra incentive to put away the umbrella and head east of the Cascades.

Accommodations

Cavanaugh's Motor Inn, 1101 N. Columbia Center, Kennewick - 1-800-THE INNS   Quality accommodations with nice rooms, pool and spa, children's play area. Adjacent to Eastern Washington's largest mall. Good Northwest wine list in Cavanaugh's Landing restaurant.

Hanford House, 802 George Washington Way, Richland - (509) 946-7611 The swankiest hotel in the area, pleasant center courtyard and a very nice dining room with an attractive wine offering.

Red Lion, 2525 N. 20th, Pasco - (509) 547-0701   Close to the Pasco-area wineries and to the Pasco airport. Just off the freeway you'll find this well-planned and well-staffed Red Lion with swimming pools, nice restaurant, etc.

Dining

The Tri-Cities has an amazingly bad reputation in the fine dining department. Deserved or not, it's a long drive to the nearest big city with fancier offerings. Hotel dining rooms are a good bet including **Cavanaugh's** or the **Hanford House** or try one of these:

Emerald of Siam, 1314 Jadwin, Richland - (509) 946-9328   When this restaurant opened, a cheer went up from many folks who had been yearning for great Thai cooking. In a converted store-front on Richland's back street. NW wine list and imported Thai beer.

Giacci's, 94 Lee Blvd., Richland - (509) 946-4855 - Italian deli and restaurant.   Lunch served Mon. - Sat., Dinner served Fri. and Sat.   Good wine list.

The Blue Moon, 21 W. Canal Dr., off Washington, (509) 582-6598 Enjoy a gourmet seven-course dinner on Friday or Saturday nights (one seating each night, book reservations early). Arguably the best meal available in the Tri-Cities. This place could become Washington's answer to Nick's Cafe in McMinnville! Local wines.

For Parents Only

There's a million things for kids to enjoy in the Tri-Cities. Try to stay at a motel with a pool so the kids can enjoy an afternoon swim.   Several riverfront parks in Kennewick and Richland offer tennis, playgrounds and other diversions. Also:

Tri-Cities Air Show - Scheduled in late June or early July, this is always a real kid-pleaser. Noise, planes, military vehicles, air races.

Columbia Center Mall - Just off the freeway in Kennewick.

Columbia Cup Hydroplane Race - Late July or early August and the Thunder-on-the-Columbia comes to town for a wild time by the river. Many nearby residents come to town to enjoy this event with their families.

Hanford Science Center - In downtown Richland, this interpretive center has many interesting displays on the history of nuclear power. If you want to get closer to the action, you can tour the WPPSS Plant 2 or the Westinghouse Fast Flux Test Facility.

Washington State

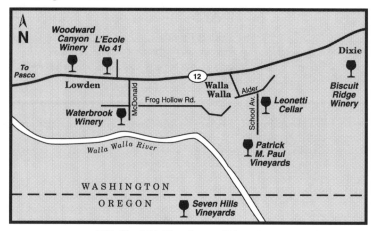

Walla Walla Area Touring

Never will you feel so at home as you do in Walla Walla. The shady, tree-lined streets seem to bring back memories of wherever you grew up and the soda shop on the corner still makes a great hamburger. Out in the Walla Walla Valley next to the onion fields and historical markers your first wineries await.

Starting in the small farming town of Lowden, your first stop is Woodward Canyon Winery across the road from the grain elevator. An insightful tasting room host pours Woodward Canyon's wines for interested wine lovers daily with varied hours in summer and winter.

Next door, L'Ecole No 41 operates out of the converted Lowden School-house with proprietors Marty and Megan Clubb often on hand to explain the history and future of this unique winery. Regular hours are Wednesday through Sunday from noon to 4 PM.

Just east of Lowden on Highway 12 is the right turn on McDonald Road for Waterbrook Winery. Owners Eric and Janet Rindal enjoy meeting wine lovers visiting the area and pouring samples of their wines. The winery is open for tasting most days from Noon to 5 PM. Schedules change so if you're coming a long way to visit, call ahead to insure someone is there to meet you.

On the east side of residential Walla Walla are Leonetti Cellar and Patrick M. Paul Vineyards. Both wineries are open by appointment only except for the annual open houses held twice a year. Leonetti Cellar is the pride and joy of Gary and Nancy Figgins. Such wide acclaim has come to Leonetti wines that production is having a hard time keeping up with demand. Popularity has been earned through many years of research, experimentation and hard work.

Nearby, Mike Paul of Patrick M. Paul Vineyards has specialized in Cabernet Franc, as well as Concord and Boysenberry dessert wines but is expanding production to include Pinot Noir, Merlot and Cabernet Sauvignon.

East of town, Jack and Helen Durham welcome visitors to Biscuit Ridge Winery everyday from 10 AM to 5:30 PM. The winery is in Dixie, 11 miles east of Walla Walla.

Biscuit Ridge Winery

Rt. 1, Box 132
Waitsburg, WA 99361
(509) 529-4986

Owner/Winemaker:
Jack D. Durham
First Year: 1987
Winery Capacity:
2,000 Gallons

Tasting Room Hours:
Daily, 10 AM-5:30 PM

Winery History:
Jack Durham retired from the Navy in Alaska in 1964 and spent the next 15 years fishing, hunting and working as a professional guide in the Alaska wilderness. As time passed, he thought he might like to try his hand at grape growing and winemaking so he packed up and moved to Walla Walla with his wife Helen. After a few years of getting started and a couple of years with bad freezes, the first grapes were harvested from his vineyard halfway between Walla Walla and Waitsburg in the town of Dixie.

A visit to Biscuit Ridge Winery
Eleven miles east of Walla Walla on Highway 12, the Durham's have installed signs pointing the way to their winery about 3/4 mile south of the highway. Helen Durham offers tastes of the winery's Gewürztraminer and other wines.

L'Ecole No 41

P.O. Box 111
41 Lowden School Rd.
Lowden, WA 99360
(509) 525-0940

Owners: Martin & Megan Clubb
Winemaker:
Marty Clubb
First Year: 1983
Winery Capacity:
10,000 Gallons
1992 Production:
9,500 Gallons

Tasting Room Hours:
Wednesday - Sunday,
11 AM to 4 PM

Winery History
A Walla Walla native with family going back several generations, Baker Ferguson and his wife Jean saved a valley landmark by converting it into a winery. The old Lowden Schoolhouse, constructed in 1915, now features stainless steel fermenters and barrel storage in the basement auditorium and cafeteria. The main floor of the school is a winery reception area and combination tasting room and banqueting hall. The classroom dimensions have been changed but the character of a schoolroom has been retained. Baker and Jean turned over operation of the winery to their daughter and son-in-law in 1989. Marty Clubb now uses his chemical engirneering degree for a slightly different purpose than he perhaps intended.

A visit to L'Ecole No 41
The interesting transformation of Lowden Schoolhouse into the L'Ecole winery makes for a fun look around. The owners or their informed assistants provide information on the wines available for tasting and also on local history and things to do. A custom restaurant-for-hire operates as Barbara's 41 with owner/chef Barbara Mastin preparing gourmet lunches and dinners for groups of 10 to 30 by prior arrangement.

Continued on next page.

Washington State

L'Ecole No 41 Winery in Lowden, Washington just west of Walla Walla.

The Wines

Learning the art of winemaking with hands-on experience, Marty Clubb has produced some very nice wines in the L'Ecole style. The Sémillon has a slightly herbaceous character - the perfect complement to seasoned fish and light meats, and the L'Ecole Merlot is fleshy and fruity offering plummy nuances. Both wines impressed our tasting panels and are reviewed in the Best of the Northwest section. Viola Walla is a Vouvray-style Chenin that sips well with light foods. Cabernet Sauvignon and Chardonnay are recent additions to the production lineup but haven't established a style or track record yet.

L'Ecole No 41's Merlot and Sémillon were enjoyed by our **Best of the Northwest** panelists and are reviewed on pages 20 and 28.

Leonetti Cellar

1321 School Ave.
Walla Walla, WA
99362 • (509) 525-1428

Owners:
Gary & Nancy Figgins
Winemaker:
Gary Figgins
First Year: 1977
Winery Capacity:
7,500 Gallons
1991 Production:
7,500 Gallons

Tasting Room Hours:
May and September
weekend open houses.
Write winery for
details.

Winery History

With the success that Gary Figgins has enjoyed as a maker of fine Cabernet Sauvignon and Merlot, many winemakers might have secured a loan and expanded production by 100 times to cash-in on the reputation. Gary hasn't done that because he realizes the quality of his wine depends on the grapes he uses and the best quality grapes are in short supply. So with small harvests from his own vineyard and select lots from other growers, Gary handcrafts rich red wines in his small winery in Walla Walla. A larger winery building added in 1988-89 helps Leonetti Cellar keep up with the demand that has come through continued success.

A fascination (bordering on fanaticism) with oak and oak barrels consumes much of Gary Figgins free time. His quest to further understand the barrel-aging process and the flavor nuances imparted by various oak types have led to experiments with locally-grown oak and different methods of coopering (barrel-making).

A visit to Leonetti Cellar

The best time to catch winemaker Gary Figgins in his winery is during one of the annual open houses which take place in May (Balloon Stampede weekend) and in September (weekend after Labor Day). Write or call for exact times and other details. Gary and Nancy are sometimes on hand at selected NW wine events and competitions.

The Wines

In the age of powerful red wines crafted with many layers of flavor – both fruit and oak – Leonetti Cellar wines are among the best in the world. Combining intensity of fruit with intensity of oak requires a finesse that few have mastered as well as Gary Figgins. French and American oak barrels of varying ages are used to augment the ripe fruit flavors of Cabernet Sauvignon and Merlot as well as other Bordeaux varietals. Wines available include regular and vineyard designated bottlings of Cabernet, Reserve Cabernet, Merlot and a red table wine Meritage-style blend. Typical Leonetti Merlot offers ripe and plummy fruit with a softer palate than the Cabernet which takes on nuances of coffee, chocolate, mint and eucalyptus. See a well-established wine merchant to find these wines or visit the winery as described above. **Best of the Northwest** reviews for Leonetti wines are on pages 15 and 20.

Washington State

Patrick M. Paul Vineyards

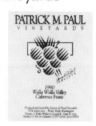

1554 School Ave.
Walla Walla, WA
99362 • (509) 522-1127

Owner & Winemaker:
Mike Paul
First Year: 1989

Winery History

Research into grape varieties and rootstocks spawned the creation of Patrick M. Paul winery. Vineyard plantings of Cabernet Franc, Pinot Noir, Merlot and Cabernet Sauvignon followed and wine production has been increasing ever since.

A visit to Patrick M. Paul Winery

An appointment is required to tour this small facility on the east side of Walla Walla near Leonetti Cellar.

The Wines

First releases of Boysenberry and Concord dessert wines found local approval but a bottling of Cabernet Franc from the 1988 vintage was the first step in establishing a reputation with a favorable review in The Wine Spectator.

Seven Hills Winery

235 E. Broadway
Milton Freewater, OR
97862
(503) 938-7710
Owners: Local Family
Shareholders
Winemaker:
Casey McClellan
First Year: 1989
Winery Capacity:
5,000 Gallons
1991 Production:
3,300 Gallons

Tasting Room Hours:
May and September
Open Houses or by
appointment.

Winery History

The development of Seven Hills Vineyard in the 1980s led to the discovery of the high quality of wines produced from the fruit by Walla Walla area wineries. Careful vineyard practice and decision making were designed to control yield and produce grapes of perfect ripeness with concentrated flavors. A winery utilizing this fruit was a logical next step. Casey McClellan cultivated his interest in winemaking while working at the vineyard in the 1980s and went on to study at U.C. Davis and work in the California and Portuguese wine industries before taking the reins at Seven Hills in 1988.

A visit to Seven Hills Cellars

Milton-Freewater is a short drive south from Walla Walla on Highway 11 through scenic hills and farmland. The winery in downtown Milton-Freewater is open during the traditional Walla Walla area May and September weekends. Other visits are by scheduled appointment.

The Wines

Richly structured Cabernet Sauvignon and Merlot are the focus at Seven Hills Winery. Intensely fruity red wines framed with toasty oak beckon the consumer to drink now but will age gracefully to further develop bottle bouquet. Other varietals are occasionally produced including Sauvignon Blanc, Chardonnay, Gewurztraminer and Riesling.

Waterbrook

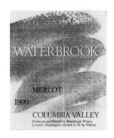

Rt. 1, Box 46
McDonald Road
Lowden, WA 99360
(509) 522-1918

Owners:
Eric and Janet Rindal
Winemaker:
Eric Rindal
First Year: 1984
Winery Capacity:
30,000 Gallons
1991 Production:
11,000 Gallons

Tasting Room Hours:
Daily, Noon to 5 PM or
by appointment.

Winery History

Out past the onion farms and wheat fields, a half-mile from Frog Hollow Road, Eric and Janet Rindal converted an asparagus storage building into an attractive little winery they call Waterbrook. Hard work and inspiration got the building cleaned up and ready for business by the 1984 crush when the first Waterbrook wines were made. The wines gained immediate popularity for clean varietal flavors and fruity character. Additional tank and barrel storage capacity was added during 1987 and 1988 to increase the variety and amount of wine produced. The planting of the winery's Cottonwood Creek Vineyard on the south side of Walla Walla promises increased production of Waterbrook's favored varietal, Chardonnay.

A visit to Waterbrook

Just a short drive south from Highway 12, a visit to Waterbrook offers the chance to meet the owners, Eric or Janet Rindal. Serious wine lovers appreciate their insightful answers and observations. Family duties sometimes call the owners away from the winery proper, so a call ahead is advised.

The Wines

Waterbrook's first releases of Chardonnay and Sauvignon Blanc won them a loyal following and the addition of Merlot and Cabernet to their lineup cemented a fondness by NW wine lovers. Chardonnay is round and rich with a reserve version made in a toasty, buttery, barrel-fermented style. Ripe and fruity reds have seen more wood in recent vintages. See **Best of the Northwest** reviews for Waterbrook Merlot and Chardonnay on pages 20 and 23.

Woodward Canyon Winery

Rt. 1, Box 387
State Highway 12
Lowden, WA 99360
(509) 525-4129

Owners: Rick &
Darcey Fugman-Small
Winemaker:
Rick Small
First Year: 1981
Winery Capacity:
13,500 Gallons
1991 Production:
13,000 Gallons

Tasting Room Hours:
Daily, 10 AM to 5 PM
(summer hours), open
to 4 PM only in winter.
Also participate in the
May and September
Walla Walla area open
houses.

Winery History

The awards came early for Rick Small, an enthusiastic and spirited winemaker who prefers to concentrate his efforts on a few varietals produced in small volume. Northwest recognition for his efforts included many gold medals, wine of the year awards, and several bests of show. Indeed the local lovers of barrel-fermented Chardonnay and ripe and toasty Cabernet Sauvignon and Merlot catapulted Woodward Canyon to fame in the 1980s.

The 1990s have seen the discovery of Woodward Canyon by the national wine press. Rick's Cabernet gained a position on the top 10 wines in the world list, and high ratings continue to drive a much accelerated demand.

A recent association with Canoe Ridge Vineyard and Chalone of California promises to add a new dimension to Rick Small's efforts. This vineyard property is located a few miles west of Paterson along the Columbia River and is just beginning to produce Merlot and other varietals.

The original Woodward Canyon vineyard, located five miles northwest of Lowden, is planted exclusively to Chardonnay. Rick Small chose the vineyard site because of a heavy concentration of limestone in the soil and has been rewarded with excellent wines from the estate grapes.

A visit to Woodward Canyon

Woodward Canyon Winery is located in a collection of small warehouse-style buildings in 'downtown' Lowden, Washington. Across the highway from the grain elevator and back through the parking lot, a small sign welcomes visitors to the tasting room where inside, Caleb Foster pours wine and explains the winery processes to visitors interested in Woodward Canyon's award-winning wines. Owners Rick and Darcey are sometimes on hand at regional wine festivals and other major events.

The Wines

Woodward Canyon's fame has come from toasty, mouth-filling Chardonnay and ripe Cabernet Sauvignon with a hearty backbone of oak. The Roza Bergé and Columbia Valley Chardonnays offer vanilla and tropical fruit and a long complex finish. Cabernets are intensely ripe and fruity. The Woodward Canyon newsletter offers winery fans insights into seasonal winery happenings and advance notice of upcoming releases. Call for info.

Walla Walla Accommodations & Dining

You won't find a place with more pioneer history than Walla Walla. As one of the end points of the Oregon Trail, the local community attracted some of the first permanent settlers in the State of Washington. The fertile Walla Walla Valley, long a prime agricultural center for a variety of crops, is now a recognized viticultural appellation.

Although opportunities for fine dining and accomodations are sparse, there are some interesting places to stay and several noteworthy restaurants. Coming to Walla Walla without visiting some of the Historical Parks would be a shame. Much of our Northwest history is echoed in events documented at Fort Walla Walla Museum and the Whitman Mission site. The Hot Air Balloon Stampede held each year on the first weekend in May is worth a special trip to visit.

Accommodations

Green Gables Inn, 922 Bonsella, Walla Walla 99362 (509)525-5501 This historic mansion has been converted into a luxury B & B with each room having its own bath. The quiet tree-lined streets for which Walla Walla is famous are yours for evening or morning strolling.

The Marcus Whitman, 107 N. 2nd - (509) 525-2200 The historic Marcus Whitman Hotel has been modernized to become one of the nice places to stay in Walla Walla. Once associated with a Black Angus Motor Inn, the hotel portion is now consolidated under one name. Restaurant, pool, air-conditioned rooms.

Dining

Patit Creek, 725 E. Dayton Ave., Dayton - (509) 382-2625 Not in Walla Walla, but the finest gourmet dining in the area. Fresh regional ingredients are innovatively prepared with care by owners Bruce and Heather Hiebert. Excellent NW wine list. Reservations required on weekends. Tues. - Sat.

The Iceburg, W. Birch at 9th, Walla Walla (509) 529-1793 Terrific hamburgers, shakes and fries. Worth a visit.

Merchants Limited, 21 E. Main - (509) 525-0900 A bright spot in town with delicious baked goods, a broad selection of fine wines and a many deli items for the hungry wine lover. Sit down dining is available upstairs.

Jacobi's, 416 N. 2nd, (509) 525-2677, The current *in* spot in town, located in the former Northern Pacific Depot. Pizza and deli fare are the draws.

For Parents Only

Bring the kids out for the Balloon Stampede! There are so many events associated with this weekend that there's bound to be something for everyone. Winery open house, too!

Pioneer Park, just east of downtown has 47 acres of shaded play area with a duck pond, kiddie pool and play equipment. Division & Alder.

McDonald's - 2130 Isaacs - East end of town. Drive-Thru, Open Sundays, all the regular McD's stuff. OR take 'em to The Iceburg (see above)

Fort Walla Walla Park - Besides the interpretive center and museum this large park has campsites and RV sites for those who prefer the great outdoors. West end of town.

Whitman Mission Memorial - The site of the Whitman Mission and the massacre that occurred there after an outbreak of measles decimated the local indian population.

111

Washington State

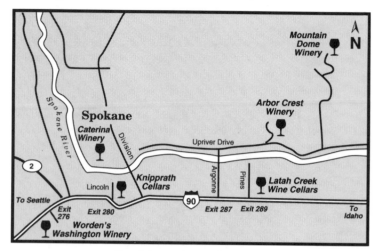

Spokane Area Touring

Whether you're traveling to Spokane for the Lilac Festival in May, a golfing vacation on some of the Northwest's finest courses in June, or for some winter skiing at Mount Spokane, you'll find some great wineries to tour.

Coming in from the west on Interstate 90 keep your eyes peeled on the right for Worden's Washington Winery. Take exit 276 and head south to Thorpe Road where a right turn leads you to the winery. The tasting room and winery offices are in a log cabin with a wonderful, lush green lawn for picnicking. Everything inside is well-appointed and Jack and Phyllis Worden are always eager to have you sample their wines.

Closer to town, Knipprath Cellars is just north of I-90 next to the historic WWP Steam Plant (take exit 280 and head north on Lincoln to 2nd St.). The winery offers tasting and sales of current releases as well as tours through the production facility. Call ahead for an appointment.

Just across the Spokane River Stephen Thomas Livingstone winery has relocated into the Broadway Dairy building and has changed both name and ownership. Call ahead for the latest news and directions.

The other Spokane wineries are several miles east of town, so get back on I-90 and drive east to exit 287. Arbor Crest Estate is reached by traveling north from the highway on Argonne to Upriver Drive. Turn right and drive to Fruithill Road which winds up the steep slope to the Estate. The remarkable mansion and grounds provide many fascinating insights into the original owner and builder, Royal Riblet. The Arbor Crest Estate is open only to persons 21 years and older.

Latah Creek Wine Cellars is located near I-90 off Pines Road. The tasting room at Latah Creek offers all manner of wine-related gift items and they encourage Christmas-shopping-weary enophiles to have a taste of wine and leisurely browse through the many treasures available for purchase.

Mountain Dome Winery produces only methode champenoise sparkling wine and is open by appointment. Call ahead and owners Michael and Patricia Manz will give you driving directions to their unique winery and home in the foothills south of Mount Spokane.

Arbor Crest Cliff House above the Spokane River.

Arbor Crest Wine Cellars

N. 4705 Fruithill Rd.
Spokane, WA 99207
(509) 927-9463

Owners: David
and Harold Mielke
Winemaker:
Mikhail Brunshteyn
First Year: 1982
Winery Capacity:
150,000 Gallons
1991 Production:
40,000 Gallons

Tasting Room Hours:
Daily, Noon to 5 PM
Must be 21 years or
older to enter the
estate.

Winery History

Owners David and Harold Mielke began Arbor Crest Winery as a brotherly project and a diversification from their fruit packing business. Their success has been complete with award-winning varietals being produced annually since the first harvest in 1982. The restoration of Arbor Crest Estate into a visitor facility is complete and the historic site is open daily for visits and wine tasting. The actual winemaking currently takes place at another Spokane location.

A visit to Arbor Crest

The Arbor Crest Estate is a remarkable structure built in 1924 by Royal N. Riblet, a wealthy Spokane businessman who created a remarkable mansion above the Spokane River. The stone structure and its accompanying gazebo and landscaped grounds make a wonderful afternoon's exploration by interested winelovers. Marmots climb the rocky cliff and chatter at intruders and the dozens of personal touches left by Royal Riblet are intriguing and, at times, mystifying. Wine tasting is offered in the lower level of the mansion where several of Arbor Crest's releases may be sampled.

The Wines

Producing a wide selection of varietals, Arbor Crest has developed a consistent style of high quality wines. Their best efforts include Merlot, Chardonnay, Sauvignon Blanc and Sémillon. See **Best of the Northwest** reviews of these excellent bottlings beginning on page 14 of this guide.

Washington State

The Caterina Winery

The Broadview Dairy
Washington St. at
North River Drive

Owners:
Caterina Trust,
Fred & Karen Hollin
Winemaker:
Michael Scott
First Year: 1993
Winery Capacity:
12,000 Gallons
**1993 Crush
(anticipated):**
75 tons

Tasting Room Hours:
To be determined

Winery History

Beginning life as the Steven Thomas Livingstone winery up the street on Division, Caterina Winery will be operated by Livingstone cellarmaster and manager Michael Scott. Purchase of the winery equipment and wine inventory was made possible through local investors with the facility being moved to the Broadview Dairy near the Spokane Riverfront Park. This historic site is shared with a milk processing plant and is being upgraded with more facilities for tourists. Caterina Winery will occupy the lower level of the building with entrance on the south side facing Cavanaugh's Inn at the Park.

A visit to Caterina Winery

Winery transfer of ownership and completion of moving tanks and equipment will take place in Fall of 1993. Call directory assistance for the winery's new phone number or visit the site after that time. A full tasting room program is planned.

The Wines

Purchase of wine inventory from Livingstone will allow a continuance of style since Mike Scott exerted considerable influence in his former position as cellarmaster/manager. Chardonnay, Sauvignon Blanc, Merlot and Cabernet Sauvignon may be joined by other varietals as production stabilizes and grape sources become available.

Knipprath Cellars

Knipprath Cellars

1991
WASHINGTON STATE
Reserve Chardonnay
Columbia Valley

S. 163 Lincoln St.
Spokane, WA 99201
(509) 483-1926

Owner & Winemaker:
Henning Knipprath
First Year: 1991

Tasting Room Hours:
By appointment only or
for special events

Winery History

"Knipprath Cellars was started in 1991 by a small circle of friends and is dedicated to producing the finest hand-crafted wines available." Henning Knipprath is the winemaker for the group and his name is carried on he winery label. The small winery operation is currently located in the "future downtown arts and entertainment district" of Spokane, near the WWP Plant!

A visit to Knipprath Cellars

Knipprath (pronounced "nip rath") Cellars offers special tastings and visits to the winery by appointment and during events announced through the winery newsletter. Write or call the winery to be added to their mailing list.

The Wines

Current releases from Knipprath include Chardonnay, Riesling, Dry Riesling, Late Harvest Riesling, White Cabernet and Knipprath Nouveau.

Latah Creek
Wine Cellars

E. 13030 Indiana
Spokane, WA 99216
(509) 926-0164

Owner & Winemaker:
 Mike Conway
First Year: 1982
Winery Capacity:
 35,000 Gallons
1991 Production:
 28,000 Gallons

Tasting Room Hours:
Daily, 10 AM - 5 PM
Sunday, Noon - 5 PM

Winery History
 Another California wine veteran, Mike Conway left his assistant winemaker's job at Parducci to come north and make wine for Jack Worden at Worden's Washington Winery. Two years later in 1982 he started his own enterprise in partnership with Mike Hogue. Today, according to the original plan, he is now sole proprietor of the winery.

A visit to Latah Creek Wine Cellars
 Styled after 'Spanish Mission' architecture, the winery is just off Interstate 90 east of Spokane on Indiana Road. The winery offers a year-round tasting room pouring samples of the broad range of wines produced here. Also on display in the tasting room is a collection of artwork by Yakima wildlife artist, Floyd Broadbent. Each vintage a different painting is featured on the Latah Creek label. The winery's well-stocked gift shop offers all manner of wine-related items for sale.

The Wines
 Latah Creek produces a delicious Chenin Blanc, Riesling and other wines but our **Best of the Northwest** Chardonnay panel found Mike Conway's Feather Chardonnay to be just the answer to overblown oaky versions so popular these days. It's nice to have a choice. Also made at Latah Creek are Merlot and Lemberger.

Mountain Dome
Winery

16315 E. Temple Rd.
Spokane, WA 99207
(509) 928-BRUT

Owners:
 Michael and
 Patricia Manz
Winemaker:
 Michael Manz
First Year: 1984
Winery Capacity:
 6,000 Gallons
1992 Production:
 6,000 Gallons

Winery History
 Up in the foothills of Mount Spokane in a beautiful forest of conifers is the dome-shaped home of Dr. Michael Manz and his family. Nearby, the winery-named-after-the-home is now completed and is equipped with the most modern gear for producing methode champenoise sparkling wine.

 Dr. Manz knows what he likes and it's not André extra dry from California. His favorite sparklers include top of the line vintage and nonvintage bruts from Champagne and his goal is to make wines of that quality.

A visit to Mountain Dome Winery
 The winery is open by appointment to those keen on taking a look at the sparkling wine operation. Two festivals are planned each year and you may write to be included on the Mountain Dome mailing list.

Continued on next page.

Patricia and Michael Manz with their youngest daughter, Rachael relax on a hot summer day in front of the winery.

The Wines of Mountain Dome Winery

Production of sparkling wine at Mountain Dome has been increasing steadily since the first small lots were laid down 'sur lie' in 1984. The grape crush in 1988 was 16 tons - 10 tons more than in 1987. Crush in 1992 was 45 tons.

The cuveé for Mountain Dome's sparkling wine is a blend of two-thirds Pinot Noir and one-third Chardonnay. The grapes are brought up from vineyards near Pasco and are picked early to achieve the sugar/acid balance necessary for flavorful Champagne-style wines. The cuveé is fermented in French oak barrels. A new disgorging line arrived from France in 1992 and the 5,000 square foot winery was busy with bottling activity for many weeks.

The first release took place in October of 1992 with Mountain Dome's Washington State Brut from the 1988 vintage. A delightful wine with aromas of toast and pear drops that shows the finesse and complexity of the finest sparkling wines.

Worden's Washington Winery

7217 W. 45th
Spokane, WA 99202
(509) 455-7835

Owner: Jack Worden
Winemaker:
  Paul Vandenburg
First Year: 1980
Winery Capacity:
  50,000 Gallons

Tasting Room Hours:
Daily, Noon to 5 PM

Winery History

The first winery to open its doors in Spokane and one of the first to begin serious winemaking in Washington, Worden's has continued to produce quality wines from fruit grown in the Columbia Valley appellation. Several noted Northwest winemakers began their careers here.

A visit to Worden's Winery

Worden's Washington Winery is nestled in a forest of pine trees on the western outskirts of Spokane. The A-frame cabin that serves as tasting room seems an appropriate structure in the quiet, woodsy setting quite remarkably close to Interstate 90. This popular stopping place is great for picnicking and relaxing under the Ponderosa pines.

The Wines

An unusual approach to red wine making (until recent years!) has been the 50/50 blending of Worden's Cabernet/Merlot. The softening effect of the Merlot makes the wine drinkable at a younger age and provides pleasant drinking for those with less of a 'red wine palate'. Chardonnay, Gewurztraminer, Riesling and Chenin Blanc are also made.

Spokane Area Accommodations & Dining

For the wine lover traveling to Spokane there are many interesting sights to fill the hours between visits to the area wineries. Spokane is Washington's second largest city and the urban center of the city offers fine restaurants and entertainment while the outlying areas provide some of the State's best golf courses as well as excellent fishing, hunting and hiking. A wonderful time to visit Spokane is the spring when the snows of winter have melted away and the flowers for which the city is famous have burst into bloom.

Accommodations

Cavanaugh's Inn at the Park, W 303 North River Dr. - 800-THE-INNS, (509) 326-8000   New hotel downtown with all the luxury amenities you can ask for. The five-story atrium lobby offers two restaurants and lounges while three heated pools, and fitness center keep you physically active. Suites with fireplaces, view rooms and rooms with balconies. $69 and up.

Cavanaugh's River Inn, N 700 Division St. - (509) 326-5577 Just north of town this hotel features a resort-like setting with tennis courts, putting green, playground, pools and sauna. Restaurant and lounge. $61 and up.

Sheraton Spokane, 322 N. Spokane Falls Court, 99220 (509) 455-9600 On the river and visible from much of downtown, this is another of Spokane's fine hotels. The atrium pool and spacious rooms and suites are but two of the quality features. Moderately priced considering the amenities.

Ridpath Hotel, W 515 Sprague - (800) 555-7122 (WA), (800) 426-0670 (USA), (509) 838-2711   A Spokane classic restored to modern splendor. Fine dining at the rooftop Ankeny's restaurant. $52 and up.

Washington State
Dining

Patsy Clark's, W 2208 Second Ave. - (509) 838-8300 A luxuriously restored mansion with unique dining rooms. restored to their original grace and charm. The menu changes seasonally with both local and exotic selections. Extensive wine list with many North-west selections.

Ankeny's, W 515 Sprague, (509) 838-6311 A wonderful view-restaurant and bar atop the Ridpath Hotel down-town. Many interesting menu items and appetizers. Complete wine list.

C. I. Shenanigan's, N 332 Spokane Falls Court - (509) 455-5072 Seafood, beef and pasta restaurant on the banks of the Spokane River. Summertime deck dining and attractive lounge. Good selection of NW wines and beers.

Milford's Fish House and Oyster Bar, N. 719 Monroe (509) 326-7251 A Spokane institution for many years, this is the choice for fine seafood from NW waters. The busy Oyster Bar offers a place to meet new people in a convivial, yet civilized, atmosphere.

Coeur d'Alene, Idaho

Beverly's at the Coeur d'Alene Resort Exit 11 off I-90, (208) 765-4000. This magnificent resort is the show-place of the region and the restaurant included as the resort's finest has a well-deserved reputation for the area's finest meals. The wine cellar at Beverly's is a masterpiece with wines spanning both globe and with a deep selection of Northwest favorites.

Spokane Area Activities - For Parents Only

In the warm, Spokane summer your kids will appreciate a motel with a pool and there are several nice ones to choose from. Also the American Hot Rod Association has an event here in August for all the young car buffs in the family.

Riverfront Park - This decade-old world's fair ground has some fancy stuff for kids to do and some nice things for Mom and Dad too. Close to downtown - just across the bridge from Cavanaugh's Inn at the Park.

Manito Park - South of I-90 off Grand, this park includes various gardens and a conservatory, not tremendously in-teresting for younger children but an enjoyable outing none-the-less.

Spokane Lilac Festival - With the coming of spring comes the blooming of Spokane's namesake flower and a parade for the enjoyment all. Third week in May.

Mirabeau Park and Walk in the Wild Zoo - N. Pines & E. Euclid - (509) 924-7220 A unique park and zoo for appreciation of animals in their natu-ral habitats.

Joggers - and their kids will enjoy the chance to participate in the Blooms-day Fun Run 12K race along with fifty thousand other like-minded hoofers. The run takes a tour of much of Spo-kane winding up and down more than one tiring hill. Over 50,000 people finish the run each year.

Riverside State Park - Northwest of the city - camping, hiking, horseback riding along the beautiful Spokane River. 100 RV hookups.

Finch Arboretum - Near downtown at W 3404 Woodland Blvd. - Take the kids out for a nature hike in this 65 acre tree preserve.

Skiing - Four major ski resorts are within a two hour drive of Spokane. Take 'em out in the snow for a change of pace.

Methode Champenoise Sparkling Wine Production

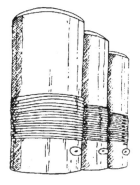

The first sparkling wines produced at l'Abbaye d'Hautvilliers prompted Dom Perignon to exclaim "I'm drinking stars!" While this certainly overstated the reality, his discovery of how to keep wine under pressure has had a profound effect on the wine drinking world. The refined process know as methode champenoise (met toad shamp in wahs) creates sparkling wine in the same bottle where the secondary fermentation and aging took place.

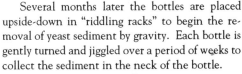

Sparkling wine begins as still wine (without bubbles) fermented in stainless steel tanks and combined into a blend or "cuvée" (koo vay). To this still wine blend is added "liqueur de tiriage," a mixture of sugar, yeast and wine, to begin the second fermentation which will untimately give us "stars" to drink. The wine is placed in champagne bottles and capped with crown caps (beer caps).

Several months later the bottles are placed upside-down in "riddling racks" to begin the removal of yeast sediment by gravity. Each bottle is gently turned and jiggled over a period of weeks to collect the sediment in the neck of the bottle.

To remove the collected sediment, the bottles are chilled and placed neck-down in a freezing brine solution which freezes a plug of wine and sediment in the neck of the bottle. This plug is "disgorged" by the pressure built up in the bottle when the crown cap is removed. A "dosage" is added (a mixture of sugar, brandy and wine) to create the final sweetness level in the sparkling wine. A month or two of rest and the sparkling wine is on its way to your celebration.

To safely open a bottle of sparkling wine, first remove the foil and loosen the wire hood holding the cork down. Remove the hood, keeping your thumb over the cork. Cover the top of the bottle loosely with a cloth napkin and grasp the cork firmly. Holding the bottle at a 45° angle, turn the bottle until the cork comes out with a small "pop."

By the way, if you'd like to win a bet at your next wine tasting, ask your friends what Dom Perignon's first name was. You'll know the answer, Pierre.

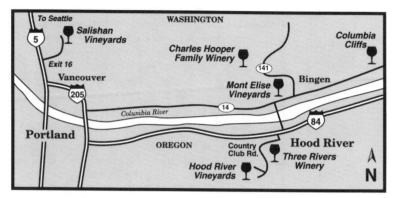

SW Washington & Columbia Gorge Wine Touring

The pastoral farmlands of Southwest Washington and the magnificence of the Columbia River Gorge are the non-enological highlights of touring this area. The icing on the cake is the collection of fine wineries found here.

The I-5 traveller can take a break from the rush of the freeway to stop and visit Joan and Lincoln Wolverton at Salishan Vineyards just northeast of the town of LaCenter. The winery and the Wolverton's home are at the edge of the vineyard with views of the Lewis River Valley and its lush pastures and orchards. The winery is open weekends, 1 - 5 PM, summer and fall.

To make the connection to the Gorge Highway follow the signs to Interstate 205 which bypasses all the congestion of the Portland area. Shortly after crossing the Columbia River you'll see signs for Hood River and The Dalles pointing you to I-84.

The Columbia Gorge Highway (I-84) was built in the 1920s and since has provided many visitors with unequalled panoramas of geologic splendor. The scenic highway bypass is worth the extra driving time for first time visitors to get a peek at the waterfalls and beautiful canyons that line the Oregon side of the Gorge.

Hood River offers two winery stops for travelling winelovers. Just off the freeway at exit 62 (you'll see the big sign) turn right to find Three Rivers Winery on Country Club Road. Farther up the road and around a few well-marked turns is Hood River Vineyards.

Across the Hood River Bridge to Washington (50¢ toll) you can visit Mont Elise Vineyards winery and tasting room in downtown Bingen. A drive up Highway 141 through White Salmon to Husum is the first half of a scenic adventure to the Charles Hooper Family Winery. The quiet forest drive and views of Mt. Hood from the winery are well worth the drive.

Further up the Washington side of the Gorge you'll find Columbia Cliffs Winery near the town of Wishram. Call ahead to be sure the winery is open if you're traveling during the week or in the winter months.

Charles Hooper Family Winery

P. O. Box 215
196 Spring Creek Rd.
Husum, WA 98623
(509) 493-2324

Owner: Hooper Family
Winemaker:
Charles Hooper
Vineyard Manager:
Chris Hooper
First Year: 1985
Winery Capacity:
3,000 Gallons

Tasting Room Hours:
Mar. - Nov., Weekends,
11 AM to 6 PM
Also summer weekdays

Winery History

While living in France, England and Germany for more than 20 years, Charles and Beverlee Hooper developed an interest in wine and viticulture. The dream of planting their own vineyard and founding a winery began to grow. With the help of their daughters Kim and Janet, son Chris and many friends, the first grapes were planted in 1979 overlooking the Columbia Gorge. With the opening of the Charles Hooper Family Winery in 1985, the dream became a reality.

A visit to Hooper Family Winery

The alpine setting of the property is complemented by panoramic views of the Gorge and of Mount Hood in the distance. As you walk among the five acres of Riesling grapevines (trained on single stakes on terraced hillsides) you can hear the wind in the nearby fir trees and imagine yourself in the Mosel or Rheingau, on the steep slopes of the famous German vineyards. The quiet alpine vineyard makes a great site for warm-weather picnics.

The Wines

The wines made at Hooper Family Winery show the owner's palate and love for German style, off-dry wines. Made in a light style, the wines are excellent for accompanying picnics and casual sipping. Each wine is true to varietal character.

Columbia Cliffs Winery

8866 Highway 14
Wishram, WA
98673 • (509) 767-1100

Owners/Winemakers:
Kenn & Linda Adcock
First Year: 1985

Tasting Room Hours:
Weekends, Apr. - Oct.,
11 AM to 5 PM, also
most summer weekdays

Winery History

Towering basalt cliffs rise 400 feet above the north side of Columbia Cliffs Vineyard giving the name to both vineyard and winery. Kenn and Linda Adcock planted the vineyard and built the small winery in 1985.

A visit to Columbia Cliffs

Located near the famous Maryhill Museum (home of several Rodin sculptures and other rare original art) and near the replica of Stonehenge, Columbia Cliffs offers a unique micro-region for the study of several academic disciplines. The grandeur of the Columbia Gorge stimulates an interest in geology, as well..

The Wines

A wide selection of wines including Merlot, Petit Sirah, Pinot Noir, Nebbiolo, Cabernet Sauvignon, Muscat of Alexandria and Sauvignon Blanc are produced.

Hood River Vineyards

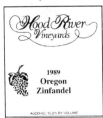

4693 Westwood Drive
Hood River, OR 97031
(503) 386-3772

Owners:
New Partnership
First Year: 1981
Winery Capacity:
10,000 Gallons
1991 Production:
7,000 Gallons

Tasting Room Hours:
Daily, 10 AM to noon,
1 PM to 5 PM
April 1 to December 1

Winery History

Orchardist and Hood River businessman Cliff Blanchette began a second career growing grapes in the hills above the Columbia River in the late 1970s and bonded his winery in 1981. The winery and tasting room provided employment for several family members during the 1980s. The winery was sold in 1993 to new investors whose plans for Hood River Vineyards are unclear.

A visit to Hood River Vineyards

Hood River Vineyards winery with the tremendous view atop the hill has been open April through the end of November welcoming winelovers for tasting or tours 7 days a week. With the new ownership, call ahead just to be sure.

The Wines

Cliff Blanchette's wines came from grapes grown in both Oregon and Washington and he always kept a supply of pear and raspberry on hand for regular customers who liked fruit wines. A Zinfandel wine crafted from local grapes is a favorite for lovers of red wine. The spicy character works well with hearty foods. New ownership may alter the mix of wines produced.

Mont Elise Vineyards

315 West Steuben
Bingen, WA 98605
(206) 493-3001

Owners: The Charles
Henderson Family
Winemaker:
Chuck Henderson, Jr.
First Year: 1975
Winery Capacity:
18,000 Gal.

Tasting Room Hours:
Daily, 11:30 AM - 5 PM

Winery History

Chuck Henderson, Sr. is one of the pioneers of fruit production along the Columbia Gorge. His efforts with Walter Clore in identifying local microclimates for winegrapes led others to plant vitis vinifera on nearby slopes. The original winery was named Bingen Wine Cellars but later changed to honor Chuck's daughter, Elise. His son, Chuck Jr., studied winemaking at U.C. Davis and has handled winemaking duties along with Chuck, Sr.

A visit to Mont Elise Vineyards

Dressed up Bavarian style, the town of Bingen on the Washington side of the Columbia Gorge plays up its German-immigrant heritage to attract the business of sightseers traveling through the area. The winery tasting room offers a picture-window view into the winery operation below. Visitors can often see some of the winemaking operations taking place or at least inspect the winery equipment while sampling a selection of Mont Elise wines. The new flow of visitors to the Gorge is due to the excellent wind surfing (board sailing) that has made the area an international mecca for the sport.

The Wines

Mont Elise Vineyards has long been hailed as one of the foremost producers of NW Gewürztraminer. The crisp, yet fruity style is not hard and tannic like Alsatian Gewürz, but offers more than just a simple sipping wine. Other varietals are well made, including the red wines Gamay Beaujolais and Pinot Noir.

The Henderson's latest project is a method champenoise sparkling wine made from Pinot Noir. Released in the fall of 1987, the wine is characterful in the French style with loads of fruit and yeasty-toasty nuances - very limited production.

Mt. Hood Winery

Government Camp
Loop Road
Mt. Hood, Oregon
(503) 272-3600

Owner: Gary Hood
Winemaker:
  Doug Whitlock
First Year: 1974
Winery Capacity;
  5,000 Gallons

Tasting Room Hours:
Winter or Summer
Mid-Season
Daily, noon to 6 PM
(later if the
night-skiing crowd demands it)

Winery History

Lester Martin, the original owner and winemaker of Mt. Hood Winery was content to make wine for 14 years from fruit of his own growing and welcome visitors to his small facility at the orchard. His successors made a bolder marketing statement by moving the winery to Mount Hood's Government Camp ski area just as the 1988 ski season got under way.

A visit to Mt. Hood Winery

Government Camp is a delightful place to start a winter or summer adventure. Winters see lots of snow for skiing, sledding and the like while the summer months see meadows of alpine wildflowers and birds chirping on every tree. Nature's change of face attracts thousands of recreational outdoors people each year. The winery to quench your thirst is right on Hwy. 26 - Government Camp Loop Road - you can't miss it!

The Wines

Mt. Hood Winery's winemaker is Vancouver, WA lawyer Doug Whitlock. Doug worked with Lester Martin to find out the secrets to making delicious fruit and berry wines and plans no drastic change from the successful recipes that have preceded him. Additional wines made from vinifera grapes have been added.

Joan Wolverton, winemaker and philosopher for Salishan Vineyards.

Salishan Vineyards

35011 North Fork Ave.
La Center, WA 98629
(206) 263-2713

Owners: Lincoln and
  Joan Wolverton
Winemaker:
  Joan Wolverton
First Year: 1977
Winery Capacity:
  10,000 Gallons
1991 Production:
  10,000 Gallons

Tasting Room Hours:
May - December, week-
ends, 1 PM to 5 PM
Tours and groups by
appointment.

Winery History

One of the original success stories for Northwest "dreams become reality" wineries, Salishan's insightful owner Joan Wolverton might add that dreams sure are a lot of hard work! The day to day struggle of coaxing grapes to ripeness, cajolling wines to perfection and chasing away flocks of hungry robins, all while raising a family must seem a great burden until she and Lincoln collect the gold medals for their hard work.

The vineyard near the tiny farming community of La Center, was begun in 1971. The intention of specializing in Pinot Noir seemed the right choice as even their earliest efforts won great praise. Today, in addition to well-received Pinot Noir, their dry Chenin Blanc and Dry Riesling get raves from consumers and wine judges alike. Wines that complement foods are their specialty.

A visit to Salishan Vineyards

Just five minutes from I-5, Salishan Vineyards is a convenient stop during the monotonous drive from Seattle to Portland. Weekend afternoons find winemaker Joan Wolverton dispensing not only award-winning wines but also wine information and insights spiced with her special sense of humor.

The tasting room is tucked away in a corner of the winery where Joan and Lincoln pour samples of popular releases. Truly a stop not to be missed!

The Wines

Salishan's early reputation came from the fine quality Pinot Noir harvested from their vineyard at the winery. The microclimate is a proven one for this varietal with a neighboring vineyard providing grapes for Columbia Winery's Pinot and also other smaller producers.

Recently, Salishan's claim to fame has turned white. Dry Riesling and Dry Chenin Blanc have jumped-in to share the spotlight with the Pinot Noir. These two wines as made by Joan Wolverton are excellent accompaniments to lighter foods and appetizers.

Three Rivers Winery

275 Country Club Road
Hood River, OR 97031
(503) 386-5453

Owner / Winemaker:
Bill Swain
First Year: 1986
Winery Capacity:
12,500 Gallons
1991 Production:
7,500 Gallons

Tasting Room Hours:
April - December -
daily, 11 AM to 6 PM,
Sunday 1 PM to 5 PM
January - March - Fri. &
Sat., 11 AM to 6 PM,
Sunday 1 to 5 PM

Winery History

Fifteen years after graduating from U. C. Davis, Bill Swain fulfilled the dream of many young enologists by opening his own winery. The experience he gained at Charles Krug Winery in the Napa Valley and at Cresta Blanca Winery in Ukiah prepared him well for the venture he now directs in Oregon. Bill first came to Washington and planted his vineyard in 1981 near the small, Columbia Gorge community of Underwood. The south facing slope and well-drained soil seemed a perfect combination for winegrapes and the five-acre plot was planted two-thirds to Riesling and one-third to Pinot Noir. The winery location across the Columbia in Hood River was chosen for marketing reasons - direct access to tourist traffic off Interstate 84.

A visit to Three Rivers Winery

The winery's tasting room is located in the 'Copper House,' a turn of the century home along Country Club Road. Bill and Ann Swain have spiffed up the living and dining rooms to act as a gift shop and tasting room. A large fireplace insert warms the rooms for winter visitors. Look for Three Rivers Winery just off exit 62 from Interstate 84.

The Wines

Bill Swain crafts easy-drinking Riesling and Gewürz with distinctive aroma and an off-dry palate. Chardonnay and Pinot Noir complement fine cooking with a dry palate and lots of fruit and complexity gained through oak aging.

SW Washington & Columbia Gorge

Accommodations

Columbia Gorge Hotel 4000 Westcliff Drive, Hood River, OR 97031 (503) 386-5566, out of state: 1-800-345-1921 This famous hotel once hosted Rudolph Valentino and other famous personalities from the 1920s upon completion by timber baron Simon Benson. The hotel today offers quiet elegance and a magnificent view of the Gorge. Immaculate garden out front for relaxing and a "World Famous Farm Breakfast" is included for guests. Expensive

Vagabond Lodge 4070 Westcliff Dr., Hood River, OR 97031 (503) 386-2992 Right next door to the Columbia Gorge Hotel and half the price! Some of the view rooms rival the best the CGH has to offer.

Lakecliff Estate 3820 Westcliff Dr., Hood River, OR 97031, (503) 386-7000 In this city of many enjoyable B & Bs, this one stands out for its history, location and view of the latest action to come down the Gorge. Friendly hosts, delicious breakfast, varied accommodations to suit all tastes.

Orchard Hill Inn Rt. 2, Box 130 - Oak Ridge Road, White Salmon, WA 98672 (509) 493-3024 Up in the hills across the valley from Charles Hooper Winery, this secluded bed and breakfast is nestled along the White Salmon River. Three rooms are available in the main house and a separate 8-bed bunkhouse with private bath and conference table offers a unique alternative. Sideboard breakfast included.

Dining

Hood River

Stone Hedge Inn, 3405 Cascade Drive, Hood River (503) 386-3940 The food and service at this elegant restaurant wins raves from locals and visitors alike. Well-prepared seafood and meats are complemented by local fresh produce and a NW/Continental cooking style. Beautiful grounds and a well-thought out collection of wines.

Peter B's, , 13th & B Streets, Hood River (503) 386-2111 Peter Bollinger's converted house near downtown is home to some of Hood River's most imaginative culinary creations. Influences from widely international sources create a lively menu and unique daily specials. Awesome desserts and a top-flight wine list.

Underwood, WA

The Partridge Inn, Cook-Underwood Road, Underwood (509) 493-2381 A dinner house in the country tradition overlooking the Columbia Gorge. Classy entrees and delicious pies for dessert. Wed. through Sun.

For Parents Only - Local Activities

Bonneville Dam, Cascade Locks, OR Come and see where electricity is made. Kids marvel at the size of the dam and the turbines in the power house. If you come in the right season you can watch salmon jumping up the fish ladder to reach their spawning grounds. A nice city park in Cascade Locks provides an opportunity for picnicing.

Maryhill Museum, Maryhill, WA Sam Hill, son-in-law of James J. Hill, built this mansion for his wife but it's now a fantastic, if lonely, art museum. A large collection of Rodin sculptures, French and American paintings and a replica of Stonehenge hold fascination for children of all ages.

Oregon
Wine Touring

Oregon

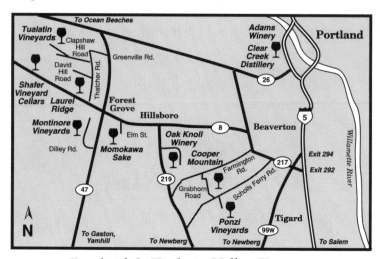

Portland & Tualatin Valley Touring

Portland, the City of Roses, is a beautiful urban environment where the citizens care very much about livability and style. The surrounding bedroom communities of Beaverton, Hillsboro and Forest Grove offer a mix of residential and farm usage with wineries one of the more recent iterations of the latter.

Right in downtown Portland is Adams Vineyard Winery. Famed for high quality Pinot Noir, the winery is open only by appointment. Their Northwet Portland neighborhood also includes Clear Creek Distillery, regionally famous maker of eau de vie. Clear Creek is open by appointment also.

A few minutes south of Washington Square in Beaverton, Ponzi Vineyards welcomes visitors on weekends from Noon to 5 PM and weekdays from 10 AM to 5 PM. Their attractive picnic area is a shady summer retreat for snacking and wine sipping. Ponzi Reserve Pinot Noir has become internationally famous.

Just northwest of Ponzi, Cooper Mountain Vineyards winery is open Friday through Sunday from Noon to 5 PM. Bob and Corrine Gross operate this growing venture featuring one of Oregon's largest plantings of Pinot Gris.

Oak Knoll Winery is a few miles further west tucked away on Burkhalter Road. Open daily from Noon to 5 PM, Oak Knoll is well known not only for Pinot Noir and other grape varietals but also for delicious fruit wines.

Four wineries (and one sake producer!) are open to the public near Forest Grove. Tualatin Vineyards is open daily at their location in the picturesque farmland north of of town. Harvey & Miki Shafer welcome visitors daily down the road in Gales Creek at Shafer Vineyard Cellars. Their shady veranda is just the spot for an afternoon rest and a picnic.

The historic site of Laurel Ridge winery on David Hill Road lays claim to being one of Oregon's oldest wine producers. The winery is open daily from Noon to 5 PM. Montinore Vineyards, southwest of town on Dilley Road, has completed their visitor center to complement their impressive 700-acre estate.

Momokawa Sake is open for tasting and sales of their unique products just off the Tualatin Valley Hiway. A not-to-be-missed learning experience for wine lovers, the explanation of the sake brewing process is most interesting.

Adams Vineyard Winery

1922 NW Pettygrove St.
Portland, OR 97209
(503) 294-0606

Owners: Peter and
Carol Adams
Winemaker:
Carol Adams
First Year: 1981
Winery Capacity:
10,000 Gallons
1991 Production:
8,000 Gallons

Tasting Room Hours:
By appointment only.

Winery History

Peter and Carol Adams added yet another dimension to their busy lives when they bonded Adams Vineyard Winery in 1981. This solidified the family's commitment to the making of fine wine in the Pacific Northwest. Their weekday schedule finds Peter most often involved in one or more of his several business interests while Carol holds down the fort at the winery and does occasional writing on the subjects of food and wine. Evenings and weekends find the family together, either at home, at the winery or at their 18 acre vineyard near Newberg in Yamhill County.

A visit to Adams Vineyard Winery

The winery offers no tasting room or tours, but the fine wines produced there are available in Northwest's larger cities and in selected national markets. Serious fans of the winery may call or write for an appointment to visit the Northwest Portland location.

The Wines

Several large tastings of Oregon Pinot Noir have revealed Adams Vineyard Pinot to be among the most age-worthy in the state. Bottling versions from both Yamhill County (the Adams estate vineyard) and Polk County, winemaker Carol Adams produces rich wines of great character. Crisp Chardonnay and Sauvignon Blanc are favorites with seafood. See **Best of the Northwest** reviews of Adams Pinot Noir on page 17.

Clear Creek Distillery

1430 NW 23rd Ave.
Portland, OR 97210
(503) 248-9470

**Owner and
Winemaker/Distiller:**
Stephen R. Mc Carthy
First Year: 1986
Production Capacity:
100,000 Gal.

Tasting Room Hours:
By appointment only.

Winery History:

Native Northwesterner Stephen McCarthy graduated from Reed College in Portland and then attended NYU law school. Success in business followed with Steve well-aligned on the fast track. Along came a trip to France in 1982 where Stephen enjoyed his first taste of traditional eau-de-vie, the 'water of life' distilled in many villages in Alsace from local fruits and berries. This was of particular interest to McCarthy because his family owned a large pear orchard in Hood River. Eau-de-vie de poire, pear brandy, seemed like the perfect answer to surplus pears.

Experiments with distillations led to purchases of more and more specialized equipment and to

Continued on next page.

Oregon

Steve McCarthy of Clear Creek Distillery.

better and better prototype eaux-de-vie. In 1987 a decision was made to finance a commercial distillery. The Oregon liquor board proved to be a friend, not an enemy, and helped secure the necessary permits to allow commercial production and sale of the brandy in state liquor outlets. Today, the Clear Creek product line includes not only eaux-de-vie, but several types of grappa as well. Grappa is a spirit that is distilled using grape pomace left over from wine production.

A visit to Clear Creek Distillery

If you are fascinated by eau-de-vie and would like to see how it is produced, Steve McCarthy will show you around his operation by appointment. The rows of barrels and gleaming copper stills are a delight to the eye. A well-informed host, Steve is a wealth of information on the history and making of eaux-de-vie.

The Spirits

The eaux-de-vie produced at Clear Creek include versions made from pear, apple, raspberry and cherry. Each of these is effusively fruity to the nose and offers a complex palate and long finish. Grappa made from Pinot Gris and Muscat are delightful "digestifs" and the Gewurztraminer "Marc" (pronounced "mar") is pungent and fiery.

Cooper Mountain Vineyards

9480 SW Grabhorn Rd.
Beaverton, OR 97007
(503) 649-0027

Owners: Robert and
Corrine Gross
Winemakers: Bob
Gross, Rich Cushman
First Year: 1987
Winery Capacity:
 5,600 Gallons
1991 Production:
 5,600 Gallons

Tasting Room Hours:
Feb. - Nov., Fri., Sat.,
Sun. - Noon to 5 PM

Winery History

A career-related move to Portland in the mid-1970s led Bob and Corrine Gross to the purchase of the Cooper Homestead located just south of Beaverton. The 1865 homestead is located on an extinct volcano and proved to have excellent potential as vineyard land. The first acres of Pinot Noir, Chardonnay and Pinot Gris were planted in 1978. Grapes flourished on the site and the Gross family was content to sell their harvests to other Oregon vintners who made award-winners by the dozens. Of course, a true winelover couldn't long resist the temptation to try his own hand at the finished product so in 1987 Bob Gross fermented both Pinot Noir and Chardonnay under the tutelage of Rich Cushman.

A visit to Cooper Mountain Vineyards

A large winery building and cozy tasting room adjoin the Cooper Mountain Vineyard at the Gross' home near Beaverton. Accessible from either Farmington or Scholls Ferry Roads, the site offers a magnificent southwest view and a grassy knoll for picnicking. Weekend hours are Noon to 5 PM.

The Wines

Regular and reserve bottlings of Pinot Noir and Chardonnay have been well received by fans of Cooper Mountain Vineyards. Pinot Gris is the favored varietal and offers a delightful alternative for pairing with seafood and lighter meats. See **Best of the Northwest** review on page 27.

Laurel Ridge Winery

David Hill Road
P.O. Box 456
Forest Grove, OR
97116 • (503) 359-5436

Owners: Corporate
 Partnership
First Year: 1986
Winery Capacity:
 25,000 Gallons

Tasting Room Hours:
Daily, Noon to 5 PM
Closed January

Winery History

This property has a long and varied history going back to the 19th century when vineyards were originally planted at the site and the farmhouse was built. The wine boom of the 1970s saw first the Charles Coury Winery in residence, then an operation named Reuter's Hill Winery gave it a go, hoping that naming the place after the original settler would bring good luck. It didn't. The Reuter's Hill wine inventory was sold off at $1 a bottle during Thanksgiving weekend of 1980.

After six years of dormancy the property was purchased and resurrected by a partnership of families already successful in various businesses, most notably grape growing.

Continued on next page.

Oregon

Sauvignon Blanc/Semillon

The current owners have spruced up the farmhouse and grounds and offer visiting winelovers a nice lawn on which to enjoy their picnic. The acres of vineyard spread out behind the winery making a restful wine country vista.

A visit to Laurel Ridge Winery

The Laurel Ridge site is just northwest of Forest Grove. Take Thatcher Road then turn left down David Hill Road. A couple of tight curves in the winery's driveway suggest that leaving the Winnebago at home might be in order, otherwise it's easy for cars to make their way. The tasting room is open daily from Noon to 5 PM.

The Wines

Several versions of methode champenoise sparkling wine are produced here along with other still varietal wines. Crisp Sauvignon Blanc and Gewürztraminer are available, as is Pinot Noir.

Momokawa Sake, Ltd.

MOMOKAWA PREMIUM SAKE

920 Elm Street
Forest Grove, OR
97116 • (503) 357-7056

Owner: Momokawa Sake, Ltd., Grif Frost
Toji: Ben Ben
First Year: 1992

Tasting Room Hours:
Daily, Noon to 5 PM

Winery History

Momokawa Sake, a famous Japanese producer has come to Oregon to try making the centuries old brewed rice "wine" with local ingredients. The sake making process is fascinating and is thoroughly explained by the well-informed tasting room staff. Appreciated like wine, a sake tasting is most revealing to many American consumers who know little of this ancient beverage. Imported Japanese sakes are poured as of press time for this book (1993) but the brewery is expected to be producing Oregon sake by 1994.

A visit to Momokawa

Just up the road from Forest Grove and Hillsboro, the Momokawa facility is located on the Tualatin Valley Highway. The traditional Japanese decor, including a small Japanese garden outside, gives the visitor a unique sense of experiencing something special. As mentioned above, the sake tasting and explanation of the sake-making process are both informative and enjoyable.

The Sake

Four versions of Momokawa Japanese sake are currently poured. Ranging from rare and expensive to traditional "everyday" sake, the products offer distinct and enjoyable differences.

132

Montinore
Vineyards

P.O. Box 560
3663 SW Dilley Road
Forest Grove, OR
97116 • (503) 359-5012

Owners:
  Leo and Jane Graham
Winemaker:
  Jacques Tardy
First Year: 1987
Winery Capacity:
  50,000 Gallons

Tasting Room Hours:
Daily, Noon to 5 PM

Winery History

Montinore (a contraction of Montana-in-Oregon) was the name coined in 1905 for the property now planted with 430 acres of vineyard two miles south of Forest Grove. The property's owner at the time was John Forbis, a former corporate attorney for Anaconda Copper and acquisitions agent for the Oregon Pacific Railroad.

In 1965 Mr. and Mrs. Leo Graham purchased the 361 acre ranch and added to the holding with purchases of land from adjacent farms. Consultant Jeffrey Lamy was retained in 1982 to study the site for development and his subsequent investigations led to a complex vineyard planting program commencing in 1983.

Almost a dozen different varietals are planted on various slopes about the property comprising 45 different vineyard blocks. Each block has been located to optimize soil type and exposure to varietal. According to research and data everything is in its proper place.

Today, the grapevines have matured, a large, modern winery is in place and a lot of wine is being made. Sales and distribution are the current focus.

A visit to Montinore Vineyards

The property's stately mansion (Leo and Jane Graham's home, once the home of John Forbis) offers a bit of elegance not often seen in this part of Oregon. The winery visitor center includes displays of grape growing and winemaking equipment as well as a large tasting room. A grand assortment of wine-related gifts are available.

The Wines

Montinore's huge vineyard provides many varietals for the winemakers to work with. Pinot Noir, Chardonnay, Pinot Gris, Riesling, Gewürztraminer, Chenin Blanc and Müller Thurgau are complemented by sparkling wines and late harvest styles.

Oregon
Oak Knoll Winery

29700 SW
  Burkhalter Rd.
Hillsboro, OR 97123
(503) 648-8198

Owner: Ron Vuylsteke
  & Marj Vuylsteke
Winemaker:
  Ron Vuylsteke
First Year: 1970
Winery Capacity:
  Over 100,000 Gallons
1991 Production:
  60,000 Gallons

Tasting Room Hours:
Daily, Noon to 5 PM
Closed major holidays.

Winery History

The 1980's have been very important to Oak Knoll Winery. After a decade of mostly fruit and berry wine production, the Vuylsteke family now concentrates their efforts on varietal grape wines (90% of production). The handwriting was on the wall when the 1980 Oak Knoll Vintage Select Pinot Noir won the Governer's Award for the best varietal in the state at the 1983 Oregon State Fair.

Some things change and some things stay the same. Almost all of the second generation Vuylstekes are involved directly with winery operations. The eldest son, Ron Jr., works for Joseph Phelps Winery in the Napa Valley, Steve Vuylsteke is now president of Oak Knoll , Doug Vuylsteke is Cellarmaster for Rex Hill Winery, and John and Tom Vuylsteke work the Oak Knoll cellar and warehouse. Ron Vuylsteke, Sr. continues as winemaker in charge assisted by Jeff Herinckx and Marj Vuylsteke is tasting room manager and director of hospitality.

Sales and distribution are up under Steve's astute leadership and Oak Knoll is now Oregon's best selling winery in state.

A visit to Oak Knoll Winery

The Oak Knoll Winery is conveniently located just off Highway 219 outside of Hillsboro. This entrance is well marked but you can also sneak in the back way on Rood Bridge Road from Farmington Road or River Road. The tasting room and gift shop at Oak Knoll are cheerful and their picnic area under the spreading oak tree is always inviting. The third weekend in July the Vuylstekes host their Bacchus Wine Festival featuring blues and jazz musicians along with special food offerings.

The Wines

A complete selection of varietals is produced at Oak Knoll including Chardonnay, Pinot Gris, Riesling, Muller Thurgau and Gewurztraminer. The Pinot Noir and Vintage Select Pinot Noir are especially good and were favorably reviewed by our Best of the Northwest tasting panel. See review on page 18. Their raspberry dessert wine, Frambrosia, is a favorite with chocolate desserts or just for sipping.

Ponzi Vineyards winery near Beaverton, Oregon.

Ponzi Vineyards

14665 SW Winery Ln.
Beaverton, OR 97007
(503) 628-1227

Owners: Dick and
Nancy Ponzi
Winemaker:
Dick Ponzi
First Year: 1974
Vineyard Established:
1970
Winery Capacity:
20,000 Gallons

Tasting and Sales:
Weekends, Noon-5 PM
Weekdays, 10 AM-5 PM

Winery History

Dick and Nancy Ponzi arrived in Oregon in the late 1960s from California. They had been working toward finding just the right property to establish a vineyard for two years and the Tualatin Valley held the answers to all their requirements. A rundown farm with excellent grape-growing potential was purchased near Portland and Nancy began planning and planting the vineyard while Dick taught engineering at Portland Community College.

All the family members pitched-in summers, weekends and most every available time. As the vineyard became winery, Dick became winemaker, drawing on his experience at home winemaking augmented with courses at U. C. Davis.

Widespread acclaim for Ponzi's Pinot Noir and Pinot Gris has the family anxiously anticipating each new vintage. The Ponzi children, Michel, Anna-Maria and Luisa, have all taken positions with the winery operation.

A visit to Ponzi Vineyards

A short drive in from Scholls Ferry Road leads alongside the original vineyard planting at Ponzi winery. The grassy picnic area in front of the winery is inviting, but most winelovers come to taste the wines for which Ponzi Vineyards has become internationally famous. Admiration for Ponzi Pinot Noir and Pinot Gris has come from all quarters.

Continued on next page.

Oregon

The Wines

Some bottlings of Ponzi Vineyard Pinot Noir and Pinot Gris are in such high demand that it is often difficult to get some without a visit to the winery. The ripe style of Pinot Noir, tempered by aging in French oak, impressed our panelists for the **Best of the Northwest** judging so much that the wine was rated the favorite Northwest Pinot. See the review on page 17. Very limited availability.

By the way . . .

Dick and Nancy Ponzi established one of Oregon's first microbreweries in downtown Portland in 1984. The Bridgeport Brew Pub is open Tuesday through Sunday.

Shafer Vineyard Cellars

6200 NW Gales Cr. Rd.
Forest Grove, OR
97116 • (503) 357-6604

Owner and Winemaker:
Harvey Shafer
First year: 1981
Winery Capacity:
20,000 Gallons

Tasting Room Hours:
Summer: daily, 11 AM to 5 PM, Winter: weekends only

Winery History

The lush vineyards spreading out behind Shafer winery were planted in 1973 and now offer the complex fruit from which the finest Pinot Noir and Chardonnay can be crafted. Harvey Shafer has been perfecting techniques to achieve the best full-bodied Pinot Noir and toasty, barrel-fermented Chardonnay. Dedication to both vineyard and winery have carried Shafer Vineyard Cellars to more than a decade of success.

A visit to Shafer Vineyard Cellars

The winery is just east of Gales Creek, a short drive from Forest Grove through quiet farmland and pastures. Most of the route is shaded by tall deciduous trees that overhang the road on both sides to form a sort of dappled-green tunnel. The tasting room offers visitors a chance to try several Shafer wines and to enjoy a picnic on the covered veranda or in the gazebo. Harvey's wife, Miki, offers handmade crafts that vary with the season.

The Wines

Many years of fine-tuning his winemaking and grape growing techniques have led Harvey Shafer to a consistent style that has many fans. In addition to the varietals named above the winery produces Riesling, Gewurztraminer, Muller Thurgau and Sauvignon Blanc.

Tualatin Vineyards

10850 NW Seavy Road
Forest Grove, OR
97116 • (503) 357-5005

Owners: Bill Malkmus
and Bill Fuller
Winemaker: Bill Fuller
First Year: 1973
Winery Capapcity:
60,000 Gallons
1991 Production:
52,000 Gallons

Tasting Room Hours:
Weekdays, 10 AM to
4 PM – weekends,
Noon to 5 PM

Winery History

Tualatin Vineyards was founded by two native Californians who staked their fortunes on the success of the Oregon wine industry. Bill Fuller and Bill Malkmus joined forces in 1973 to establish a small pioneer winery and vineyard 30 miles west of Portland, near Forest Grove.

Bill Fuller, whose credentials include a Master's Degree in enology and 9 years experience at Louis Martini Winery, has been resident overseer and winemaker at Tualatin. Bill Malkmus maintained his investment banking business and handled national distribution for Tualatin from his office in San Francisco.

At press time of this book, changes were taking place in the ownership and management of Tualatin Vineyards. Hopefully this will not affect the high quality of the wines and welcome at the winery.

A visit to Tualatin Vineyards

Follow Highway 47 or Thatcher Road south from Forest Grove and watch for signs indicating a left turn to Tualatin Vineyards. Turns onto Clapshaw Hill Road and Seavey Road are less well marked. Drive slowly and keep your eyes peeled. Once at the winery, you'll enjoy the spacious tasting room, umbrella'd picnic tables and quiet country surroundings.

The Wines

Tualatin's 85 acre vineyard is now in full production so all wines are now 'estate bottled' – made only from grapes grown on winery property. This gives the winemaker greater control over the wine styles and allows split-second decision making at harvest time. Featured varietals include Chardonnay, Gewürztraminer, White Riesling and Pinot Noir while small plantings of other varieties (Flora, Müller-Thurgau) allow the winery to release small lots of these unusual wines, often for sale at the winery only. The rich and powerful Chardonnay and spicy Gewurztraminer made by Tualatin were favorites of our **Best of the Northwest** panels. See reviews beginning on page 14.

Oregon

Portland Area Accommodations & Dining

The Portland area has long been a favorite of many winelovers who like an urban environment but perhaps not as fast-paced as Seattle. Portland's many parks and the close proximity of wineries AND vineyards make for a relaxed touring trip with endless picnic opportunities.

Accommodations and dining in this part of Oregon are without equal elsewhere in the state. Many superb restaurants and all manner lodgings are scattered about Portland and the surrounding countryside.

Accommodations

The Westin Benson, SW Broadway at Oak - (503) 228-2000 The elegance and consistent good service at this Portland landmark have diminished not at all since its acquisition by the Westin Hotel goup. The London Bar and Grill maintains one of the city's best wine cellars with choices for every taste.

Hotel Vintage Plaza, 422 SW Broadway. - (503) 228-1212 Portland's own hotel dedicated to the Oregon wine industry. Complimentary wine tasting each evening in the lobby, each room is named after an Oregon winery or vineyard, and attentive service to every detail. Pazzo Ristorante offers Northern Italian cuisine and an impressive wine cellar.

Riverplace Alexis, 1510 SW Harbor Way - (503) 228-3233, (800) 227-1333 If you can afford the best, then you will find it at this showplace on the Willamette River. Superb service and unbeatable ambiance. The Esplanade Restaurant features regular winemaker dinners with Oregon's finest.

Mallory Hotel, 729 SW 15th Ave. - (503) 223-6311, (800) 228-8657 Close to downtown location offers convenience to shopping, etc. Inexpensive, full service, quality accommodations.

Northwest Bed and Breakfast, Portland - (503) 243-7616 A reservations agency for many attractive B & B's in the Portland area and around the Pacific Northwest.

Dining

The Heathman (Hotel) SW Broadway at Salmon St. (503) 241-4100 Great lunches and dinners feature wonderful NW specialties. Szechuan salmon and Oregon lamb are two favorites. Extensive NW wine list is sure to please.

Genoa, 2832 SE Belmont St., (503) 238-1464 This price-fixed Italian dinner should answer all your questions about Northern Italian cuisine. Courses are described as served and include Northwest ingredients in classical and contemporary preparations. Great desserts. Expensive but worth every penny for the experience.

Zefiro, 500 NW 21st Ave., (503) 226-3394 The NW Portland scene continues to impress with fine meals and innovative international melange. This hot spot will have to prove it can survive, but for now it's THE place to be. Excellent wine list. Moderate.

Ron Paul Charcuterie, 1441 NE Broadway (503) 284-5347 Great new-American cuisine featuring the finest local ingredients and an unyielding emphasis on quality in preparation and service. The owner's love affair with local wine shows with the carefully selected offerings on the trim wine list.

Jake's Crawfish House, 401 SW 12th -(503) 226-1419 Impeccably fresh seafood served best when unadorned. Locals and tourists mingle in the bar before dinner. A deservedly fine reputation for service and quality.

Atwater's, 111 SW 5th Ave., 30th Floor (503) 275-3600 Enjoy the view superb preparations by Mark Gould, the NW's latest wunderkind chef. Dang, it's nice to have a MALE wunderkind to write about for a change! He's great, watch out Cappy!

McCormick & Schmick's Seafood Restaurant, 235 SW 1st Ave. -(503) 224-7522 The decor is more along the lines of a bar and grill, and the management's decision to recently allow a cigar "tasting" in the bar is questionable, but when the food comes out of the kitchen, all is forgiven. Portland's haven for oyster lovers and also for those who covet single malt Scotches. Enjoy dinner daily and lunch with local ad-types Monday - Friday.

Portland-Area Activities for Young or Old

Portland Zoological Gardens - Above Washington Park in quiet suburban surroundings, the Portland Zoo is a nice outing on a sunny day or even an overcast one. The children's petting zoo is open weekends during the spring and summer. A narrow-guage train runs between the zoo and Washington Park during the warm weather months.

Washington Park - In the hills above Portland is this forested quiet zone with trails for walking, playgrounds for the kids and picnic tables for hungry winelovers. The Portland Rose Test Garden provides a marvelous display in spring and summer. Hoyt Arboretum gives tree cheers for green-minded Northwesterners.

OMSI - Oregon Museum of Science and Industry - The new location in the shadow of the Marquam Bridge has brought new vitality to this impressive science education center. Let the youngsters play with computers, save an ecosystem or just hang out in a replica space station. 1945 SE Water Avenue.

The Spirit of Oregon Dinner Train (503) 324-1919. Like the Spirit of Washington Dinner Train in Seattle (ownership not at all related) The Spirit of Oregon hauls a trainload of passengers up and down the tracks while serving a brunch or dinner along the way. The destination has been the abandoned timber town of Cocheran in the Coast Range Mountains. Views of the local Washington County farmland and stands of timber in the foothills are punctuated by picturesque woodland streams and occasional wildlife. This enterprise is just getting started and it should find its identity soon. $50 to $65 per person.

Saturday (and Sunday) Market - Near Portland's Willamette River waterfront gather the craftsmen and women, the street entertainers and muscians, ethnic food sellers and many other strange folks every Saturday and Sunday. Under the Burnside Bridge at 1st is where the action begins at 10 or 11am.

Breweries Find yourself a thirst and head down to BridgePort Brewery at 1313 NW Marshall, Portland Brewing Co. at 1339 NW Flanders, or Widmer Brewing in the Heathman at 901 SW Salmon for a taste of Northwest microbrewing history.

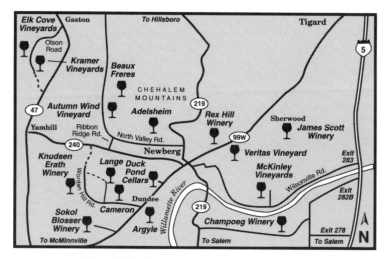

Yamhill County Touring – North

Yamhill County has virtually filled up with wineries over the past few years to the point where it takes several days to visit every stop. If you're traveling on one of the holiday weekends when ALL the wineries are open, you really have a lot of touring to do. Take your time and drive carefully.

Elk Cove Vineyards and Kramer Vineyards, are just off Highway 47 near Gaston. Don't miss either of these two stops. At Elk Cove, the tasting room commands a view of the vineyard while at Kramer Vineyards, Trudy Kramer delights and enlightens the customers with her wit and enological expertise.

Autumn Wind Vineyard is located west of Newberg on North Valley Road. This area, called Ribbon Ridge, has become more and more developed by in-the-know grape growers. Autumn Wind is open weekends for tasting and sales.

Just north of Newberg, Rex Hill Vineyards and Veritas Vineyards are on opposite sides of Highway 99W and are open daily for tasting and sales. The expansive grounds at Rex Hill make a grand location for an al fresco picnic. Two nearby wineries, James Scott and McKinley Vineyards are open by appointment, while Champoeg Winery across the river is open daily.

South of Newberg, in and around the town of Dundee, several more wineries are open daily for visits and tasting. Duck Pond Cellars is just north of town and the satellite tasting room for Elk Cove is right on the highway. Lange Winery up the hill is open daily dispensing "dry wine and dry humour." Two miles west near Crabtree Park is the Knudsen Erath Winery and south of Dundee just up the hill from the highway you'll find Sokol Blosser Winery. Both Knudsen Erath and Sokol Blosser have wonderful selections of gifts and goodies as well as nice picnic areas for snacking.

In the town of Dundee stands the stately Victorian that is tasting room and offices for Argyle. There is a small charge for tastes of their sparkling wines.

Adelsheim Vineyard, located just west of Newberg and Cameron winery, just west of Dundee keep no formal tasting room hours but are often open during holiday weekend events.

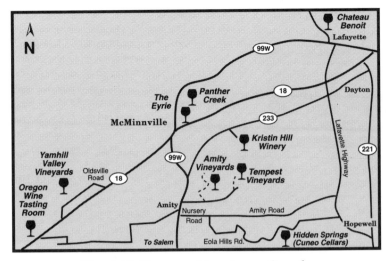

Yamhill County Touring – South

Heading south from Dundee on Highway 99W you'll discover the wineries of southern Yamhill County. Your first stop might be Chateau Benoit, open daily just a couple of miles west of Lafayette. The view from the winery and banqueting hall are grand.

Continuing down 99W to McMinnville you can visit Panther Creek Cellars and The Eyrie winery only on the special Yamhill County weekend events on Thanksgiving and Memorial Day. (Eyrie on Thanksgiving only.)

South of McMinnville on Highway 18 you'll find Yamhill Valley Vineyards. Open daily, YVV offers tasting of their fine wines and an opportunity to enjoy your picnic on a shady deck overlooking their expansive vineyard.

Over on the eastern side of the county Amity Vineyards and Kristin Hill Winery are open daily for tastings and informal tours. Amity is one of the area's original winery and vineyard operations while Kristin Hill is one of the newest. Madrona View Vineyards is headquartered in this same area but is open only by appointment at this time.

Up the windy, steep (but worth the drive) Eola Hills Road, Gino Cuneo has taken over the former Hidden Springs Winery to create Cuneo Cellars. His dedication to red wine should be a beacon to many wine lovers who seek the rich and robust in their glass. Hours are yet to be decided.

By the way . . . when you're near McMinnville, take the short drive to the Oregon Wine Tasting Room at the Lawrence Gallery just north of Sheridan. Patrick, the resident wine expert and wit, serves a little cabaret with the Cabernet and Pinot Noir. How can one man keep track of 15 tasters (or more) while washing glasses, opening bottles and ringing up sales? Catch the act daily and be prepared for a good time.

Oregon

Adelsheim Vineyard

22150 NE Quarter Mile
Lane
Newberg, OR 97132
(503) 538-3652

Owners: David and
  Ginny Adelsheim
Winemaker:
  Don Kautzner
First Year: 1978
Winery Capacity:
  31,000 Gallons
1991 Production:
  31,000 Gallons

Tasting Room Hours:
No tasting room, but
open Memorial Day
Weekend and
Thanksgiving Weekend
Open Houses

Winery History

David Adelsheim has studied winemaking and grape growing in several locations around the world. He has selected the burgundian grape varieties of Pinot Noir and Chardonnay to be his enological focal point while also producing White Riesling, Pinot Blanc and Pinot Gris from the estate vineyard. The vineyard was planted in 1971, following David Adelsheim's acquaintance with Yamhill County vinifera pioneer, David Lett.

Marketing of the wines has not escaped the scrutiny of the Adelsheim family as David's wife, Ginny, has used her artistic talents to design fanciful labels featuring portraits of family members and close friends. These popular works of art on the bottle have become some of the Northwest's classic images for label art.

A visit to Adelsheim Vineyard

Adelsheim Vineyard is not open for public tours or wine tasting but they participate in the Wine Country Thanksgiving the last weekend in November and often join in the Memorial Day Weekend celebration "Match Made in Heaven" sponsored by the Yamhill County Wineries Association.

The Wines

Several excellent Adelsheim Pinot Noirs are produced. In addition to an Oregon appellation, some vineyard-designated versions have been made from grapes harvested in the Eola Hills from sites that David Adelsheim feels have unique qualities. Elizabeth's Reserve, a blend of lots that exhibit the finer qualities of Pinot Noir is named for David and Ginny's daughter. Adelsheim wines are often hard to find and a visit to a well-connected Portland or Seattle wine merchant may be necessary to secure a supply. Chardonnay, Pinot Blanc and Pinot Gris are excellent but are similarly in short supply. Adelsheim Merlot also has a long and impressive reputation. Some Adelsheim wines are available for tasting at the Lawrence Gallery tasting room in Sheridan or at the Elk Cove tasting room in Dundee.

Amity Vineyards

18150 Amity Vnyds. Rd.
Amity, OR 97101
(503) 835-2362

Owners: Myron
Redford, Janis
Checcia, Ione Redford
**President and
Winemaker:**
Myron Redford
First Year: 1976
Winery Capacity:
24,000 Gallons
1991 Production:
21,000 Gallons

Tasting Room Hours:
Daily, May1 - Nov. 1,
Noon to 5 PM, winter
hours: weekends only
Several festivals are
offered each year. Write
or call the winery to
receive mailings.

Winery History

Myron Redford began his career in 1970 as a cellar worker for the old Associated Vintners winery in Seattle. As he dreamed of having his own winery, he learned his lessons well and persevered until the opportunity came his way. With the help of his mother, Ione, and close friend Janis Checchia he brought Amity Vineyards to a place of respect and prominence in the circles of Northwest wine.

Expansion of the winery in 1984 enabled a production increase from 10,000 to over 20,000 gallons. Other improvements to the property are planned as possible. Meanwhile, continued study of grape growing and winemaking techniques have kept Amity Vineyard wines on the plateau of high quality.

A visit to Amity Vineyards

Take your time heading up Amity Vineyards Road. It is bumpy and full of twists and turns, but the trek is worthwhile. Amity does not have the fanciest tasting room in Oregon, but continued improvements have made for a comfortable visit while maintaining the rural character. The tasting bar is in the corner of the winery offers a view of the operation in stasis. A selection of Amity wines are offered for tasting and a broader selection is available for sale. Purchase of some of the harder-to-find bottlings is only possible at the winery.

The Wines

Myron Redford does not prefer over-oaked Pinot Noir. His Pinots are aged in used French oak and offer complexity gained from the additional bottle age he insists upon. The Winemaker's Reserve is a very fine bottling. The planting of true Gamay noir a jus blanc (the true grape of Beaujolais) at Amity was a milestone in Oregon viticulture. Myron's research and dedication to this project has finally yielded results in the fruity, characterful wine made from these grapes. Dry Gewurztraminer, Chardonnay, Riesling and a sulfite-free "Ecowine" are also made. See laudatory reviews in the **Best of the Northwest** section of Myron's Gamay Noir (page 22) and Winemaker's Reserve Pinot Noir (page 17).

Argyle – The Dundee Wine Company

691 Highway 99W
P.O. Box 280
Dundee, OR 97115
(503) 538-8520

Owners: Brian Croser,
 Cal Knudsen
Winemaker:
 Rollin Soles
First Year: 1987
Winery Capacity:
 105,000 Gallons
1991 Production:
 62,000 Gallons

Tasting Room Hours:
Daily, 11 AM to 5:30 PM
Tasting fee

Winery History

Argyle was founded in 1987 by Australian vintner Brian Croser. Originally cloaked in secrecy, the operation produced several vintage cuvées for sparkling wine before releasing their first wine and opening their doors to the public. The wait was worth it. Quality methode champenoise sparkling wine from Argyle has become a signature item for anyone wanting to experience the spectrum of Northwest wine. A delightful Victorian house has been outfitted as a visitor center and tasting room in downtown Dundee complete with picket fence and flower garden.

A visit to Argyle

Just off Highway 99W in Dundee you'll find the quaint tasting room tucked into the parlor of a pretty Victorian house. The bright and airy front room is a great place to enjoy samples of Argyle sparkling wine and the two still wines made here. A nominal tasting fee is required, but you are tasting expensive, high quality sparkling wine. Toast your partner with this visit as your first or last stop of the day! A selection of gifts and accessories is offered.

The Wines

Methode champenoise sparkling wine is the focus at Argyle and the owners have developed relationships with area vineyards to provide grapes at the proper ripeness levels for sparkling wine production. Crisp Brut, Rose Brut and Blanc de Blancs offer forward fruity character that defines Argyle's Northwest style. See reviews of Argyle Brut and Rose Brut in the **Best Northwest Wines** section on page 36.

Arterberry Cellars

P.O. Box 772
905 East 10th Ave.
McMinnville, OR
97128 • (503) 472-1587

Winery History

The tragic death of winemaker Fred Arterberry, Jr. in 1990 was a devastating blow to the Arterberry family but the winery continued to produce wine until 1993. Equipment and unbottled wine were sold to one Oregon winery while another fledgling winery offered to take over the production facility beginning with with 1993 crush. Stay tuned.

Autumn Wind Vineyard

15225 NE
North Valley Road
Newberg, OR 97132
(503) 538-6931

**Owners &
Winemakers:**
Tom & Wendy
Kreutner
First Year: 1987
Winery Capacity:
6,000 Gallons
1991 Production:
6,000 Gallons

Tasting Room Hours:
Weekends, April - Nov.
Noon to 5 PM
Other times by
appointment.

Winery History

Tom and Wendy Kreutner are financial executives who packed their bags and moved to Oregon from Los Angeles in 1977 to satisfy their love for the outdoors. After a short time in the Northwest, the excitement of being involved in the emerging Oregon wine industry proved too appealing to pass by. For two years they studied the Willamette Valley real estate scene until just the right piece of property caught their eye in 1983 - a 52 acre farm near Newberg.

"We worked ourselves silly to plant the first vines in 1984," says owner Wendy Kreutner. "The first plot of land was cleared of cherry trees and prepared for vineyard in just a year." There are now 13 acres of vines and three more acres will be added each year until a total of about 40 acres is reached.

A visit to Autumn Wind Vineyards

The small winery in the hills above Newberg offers tasting room facilities in the corner of the winery. Visitors can stroll among the oak barrels and stainless tanks while enjoying samples of Autumn Wind wines. Outside, picnics at umbrella'd tables are encouraged and sunny-day walks through the vineyard are a relaxing diversion.

The Wines

Autumn Wind Vineyard's wines are achieving the consistent style sought by owners Tom and Wendy Kreutner. The spicy and toasty Chardonnay and the rich and earthy Pinot Noir were both well liked by our **Best of the Northwest** panels. See reviews on pages 17 and 23. Müller Thurgau, Sauvignon Blanc and Pinot Gris are also made.

Beaux Freres

Owners:
Michael & Jackie
Etzel, Patricia Parker
Robert Parker, Jr.,
Robert Roy
Winemaker:
Michael Etzel
First Year: 1991
Winery Capacity:
7,500 Gallons
1992 Production:
2,400 Gallons

Winery History

Just around the corner of Ribbon Ridge in the Chehalem Mountains from Autumn Wind Vineyard, this new operation was begun in 1988 with a sixteen-acre planting of Pinot Noir. The first harvests were custom-crushed at Ponzi Vineyards in 1991 and 1992 and a winery building on site will handle future vintages.

Partial ownership by Wine Advocate publisher Robert M. Parker, Jr. has created excitement for the project greater than would be seen for a new winery operation of its size. The first wines will be released in 1993-94.

Oregon

Chateau Benoit

6580 N.E Mineral
  Springs Road
Carlton, OR 97111
(503) 864-2991
Quality Factory Village
Hwy. 101, Lincoln City

Owners:
  Fred and Mary Benoit
Winemaker:
  Fred Benoit
First Year: 1979
Winery Capacity:
  55,000 Gallons
1991 Production:
  40,000 Gallons

Tasting Room Hours:
Daily, 10 AM to 5 PM
Closed major holidays.

Winery History

As part of the early beginnings of the Oregon wine rush, physician Fred Benoit and his wife Mary began a project to create a winery steeped in French tradition including the making of sparkling wine by the methode champenoise.

Today Chateau Benoit stands like a French chateau above vineyard and farmland, an imposing structure dominating the skyline as you approach from the valley floor. Expansion of the original facility now allows for special events as well as use of the winery reception hall for weddings, parties and celebrations of all kinds.

A visit to Chateau Benoit

The spectacular hilltop winery and chateau offer a fabulous view of Yamhill County and a grand opportunity to picnic on sunny days. The welcome is warm and friendly. When you're visiting the Oregon Coast, stop by the Chateau Benoit Wine and Food Center (a nifty cafe/tasting room combination) at Lincoln City's factory outlet mall.

The Wines

The original claim to fame of Chateau Benoit was methode champenoise sparkling wine but most bottlings are now varietal still wines, although a non-vintage Brut is yet part of the lineup. Chardonnay, Riesling, Sauvignon Blanc and Pinot Noir are distributed regionally. Pinot Gris, Dry Gewurztraminer, dessert wines and the sparkling Brut are available at the winery or the Lincoln City tasting room. Our **Best of the Northwest** panel found Chateau Benoit's Reserve Pinot Noir to be quite rich and appealing, see review on page 18.

Cameron

Winery History

Veteran enologist John Paul chose Oregon for his winery after working in three other famous viticultural regions. After studying winemaking in Burgundy, John took the helm of the Napa Valley's Carneros Creek Winery for three years before heading to New Zealand for experience in a different climate and setting. He brought to Oregon definite ideas about the wine he wanted to make.

He began in a small warehouse across the street from Arterberry Winery and The Eyrie but in 1987 moved into a new structure built in the hills above Dundee, Oregon. A partnership with grape grower

P.O. Box 27
8200 Worden Hill Rd.
Dundee, OR 97115
(503) 232-6652

Owners: John Paul,
 friends and family
Winemaker: John Paul
First Year: 1984
Winery Capacity:
 10,000 Gallons
1991 Production:
 8,800 Gallons

Tasting Room Hours:
By appointment only.

Bill Wayne led John to look for quarters closer to the viticultural origin of his wines. The winery features a cool, subterranean barrel cellar as well as room to expand production when the need arises.

A visit to Cameron Winery

Cameron Winery produces only small quantities of wine and the distribution is mostly local. The winery has no regular tasting room hours, but visitors are welcome by appointment or at the Wine Country Thanksgiving event in November.

The Wines

Cameron Pinot Noir and Chardonnay are unique bottlings made in the personal style of winemaker John Paul. Toasty, buttery Chardonnay with complex aroma and flavor is made in both a regular and reserve version. Similarly, two or more bottlings of Pinot Noir provide a choice for consumers. Cameron Reserve Pinot Noir was well liked by our **Best of the Northwest** panel. Review on page 17.

Champoeg Wine Cellars

10375 Champoeg Rd. NE
Aurora, OR 97002
(503) 678-2144

Owners: Pitterle, Killian
 and Myers families
Winemaker:
 Elise Pitterle
First Year: 1990
Winery Capacity:
 10,000 Gallons

Tasting Room Hours:
May - October, Daily
11 AM to 6 PM, winter:
Weekends, 12 to 5 PM

Winery History

From a vineyard planted in 1974, the partnership of families owning Champoeg Wine Cellars made their first wines in 1990. Previous harvests were sold to other Willamette Valley wineries from 1978 to 1989. The vineyard is planted on the south-facing slope of "La Butte" above the Willamette River near the historic Champoeg State Park. In 1992 the winery was built and the first estate bottled wines were made.

A visit to Champoeg Wine Cellars

By following signs to Champoeg State Park (pronounced "sham poo ick"), the winery is easily reached from Highway 219 near Newberg or from I-5 (Exit 282). You can view the vineyard and winery from the tasting room and enjoy an alfresco picnic on the property. Although technically in Marion County, this operation is closest to other wineries in the Yamhill County touring region.

The Wines

Pinot Noir, Chardonnay and White Riesling are current releases with Muller Thurgau soon to be released and Pinot Gris planned for future vintages.

Oregon

Chehalem

703 North Main St.
Newberg, OR 97132
(503) 538-4700

Owner/Winemaker:
 Harry Peterson/Nedry
First Year: 1993
Winery Capacity:
 5,000 Gallons

Tasting Room Hours:
By appointment only

Winery History

Wine writer Judy Peterson-Nedry and her husband Harry have been carefully tending their Ridgecrest Vineyard in the Chehalem hills northwest of Newberg since its planting in 1980. Providing grapes to other vintners for eight vintages and seeing the quality of the resulting wines convinced Harry that the time was right to bond his own facility.

A visit to Chehalem winery

The production facility for this promising operation is small and interested visitors are encouraged to phone ahead for an appointment. Plans are to participate in the Memorial Day and Thanksgiving weekend open house events. The winery is at the Peterson-Nedry residence in Newberg.

The Wines

An intensely berry-and-spice Pinot Noir heads the line with a barrel-fermented Pinot Gris also a favorite. Small lots of Chardonnay and Gamay Noir are also made.

Domaine Drouhin - Oregon

P.O. Box 700
Dundee, OR 97115
(503) 538-7485

Owner:
 Joseph Drouhin
Winemaker: Véronique
 Jousset-Drouhin
First Year: 1988
1991 Production:
 12,500 Gallons

Tasting Room Hours:
None. The winery does not have facilities for visitors. Wines are available nationally.

Winery History

When the Drouhin family of Burgundy decided to buy land in the Willamette Valley it created such a stir that Oregon's governor made a special announcement and the whole Oregon wine industry was temporarily stunned by the event.

The vindication of belief in Oregon's climate seemed now to be complete. An experienced and successful Burgundian producer had staked his reputation on Oregon as a region where fine Pinot Noir wines could be made.

Robert Drouhin and his daughter Véronique visited the area several times and then made arrangements for their first crush in 1988. In 1989, the crush took place in the new Drouhin winery, built on four levels comprising 8-1/2 stories. The hillside construction takes advantage of natural coolness of the earth and permits processing by gravity. The facility is singularly designed to produce Pinot noir.

Véronique Drouhin is a skilled enologist, trained in her family's firm in Burgundy and a veteran of several vintages. She spends the harvest months

Robert and Veronique Drouhin sample a new vintage at Domaine Drouhin Oregon.

each year in Oregon but her permanent home remains in France. Winery manager Bill Hatcher oversees the maintenance of wines during the aging period before bottling with consultation from the Drouhins as necessary.

The 180 acre parcel of land that was purchased atop the Dundee Hills offers a great site for growing Pinot Noir. Of the 130 acres that are plantable, 36 acres have been planted.

A visit to Domaine Drouhin Oregon

The Drouhin winery does not have facilities for visitors and does not offer tours or tastings. You can get a nice view of the winery from the crush pad at Sokol Blosser or if you drive around the back roads of the Dundee Hills.

The Wines

There is but one wine at Domaine Drouhin, the estate Pinot Noir. Each vintage has been well received and our Pinot Noir panel for **Best of the Northwest** enjoyed the current release. Review appears on page 18.

Duck Pond Cellars

23145 Hwy. 99W
P.O. Box 429
Dundee, OR 97115
(503) 538-3199

Owners:
The Fries Family
Winemaker: Keri
Norton, Greg Fries
First Vintage: 1989
Winery Open: 1993

Winery History

Duck Pond Cellars was founded by Doug and Jo Ann Fries with the first vineyard planted in 1986 in Dundee. Close plant spacing (one meter by two meter) yielded 2,000 vines per acre which will allow a light crop load per vine. Several members of the Fries family are involved with the operation including daughter Lisa Fries (sales and marketing), sons Greg Fries (winemaker) and Matt Fries (vineyard and cellar assistant).

A visit to Duck Pond Cellars

This new winery is located on Highway 99W just north of Dundee. The new winery is currently the only outlet for Duckpond's wines which include Chardonnay, Pinot Noir and Cabernet Sauvignon.

The Wines

An intention to make Burgundian-style wines is leading to barrel-fermentation of Chardonnay and aging of Pinot Noir in new French oak.

Elk Cove Vineyards

27751 NW Olson Road
Gaston, OR 97119
(503) 985-7760

Owners/Winemakers:
Joe and Patricia
Campbell
First Year: 1977
Winery Capacity:
40,000 Gallons
1991 Production:
36,000 Gallons

Tasting Room Hours:
Daily, 11 AM to 5 PM,
Tours and tour groups
by appointment.
Dundee Tasting Room -
Daily, 11 AM to 5 PM

Winery History

Like many Oregon wineries, Elk Cove Vineyards began as a dream of country life and the pursuit of fine winemaking. Both owners pitched-in on weekends to make the operation succeed. Currently, Pat is still full-time at the winery and vineyard. Joe has not yet retired from the medical profession though he spends much more time these days working the grapes. The success Elk Cove has enjoyed includes wines from many varieties. Pinot Noir, Chardonnay, Pinot Gris, Gewürztraminer and Riesling have all provided medals to hang on the tasting room wall.

A vineyard expansion in 1985 led to founding a new label, La Bohème. Special grapes from this special site west of the estate vineyard created the opportunity for a special, super-premium brand of Pinot Noir and Chardonnay.

A visit to Elk Cove Vineyards

Easiest access to Elk Cove Vineyards is by Highway 240 from Newberg or Highways 8 or 26 from Portland to Highway 47. The Elk Cove tasting room offers a mini-panorama of the 'cove' filled

with vineyard and the helpful tasting room staff offers a wide selection of Elk Cove wines to traveling wine tasters. For the winelover lacking wanderlust, the Campbells have a tasting room in Dundee. The winery sponsors Jazz concerts during the summer months. Call for information.

The Wines

Stylistically these wines demand food. The white wines offer crisp acidity and full-fruitiness to complement a wide range of seafoods as well as appetizers and lighter meats. The Pinot Noir is a classic Burgundian treasure of texture and spice that has been greeted with accollades from consumers and wine competitions alike. White varietals include Chardonnay, Pinot Gris, Gewurztraminer and Riesling. Reds include Pinot Noir (several different vineyard bottlings) and Cabernet Sauvignon. See **Best of the Northwest** reviews on pages 15, 17 and 18.

The Eyrie Vineyards

P.O. Box 697
Dundee, OR 97115
935 E. 10th
McMinnville, OR
97128 • (503) 472-6315

Owners: David
and Diana Lett
Winemaker:
David Lett
First Year: 1970
Vineyard Planted:
1966
Winery Capacity:
30,000 Gallons
1991 Production:
24,000 Gallons

Tasting and Tours:
By appointment only
Thanksgiving Open
House

Winery History

David Lett is in the wine business to make wine. First and foremost his goal is to produce the best possible bottle of wine from the best grapes he can grow. In the world of storybook, castle wineries with views across the vineyards and flocks of eager tour guides, David Lett prefers his quiet back street in McMinnville where he can make his wine.

Since the mid-1960s he has been the proponent and champion of winegrowing in Western Oregon. A decade of grapegrowing separates him from almost every other Oregon winery and he has tried hard to make the time work to his advantage. He stimulated the recent flurry of Pinot gris planting when he grafted over his White Riesling vines to the French variety. At times he seems obsessed with the matching of varietal clones to the challenging cool of the Willamette Valley. His style is intense and focused.

A visit to The Eyrie Vineyards

A drive to McMinnville on Thanksgiving Weekend can reward you with a glimpse of this master out of his element. For these few days he welcomes admirers and strangers without appointment to share his wines and enjoy music and warm conversation. His twinkling eyes and white beard are temporarily in the public domain as he wins many new friends. *Continued on next page.*

151

Oregon

Diana and David Lett, owners of The Eyrie Vineyards.

After the holidays it's back to work. David and Diana Lett's dedication is complete, their commitment total. Their satisfaction is in knowing that they've made the best wine they can make. Incidentally, David Lett was instrumental in helping Burgundy wine producer Robert Drouhin purchase land in Oregon in mid-1987. The expansion of French winemaking to Oregon affirms David Lett's belief in the state's winegrowing potential.

The Wines

David Lett has had very few failures when it comes to making Pinot noir. Recent tastings going back to his first vintages reveal a combination of luck and skill in creating wines that gain complexity and character with age while holding off the negative effects of time. Nuances of cherry, spice and plum in the aroma yield to toasty fruit and spice in the mouth. Almost to a wine the results have been spectacular. Eyrie wines are best appreciated with characterful cuisine - especially in their youth. Muscat Ottenel, Pinot Gris, Pinot Meunier and Chardonnay are also made. A **Best of the Northwest** review of Eyrie Pinot Noir appears on page 18.

Hidden Springs/ Cuneo Cellars

9360 S.E. Eola Hills Rd.
Amity, OR 97101
(503) 835-2782

Owner: Gino Cuneo
First Year: 1980
Winery Capacity:
  15,000 Gallons

Tasting Room Hours:
To be determined.

Winery History

Hidden Springs winery was a joint venture between Don Byard and Al Alexanderson that evolved from their amatuer winemaking ventures during the 1970s. The mountaintop site seems to be well-suited to Pinot Noir, always a rich and flavorful wine from the estate vineyard. Hidden Springs winery was the first winery to be located in the now famous Eola Hills wine growing area located between the Salem-area wineries and the Yamhill County wineries. After a period of being leased to another Oregon winery, Hidden Springs was sold in 1993 to Seattle winemaker Gino Cuneo.

A visit to Hidden Springs winery

A warm welcome always greeted wine lovers at Hidden Springs. The new owners plan to maintain regular tasting room hours when re-organization of the winery is completed. The view from the hill-top site of the surrounding countryside is fabulous.

The Wines

Pinot Noir and other Oregon varietals were the favorites of the original owners. Gino Cuneo also intends to produce his ultra-premium Cabernet named Cana's Feast at the winery.

James Scott Winery

27675 SW Ladd Hill Rd.
Sherwood, OR 97140
(206) 896-9869

Owner/Winemaker:
  James Scott Howard
First Year: 1992
Winery Capacity:
  5,000 Gallons
1992 Production:
  1,400 Gallons

Tasting Room Hours:
By appointment only.

Winery History

James Scott Howard discovered the joys of wine through his travels in the military with extended stays in Europe and California. Discussions with noted California winemakers and short-courses at U.C. Davis prepared him for his ultimate goal of bonding his own winery. James Scott Winery is located northeast of Newberg on Ladd Hill Road.

A visit to James Scott Winery

Winemaking and wine distribution (while still holding down full-time accounting work in the Army) take up most of the winery owner's time. An appointment is necessary to visit the winery . (Take Ladd Hill Road 3.5 miles east of Hwy. 99W.)

The Wines

Selection of old-vine Pinot Noir and dedication to small lot production were key to the great success of the first James Scott wines. Plans include production of Cabernet Sauvignon, Merlot, Riesling and Chardonnay, in addition to Pinot Noir.

Dick Erath of Knudsen Erath Winery in Dundee, Oregon.

Knudsen Erath

17000 NE Knudsen Ln.
off Worden Hill Road
Dundee, OR 97115
(503) 538-3318

Owners:
  Dick and Joan Erath
Winemaker: Dick Erath
First Year: 1972
Winery Capacity:
  102,000 Gallons
1991 Production:
  62,000 Gallons

Tasting Room Hours:
Daily, 10:30 AM to
5:30 PM (5/15-10/15)
Daily, 11 AM to 5 PM
(10/16-5/14) Tours and
groups by appointment.

Winery History

Originally a partnership between winemaker Dick Erath and lumberman Cal Knudsen (who provided capital to expand the winery/vineyard operation at the beginning), Dick Erath acquired sole ownership of the winery in 1988. Vineyard property still owned by Cal Knudsen continues to provide grapes for the Knudsen Erath winery - currently one of the largest in Oregon.

Dick Erath is one of the state's most experienced, and innovative, vineyardists and winemakers. Recent experiments in the winery include barrel-fermented Riesling and cooperage made from native Oregon oak.

A visit to Knudsen Erath Winery

If you enjoy award-winning Pinot Noir and other varietals, Knudsen Erath is an important tasting room to visit. Friendly staff know the wines and the proprietors have thoughtfully stocked a complete line of gifts and logo-ware. Also a nice picnic patio among the oaks and vineyards is provided. Drive into the Red Hills of Dundee on Worden Hill Road to the find the winery near Crabtree Park. Let the kids run off some energy at the park before heading on to the next stop.

The winery is always looking for a reason to have a party and their Harvest Festival on the last weekend in August is legendary. Call for details.

The Wines

Knudsen Erath has, from the beginning, had a reputation of being the producer of one of Oregon's finest Pinot Noirs. The Vintage Select designation signifies a reserve-style lot that offers depth and complexity along with ageability for the long haul. Cuisine-friendly Dry Gewürztraminer and Dry Riesling have proven very popular. Also produced are Chardonnay, Cabernet Sauvignon and late harvest Riesling and Gewürztraminer. See **Best of the Northwest** reviews of K-E Pinot Noir and Dry Riesling on pages 18 and 30.

Kramer Vineyards

26830 NW Olson Rd.
Gaston, OR 97119
(503) 662-4545

Owners: Trudy and
Keith Kramer
Winemaker:
Trudy Kramer
First Year: 1989
Winery Capacity:
6,500 Gallons
1991 Production:
6,500 Gallons

Tasting Room Hours:
Friday through Sunday,
Noon to 5 PM

Winery History

Kramer Vineyards is a labor of love for Keith and Trudy Kramer. Gold medals at the state fair for Trudy's homemade raspberry wine started the Kramers thinking that winemaking wasn't all that hard. Vineyard tending didn't seem too hard either and now they have 12 acres at their home/winery estate. Keith Kramer continues to work as a pharmacist (taking the occasional vacation day to work the vineyard or a week or two during crush). Trudy takes care of family matters and handles the day to day chores around the winery. Just a few years of commercial production have shown these energetic entrepreneurs the path to success.

A visit to Kramer Vineyards

Just up Olson Road from Elk Cove, Kramer Vineyards welcomes wine lovers with their own style. The knight of the vineyard guards the parking lot and the tasting room is informal and airy. Enjoy the wines of your choosing. Whether you're partial to delicious fruit wines or well-structured grape varietals, Trudy Kramer has something to please you. Special events are plentiful here – try the Weird Foods Festival or the Berry Social. Call the winery for a recording detailing upcoming events.

The Wines

Kramer Vineyards' Pinot Gris, Gewurztraminer and Raspberry Wine are among the favorites made here. Our Best of the Northwest panelists rated these among the Northwest's finest - see reviews beginning on page 14. Other varietals include Pinot Noir, Chardonnay, Riesling and Muller Thurgau. Fruit wines vary with the season.

Oregon

Kristin Hill Winery

3330 SE Amity-Dayton Highway
Amity, OR 97101
(503) 835-0850

Owners: Aberg Family
Winemaker: Eric Aberg
First Year: 1990
Winery Capacity:
  1,200 Gallons

Tasting Room Hours:
Daily, May - October,
Noon to 5 PM
Nov. - April, weekends
only, Noon to 5 PM

Winery History

Linda and Eric Aberg are both retired from the U. S. Army and fell love with wine while stationed in Europe. With some home winemaking experience, the Abergs began to dream of owning their own winery. A search for vineyard land ended in the Willamette Valley where the first vines were planted in 1985. The winery was bonded in 1990 and small lots of selected varietals are produced annually. The grand opening of their tasting room took place in May of 1993.

A visit to Kristin Hill Winery

The Amity-Dayton Highway (233) cuts off from Hwy. 99W just south of Dundee, heading southeast toward Amity. Kristin Hill is just east of this road near Amity. Relaxed atmosphere is the order of the day at Kristin Hill where visitors can play catch with winery dog Pinot Gris and most often meet the owners for some barrel tasting.

The Wines

Kristin Hill produces Pinot Noir, Chardonnay, Riesling, Gewurztraminer and a methode champenoise sparkling wine.

Lange Winery

18380 NE Buena Vista
P.O. Box 8
Dundee, OR 97115
(503) 538-6476

Owners: Wendy
  and Don Lange
Winemaker:
  Don Lange
First Year: 1987
Winery Capacity:
  10,000 Gallons
1991 Production:
  6,500 Gallons

Tasting Room Hours:
Daily, 11 AM to 6 PM

Winery History:

Don and Wendy Lange moved to the Willamette Valley from Santa Barbara, California and have followed the lead of other area residents by taking a leap into winemaking. Six acres of Pinot Noir are now in place at the winery above Dundee and a large winery building has facilitated moving barrels and equipment out of the Lange's home.

A visit to Lange Winery

Drive up Worden Hill Road from Dundee and watch for your right turn marked by a sign for Lange Winery. A few twists and turns lead to the attractive home where Lange Winery's tasting room is in the daylight basement overlooking the vineyard. Owner Wendy Lange is often on hand dispensing "dry wine and dry humour." A great visit.

The Wines

The wines created from the 1987 harvest included Pinot Noir, Chardonnay and Pinot Gris. The Pinot Gris is the first release and offers a

contrast to the style of wine created by other Willamette Valley producers. This Pinot Gris was barrel-fermented in French oak and offers nuances of toast and butter to accompany the fruitiness of the young wine.

Madrona View Vineyards

17751 Amity Vnyd. Rd.
Amity, OR 97101
(503) 835-2362

Owners/Winemakers:
Michael Strauss,
William Mikey Jones

Winery History

This unusual pair of entrepreneurs have produced a wide variety of wines from fruit harvested at the estate vineyard in Amity and from fruit purchased from sources far and wide. In addition to Cash Flow Chardonnay and Pinot Noir, more substantial bottlings are made. Dessert wines of most remarkable origin round out the eclectic line. Tasting at the former Hidden Springs facility will be discontinued with the new ownership.

McKinlay Vineyards

7120 Earlwood Rd.
Newberg, OR 97132
(503) 625-2534

Owners:
Matt & Holly Kinne
Winemaker:
Matt Kinne
First Year: 1989
Winery Capacity:
4,400 Gallons
1992 Production:
4,400 Gallons

Tasting Room Hours:
Memorial Day and
Thanksgiving weekend
events and by
appointment.

Winery History

Matt Kinne is doing what he wants to do. The challenge of making high quality wine and establishing a small vineyard is a good complement to his family life. Winery, home and vineyard are located on a thirty-acre plot just above the Willamette River near Newberg. Matt's U.C. Davis training and experience in the California and Oregon wine industries prepared him well for his independent operation. He looks forward to slowly increasing production and beginning to make wine from grapes grown at the winery's ten-acre vineyard.

A visit to McKinlay Vineyards

Following the Wilsonville Road from either I-5 or its junction with Hwy. 219, you find Earlwood Road on the north side at about 6 miles distance. McKinlay Vineyards is open for the traditional Oregon wine industry celebrations (see left) and by appointment. Matt Kinne encourages visitors to give a call and come out for a visit.

The Wines

Pinot Noir and barrel-fermented Chardonnay are currently produced from grapes purchased in Yamhill and Polk Counties. The winemaker believes in diversity of both site and cooperage to make the most interesting, complex wines.

Oregon

Panther Creek Cellars

455 North Irvine
McMinnville, OR
97128 • (503) 472-8080

Owners: Ken Wright,
Steve & Martha Lind
Winemaker:
Ken Wright
First Year: 1986
Winery Capacity:
15,000 Gallons
1991 Production:
14,500 Gallons

Tasting Room Hours:
By appointment only.

Winery History

Ken Wright came to Oregon in search of success producing fine Pinot Noir. He brought along 10 years experience in the California wine industry including stints at Stevenot, Ventana Vineyards and Robert Talbott wineries. Prior to his winery experience Ken learned to match food and wine through extensive work in the restaurant business. After deciding that wine held more interest than waiting tables, he left the midwest to attend U.C. Davis. Ken operates his winery from a small building in McMinnville not far from The Eyrie and Arterberry Cellars. The original power plant for the city of McMinnville, the 8,000 square foot building was built in 1924.

A visit to Panther Creek Cellars

Generally, the winery is not open to the public except by appointment. However, Ken often opens for Memorial Day Weekend and Wine Country Thanksgiving events. By the way, Panther Creek Cellars is named for a creek which runs from the Coast Range north of McMinnville.

The Wines

Ken Wright concentrates on intense, powerful Pinot Noir utilizing longer-than-usual skin contact times and perfectly ripe grapes. Our Beswt of the Northwest Pinot Noir panel found it delicious. (See review on page 18.) Ken also makes the only Melon in Oregon. This little-known white French varietal is made in a light and flavorful style that complements fine cuisine.

Rex Hill Vineyards

Winery History

Attention to detail and dedication to quality show through in every aspect of Rex Hill Winery. Owners Paul Hart and his wife Jan Jacobsen have produced a splendid facility from a historic nut processing plant just off Highway 99W north of Newberg. Completely refurbished, the building looks from the highway to be a new structure but with the grace and line sof traditional turn of the century architecture. Winemaker Lynn Penner-Ashe came on board in 1988 and has definitely influenced Rex Hill's wine styles. Greater responsibility was added to her position when she was named President and CEO in 1993.

The Rex Hill Winery and picnic area with the Willamette Valley beyond.

REX HILL
1991
OREGON
PINOT GRIS

PRODUCED AND BOTTLED BY REX HILL VINEYARDS
NEWBERG, OREGON
ALCOHOL 12.9% BY VOLUME

30835 N Highway 99W
Newberg, OR 97132
(503) 538-0666

Owners: Paul Hart
  and Jan Jacobsen
President/Winemaker:
  Lynn Penner-Ash
First Year: 1983
Winery Capacity:
  75,000 Gallons
1991 Production:
  48,000 Gallons

Tasting Room Hours:
Daily, April - Dec.,
11 AM to 5 PM
Feb. and March, Friday,
Saturday and Sunday
Closed January

A visit to Rex Hill Vineyards

The tasting room at Rex Hill makes visitors feel at home with elegant decor and a helpful staff. Expansion of the tasting area and the construction of an outside terrace for picnics and musical events add to the enjoyment of a visit to Rex Hill.

The Wines

Rex Hill Pinot Noir has established a very fine reputation for complex aroma and a rich and mouthfilling palate. Vineyard designated Pinots are excellent but limited in production. The Rex Hill Chardonnay and Pinot Gris offer unique styles with barrel-fermentation lending a toasty quality to the wine. A second label, King's Ridge, offers quality, non-vintage Pinot Noir and Chardonnay at a lower price level. See **Best of the Northwest** review of Rex Hill Pinot Noir on page 18.

Oregon

Bill and Susan Sokol Blosser of Sokol Blosser Winery in Dundee, OR.

Sokol Blosser Winery

5000 Sokol Blosser Ln.
P.O. Box 399
Dundee, OR 97115
(800) 582-6668

Owners:
Bill and Susan Blosser
Winemaker: John Haw
First Year: 1977
Winery Capacity:
60,000 Gallons

Tasting Room Hours:
Daily, 11 AM to 5 PM
Free tours of winery

Winery History

Over the last 15 years, Bill and Susan Sokol Blosser have used their vision of producing world-class wines to build one of Oregon's largest and best known wineries. They both hold prestigious degrees from well-respected universities though neither has a background in chemistry or winemaking. Indeed it was the romance of wine and the challenge of operating a successful winery program that lured them to the vineyard. John Haw was named winemaker in 1988 upon the departure of Bob McRitchie who had served as winemaker since the first vintage in 1977.

A visit to Sokol Blosser

This winery was among the first in Oregon to bring wine to the consumer with expanded tasting room hours and a friendly, informative manner. The staff provides answers to all questions along with an informative tour of the winery. The Sokol Blosser tasting room is well-stocked with unusual and unique wine-related gifts and food stuffs.

The Wines

Two styles of Pinot Noir and Chardonnay are offered at Sokol Blosser. The Yamhill County designation is the "front line" of wines made in a lightier, fruitier style. "Redland" designates the

160

reserve style bottlings of these two varietals. Riesling, Gewurztraminer and Muller Thurgau are also produced. See the **Best of the Northwest** reviews for Sokol Blosser Redland Chardonnay and Gewurztraminer (reviews begin on page 14).

Tempest Vineyard

6000 Karlas Lane
Amity, OR 97101
(503) 252-1383

Owner/Winemaker:
Keith Orr
First Year: 1988
Winery Capacity:
7,000 Gallons

Winery History

As part of the City of Portland maintenance team that repairs traffic signals, Keith Orr needed a creative outlet. Winemaking and grape growing proved just such an escape and Tempest Vineyard was born. After several years production in a leased facility, a new winery was built in 1993 near Amity.

A visit to Tempest Vineyards

Visits to the new winery are by appointment only except on the Memorial Day and Thankgiving weekend open houses.

The Wines

Keith Orr crafts Pinot Noir, Chardonnay, Pinot Gris and Gamay Noir from purchased grapes. Plantings at the new winery will include the above varieties and also Pinot Blanc.

Veritas Vineyard

31190 NE Veritas Ln.
Newberg, OR 97132
(503) 538-1470

Owners: John and
Diane Howieson
Winemaker:
Dr. John Howieson,
John Eliassen
First Year: 1984
Winery Capacity:
18,000 Gallons
1991 Production:
11,000 Gallons

Tasting Room Hours:
Daily, 11 AM to 5 PM -
(June through Sept.)
Fall and spring, Friday,
Saturday, Sunday only.
Closed mid-December
through February.

Winery History

John Howieson is one of several Oregon physicians to have been bitten by the winemaking bug. His five years as an amateur winemaker led him down the path to bonding his own winery with an initial production of just 600 gallons of Pinot Noir. With production now over 10,000 gallons, the future looks promising for Veritas Vineyard. The winery's 30 acre vineyard is designed for soil conservation and is planted to Pinot Noir, Chardonnay, Pinot Gris, Riesling and Müller-Thurgau.

In addition to brief study of enology at U. C. Davis, John received some on-the-job training during crush at Adelsheim Vineyard. Veritas' associate winemaker John Eliassen is a native Oregonian who received training at the University of Dijon, France. His responsibilities at Veritas include both winemaking and general operations.

Oregon

A visit to Veritas Vineyards

The rustic winery and tasting room is located one-quarter mile off Highway 99W, 2.5 miles northeast of Newberg. A wonderful opportunity to visit Veritas Vineyard is during the Yamhill County Wine Country Thanksgiving celebration in late November or the Memorial Day weekend event.

The Wines

Veritas Vineyard's wines offer rich and earthy components that pair well with many hearty dishes. Varietals produced include Pinot Noir, Chardonnay, Dry Riesling and Pinot Gris. Müller Thurgau impressed our **Best of the Northwest** panel with its delicate aroma and food-friendly palate.

Yamhill Valley Vineyards

16250 SW Oldsville Rd.
McMinnville, OR
97128 • (503) 843-3100

Owners: Denis Burger,
Elaine McCall,
David & Terry
Hinrichs
Winemaker:
Stephen Cary
First Year: 1983
Winery Capacity:
24,000 Gallons
1991 Production:
24,000 Gallons

Tasting Room Hours:
Daily, 11 AM to 5 PM
(June through Nov.)
Weekends only,
(March through May)
Closed in winter.

Winery History

A partnership between a pair of Portland immunologists led to the building of one of Yamhill County's most attractive wineries. Combining a 100 acre vineyard planted to Pinot Noir, Chardonnay, Pinot Gris and White Riesling with a state-of-the-art winery and visitor center, Yamhill Valley Vineyards is a well-planned venture. The Yamhill Valley Vineyards label features both the Oregon State bird and the Oregon State flower. The Western Meadowlark has never before been so honored with its perch on the Oregon Grape plant.

A visit to Yamhill Valley Vineyards

Yamhill Valley Vineyards is tucked away at the south end of Yamhill County on a 300 acre estate in the foothills of the Yamhill County Coast Range. The well-marked route to Oldsville Road leads to the long driveway through the vineyards to the winery. A visit to the facility includes a tasting of the current release wines and a brief tour of the winery. The expansive deck offers a chance to relax and picnic with a view of the vineyard under shady old oak trees that grow right up through the structure.

The Wines

The initial vintages of Yamhill Valley Vineyards established a reputation for hearty Pinot Noir with full body and ripe flavors and aroma. White Riesling and Chardonnay are also produced. The mineral-scented, bronze-colored Pinot Gris was well liked by our **Best of the Northwest** panel. See the review on page 27.

Yamhill County Accommodations

Newberg

Springbrook Farm B & B 30295 N. Highway 99W, (503) 538-4606 The McClure family welcomes you to their hazelnut orchard estate with pool, tennis, pond and gardens. Carriage house available for families, small groups.

McMinnville

Vineyard Inn Motel 2035 S. Hwy 99W - (503) 472-4900 Indoor pool, spa, air-conditioned, convenient to local wineries, continental breakfast

Mattey House, 10221 NE Mattey Lane, (503) 434-5058 Owners Jack and Denise Seed traveled the four corners of the world before becoming innkeepers at this delightful Victorian. Located on 10 acres near Lafayette.

Steiger Haus, 360 Wilson St., McMinnville 97128, (503) 472-0821 "A wool and wine country inn." Doris & Lynn Steiger offer elegant accommodations in their new home south of downtown. Private baths, landscaped grounds and a gourmet full breakfast!

Youngberg Hill Farm B & B, 10660 Youngberg Hill Rd., (503) 472-2727 A working farm and vineyard on 700 scenic acres. Private baths, wine country hospitality, delicious meals. Your hosts: Eve and Norman Barnett.

Yamhill

Flying M Ranch 23029 NW Flying M Ranch Rd., 97148 (503) 662-3222 Take a trail ride into the Coast Range or relax in a romantic cabin by the river. Also camping and horse corrals.

Dining - McMinnville

Nick's Italian Cafe, 521 E. Third St. - (503) 434-4471 Nick's is famous all over Oregon for the fine Northern Italian food and wine country atmosphere. An extensive selection of Oregon wines goes back to the 1970s. Dinner served Tuesday - Sunday.

La Maison Surette, 729 E. 3rd St. - (503) 472-3787 This country- elegant French restaurant in a charming house near downtown offers price fixed dinner on Friday and Saturday. Reserv.

Dundee

Tina's, 760 Hwy. 99W, (503) 538-8880 Local game, fresh seafood and other fine ingredients creatively prepared and elegantly served. Lunch Tue.-Fri.; dinner, Tue.-Sun. Reserv.

Yamhill County Activities for Young or Old

Champoeg State Park, Across the Willamette from Newberg A full service park with boat access to the river, picnic tables, historic landmarks, fishing, etc. Champoeg winery nearby.

Crabtree Park, Up Worden Hill Road from Dundee. Adjacent to Knudsen Erath Winery. Nice Picnicing.

McMinnville City Park, 3rd and Adams A well-kept, quiet oasis amid the hustle and bustle of McMinnville. Two play areas, open spaces, a small creek, picnic tables and clean restrooms.

Hot Air Ballooning - See the wine country from the air and enjoy a sparkling touchdown when the adventure comes to an end! Two companies available: Partridge Farm B & B, (503) 538-2050 and Vista Balloon Adventures, (503) 625-7385.

Lawrence Gallery, Augustine's Hwy. 18 at Sheridan, Fine art to browse after sipping some prime vintages at the adjacent Oregon Wine Tasting Room. Augustine's Restaurant features fine Oregon cuisine.

Oregon

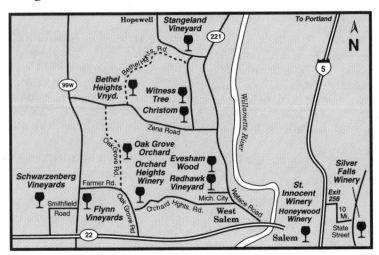

Salem Area/Polk County Touring - North

The Salem area and the Eola Hills winegrowing region west of Salem are home to some of the Oregon's finest vineyards and many interesting wineries.

In downtown Salem, Honeywood Winery on Hines St. offers tasting daily of varietal and fruit wines. Their tasting room offers a great selection of wine-related gifts. St. Innocent Winery is open only by appointment.

Follow State St.east of Salem for 10 miles to Cascade Highway and turn right to find Silver Falls Winery in the scenic Marion County farmland..

As you leave downtown Salem follow the signs for Highway 22 (Marion Street Bridge) heading west toward the ocean beaches. You'll cross the Willamette River and continue on the four-lane highway for less than a mile to the exit for West Salem. A right turn on Wallace Road (Highway 221) leads north to a left turn on Michigan City Avenue and a visit to Tom Robinson's Redhawk Vineyard. A friendly welcome in the tasting room and a wide selection of wines (many reds available!) make for a fun stop. Next door, Russ and Mary Raney operate Evesham Wood winery which is open for special events like Memorial Day weekend Tastevin Tour and by appointment.

Continue north on Wallace Road (Hwy. 221) and turn left on Zena Road. Travel west about 1.5 miles to Spring Valley Road (right turn) and a stop at Witness Tree Vineyard. Open weekends only for tasting and sales. You will have passed the former Mirassou winery a half-mile back, but it is currently open by appointment only under its new ownership and name, Christom Vineyards. Continue north on Spring Valley Road to find Stangeland Vineyard at the junction of Spring Valley with Hopewell Road. Open weekends, noon to 5.

Back on Zena Road, head west for a mile or two until you see the sign for Bethel Heights Vineyard. Members of the Casteel families are often on hand to welcome visitors to their facility. A grassy strip next to the vineyard is provided for spread-your-blanket style picnics or wine sipping.

A little cross country navigating on Oak Grove Road leads you to Oak Grove Orchards Winery and Orchard Heights Winery nearer Highway 22. Both wineries are open noon to 5 PM Tuesdays through Sundays.

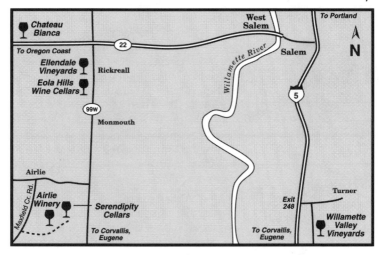

Salem Area / Polk County Touring - South

South of Salem the wineries are a little more spread out. Continuing westbound travel on Highway 22 as before, you come to a stoplight on the freeway at Highway 99W. Turn right and travel 2 miles north to the turn for Flynn Vineyard. Specializing in methode champenoise sparkling wine, Schwarzenberg Vineyards is reached by traveling west on Smithfield Road from its juction with 99W, 4.5 miles north of Highway 22.

Ten miles west of 99W and right on Highway 22 is Chateau Bianca run by the Wetzel family. A nice stop on your way to the beach!

Retrace your steps to 99W and head south to Ellendale Vineyards' tasting room in Rickreall - a great opportunity to try the wines produced by Robert Hudson. A block south, Eola Hills Wine Cellars is open for informal tours and wine tasting. They've added a special wine tasting brunch on Sundays!

Continue south on 99W through Monmouth then turn right for the town of Airlie (6 miles). Make a left turn in Airlie and travel for another 3 miles to Dunn Forest Road, home of Airlie Winery and Serendipity Cellars.

Dunn Forest Road is a one-lane, gravel driveway so take it slow for safety and courtesy's sake. At the top of the hill, Glen and Cheryl Longshore welcome you to Serendipity Cellars. Glen is the master of the Maréchal Foch grape from which he makes a delightfully fruity and spicy red wine.

Down the hill Larry and Alice Preedy welcome you to Airlie Winery. Retiring from the farm life in Kansas was too relaxing so the Preedy's decided to try their hand at grape growing and winemaking.

Back on I-5 you'll find a special reason to pull off for a stop at exit 248. Willamette Valley Vineyards is Oregon's original publically-owned winery and makes a great effort to welcome visitors to their facility. Picnic with a view of the valley and enjoy the wide selection of wines and gifts in the tasting room.

Oregon
Airlie Winery

15305 Dunn Forest Rd.
Monmouth, OR 97361
(503) 838-6013

Owners:
Larry & Alice Preedy
Winemaker:
Larry Preedy
First Year: 1986
Winery Capacity:
15,000 Gallons
1991 Production:
15,000 Gallons

Tasting Room Hours:
Weekends, 12 to 5 PM

Winery History

Transplanted to Oregon's coast range from the flat Kansas farmlands , Larry and Alice Preedy have been growing grapes in their Dunn Forest Vineyard since 1983. Thirty-five total acres are planted to Riesling, Muller Thurgau, Gewurztraminer, Chardonnay, Pinot Noir and Marchel Foch.

In 1986 the Preedys began their winemaking career by producing 4,000 gallons of wine. The winery was constructed in the same year – dug into a hillside to provide a year 'round cellar temperature of 55˙F.

A visit to Airlie Winery

Alice and Larry are often your tasting room hosts for weekend visits to Airlie Winery. They're easygoing and really kind folks who enjoy the wines they make and enjoy talking about them. The Memorial Day Weekend Blue Grass Festival is Airlie Winery's contribution to fun in the wine country each year. The Sawtooth Mountain Boys play from a bandstand by the pond and can be heard all around the winery property. Parking can get a little tight, so come early.

The Wines

Award-winning Muller Thurgau and Chardonnay are joined by Pinot Noir, Gewurztraminer, Riesling, and a tasty Marechal Foch (see Best of the Northwest review on page 22).

Bethel Heights Vineyard

6060 Bethel Heights
Road NW
Salem, OR 97304
(503) 581-2262

Owners: Terry & Ted
Casteel, Marilyn
Webb, Pat Dudley
Winemaker:
Terry Casteel
First Year: 1984
Winery Capacity:
16,000 Gallons

Tasting Room Hours:
Tues.-Sun., Mar.-Dec.,
11 AM to 5 PM

Winery History

A trip to France, a love of wine, and close ties to the Pacific Northwest led the Casteel brothers, Ted and Terry (and their families), to the Willamette Valley in the late 1970s to try their hand at grapegrowing and winemaking. The families acquired one of the most desirable vineyard sites in the Eola Hills, just northwest of Salem. Fourteen acres of first-year vines came with the property, now 51 acres are planted with Northwest varietals.

As the vines grew and as early harvests were sold to other wineries, the owners discovered what an ideal microclimate they had found. Grapes from the Bethel Heights Vineyard have made some of the Northwest's best Pinot Noir and Chardonnay wines as well as other varietals. In 1983 the time was right to build their own winery and begin production of the first estate wines.

Marilyn Webb, Terry Casteel, Pat Dudley and Ted Casteel of Bethel Heights.

A visit to Bethel Heights Vineyard

Following signs from Highways 99W or 221, turn onto Zena Road for the 3-plus mile ride to Bethel Heights Road. A picnic at Bethel Heights Vineyard offers a relaxed and quiet setting with views of the rolling hills of vineyard and farmland. Picnic tables are provided for alfresco dining.

Inside, one of the owners or their regular staff pours samples of Bethel Heights wine and offers insights into the vine-to-wine transformation that takes place each year at this vineyard-and-winery facility.

The Wines

Crisp acidity in white wines and a nice balance of fruit and toasty oak on the Pinot Noirs are a hallmark of Bethel Heights wines. Recent vintages have seen more variety in special releases including Pinot Noirs from exclusively "Old Block" and "Flat Block" sections of the vineyard. These special wines are usually available only at the winery. Crisp Chardonnay and flavorful Chenin Blanc, Gewurztraminer and Riesling are also made. See **Best of the Northwest** reviews for Bethel Heights Pinot Noir and Chenin Blanc.

Oregon

Chateau Bianca

17485 Highway 22
Dallas, Oregon 97338
(503) 623-6181

Owners:
Helmut Wetzel
Winemaker:
Helmut Wetzel
First Year: 1991
Winery Capacity:
3,500 Gallons
Tasting Room Hours:
Daily, Noon to 6 PM

Winery History

Helmut Wetzel has been involved in the Oregon wine industry as an investor for over 20 years. His new venture creates a unique opportunity for he and his family to grow grapes, make wine and market the finished product right on one of Oregon's busiest tourist routes. The 10-acre vineyard, winery and tasting room/gift shop are a complete package for the selling of Chateau Bianca wine and wine-related gifts.

A visit to Chateau Bianca

The winery is located on Highway 22, 10 miles west of Highway 99W. Members of the Wetzel family are often on hand to pour the wines and converse about their growing operation.

The Wines

Current releases include Pinot Noir, Chardonnay, Riesling and Gewürztraminer. Sparkling wines are offered in a Brut style and a Cuvée Blanc. Pinot Blanc will be joining the lineup soon.

Christom Winery

6785 Spring Vy. Rd. NW
Salem, OR 97304

Owner: Paul Gerrie
Winemaker:
Steve Doerner
First Year: 1992
Winery Capacity:
40,000 Gallons
1992 Production:
3,000 Gallons

Winery History

The original owners of this property are relatives of the California Mirassous of winery fame. The Oregon venture known as Pellier-Mirassou developed the property and made wine from 1985 until 1991. The winery closed in 1991 and was purchased by Pennsylvania oil exploration expert Paul Gerrie. Gerrie is a lover of fine Burgundy and thought this would be a fine opportunity to try his hand at creating some wines in the style of those he admires from France. Recruiting winemaker Steve Doerner from Calera Winery in California and vineyard manager Mark Feltz from Chalk Hill, Gerrie's team has begun the task of replanting vineyards, experimenting with various lots of Pinot Noir made from purchased grapes, and generally restoring the winery to order.

A visit to Christom Winery

Just next door to Witness Tree winery on Spring Valley Road and around the corner from Bethel Heights, Christom is poised geographically to welcome visitors. Wine is still in cask at press time and to invite the public in with no wine to taste or sell is unwise. Watch for a future announcement of tasting room hours.

Ellendale Vineyards

300 Reuben Boise Road
Dallas, OR 97338
(503) 623-5617

Owners: Robert and
Ella Mae Hudson
Winemaker:
Robert Hudson
First Year: 1981
Winery Capacity:
10,000 Gallons
1991 Production:
9,000 Gallons

Tasting Room Hours:
May through October:
Daily, 10 AM to 6 PM
Nov. through April:
Mon. - Sat., 10 AM to
6 PM, Sun. 12 to 5 PM

Winery History

Winemaker and landscape artist Robert Hudson retired as a major from the Air Force in 1975 with the intention of making sparkling wine. Today his sparkling wine dream has come true with the release of "Crystal Mist" Brut. Ellendale Vineyards forged their dream from the sales of many types of wine popular with local residents. Fruit wines have given way to mostly grape wines save one with the following story:

Davy Crockett once described himself as "a real woolly booger who could climb a cactus backwards with a wildcat under each arm and never get a scratch!" This description and the image it conjures up intrigued Robert Hudson to the point where he wanted to name a wine 'Woolly Booger.' The name is hardly fitting for most Northwest varietal wines but it seemed just right for a blend of blackberry, loganberry and cherry wine served up at Ellendale to "just friends" and hired help. It soon caught on and the illustration of a woolly caterpillar with the face of a backwoods, sourdough prospector has made it a Northwest legend in its own time.

A visit to Ellendale Vineyards

The new Ellendale tasting room in Rickreall is the art gallery for Robert's oil paintings of Oregon landmarks as well as pottery, jewelry and grapevine wall hangings. This new facility specializes in the production of Mead (honey wine).

Located right on Highway 99W just a quarter-mile off Highway 22, this tasting room is convenient to many travelers coming to and from many destinations. Stop by for some enjoyable wines and a browse through the gifts and knick-knacks.

The Wines

In addition to the fun "Wooley Booger" described above, Ellendale makes Pinot Noir, Chardonnay, Gewurztraminer, Riesling, Mead and other blended wines.

Oregon

Tom and Bill Huggins host the tasting bar at Eola Hills Wine Cellars.

Eola Hills Wine Cellars

501 S. Pacific Highway
W. (99W)
Rickreall, OR 97371
(503) 623-2405

Owner: Corp. Investor
Group, Tom Huggins,
General Manager
Winemaker:
   Kerry Norton
First Year: 1986
Winery Capacity:
   45,000 Gallons
1991 Production:
   45,000 Gallons

Tasting Room Hours:
Daily, Noon to 5 PM

Winery History

A partnership headed by Tom Huggins is the driving force behind this Polk County winery. Owners of the 70 acre Oak Grove Vineyard in the Eola Hills, the winery has access to excellent Pinot Noir, Chardonnay, Cabernet Sauvignon, Sauvignon Blanc and Chenin Blanc. These varietals were made beginning with the 1986 vintage and the winery opened in June of 1988.

A visit to Eola Hills Wine Cellars

Just south of the junction of highways 99W and 22, Eola Hills' new facility offers winelovers a chance to relax indoors or out, with a picnic area outside and a cafe-style tasting room inside. The proximity of the tasting room to the working winery makes it possible to enjoy a mini-tour without leaving the tasting bar. Frequently hosting the tasting room is Tom Huggins' father, Bill. A friendly welcome with the family touch! A recent innovation is Sunday Brunch served at the winery - call for details.

The Wines

Rich and hearty reds including Pinot Noir, Cabernet Sauvignon and Gamay Noir offer great appeal for red wine lovers. White wines are varietally true, crisp and clean with Sauvignon Blanc, Pinot Gris, Chenin Blanc and barrel-fermented Chardonnay leading the way. Late harvest style Riesling is crafted when the fruit dictates.

Evesham Wood
Vineyard

4035 Wallace Rd. NW
(Mail)
West Salem, OR 97304
(503) 371-8478

Owners: Russell and
  Mary Raney
Winemaker:
  Russ Raney
First Year: 1986
Winery Capacity:
  7,500 Gallons
1991 Production:
  6,500 Gallons

Tasting Room Hours:
By appointment only

Winery History

Russ and Mary Raney are pursuing a Northwest dream with a small vineyard and a small winery on their property near Salem. The first crush in 1988 included Pinot Noir and Chardonnay. Russ' background includes a degree in viticulture and enology from the German wine institute at Bad Kreuznach. He sold wine retail and wholesale for five years in St. Louis before locating to Oregon and worked as winemaker for Adams Vineyard Winery in Portland in 1984-85. Mary Raney studied horticulture at Southern Illinois University adding needed experience to the grape growing adventure that accompanies small winery operations.

By the way, the Evesham Wood name was derived from a fruit growing area of England that Russ and Mary visited on their honeymoon in 1984.

A visit to Evesham Wood Vineyard

The current Evesham Wood winery is adjacent to the original property where a co-op winery was shared by Evesham Wood and Redhawk Vineyard. Plans for the new facility include the building of Russ and Mary's home above the almost-entirely underground current structure. The winery is open during the Memorial Day and Thanksgiving open houses. Other times by appointment.

The Wines

Pinot Noir, Chardonnay and Pinot Gris are the varietals produced at Evesham Wood. Accollades in the national wine press have brought these wines more into the limelight in recent vintages. Our **Best of the Northwest** panel enjoyed Evesham's fine Pinot Gris and a review appears on page 27.

Oregon

Flynn Vineyards

2095 Cadle Road
Rickreall, OR 97371
(503) 623-6505

Owners: Wayne Flynn,
Mickey & Jeanne
Flynn
Winemaker:
Rich Cushman
First Year: 1984
Winery Capacity:
28,000 Gallons
1991 Production:
16,000 Gallons

Tasting Room Hours:
Tues. - Sun., 12 - 5 PM
$1.00 tasting fee.

Winery History

The first Flynn Vineyard site was purchased and planted in 1982 when Wayne Flynn acquired 50 acres in the southwest Eola Hills. The entire plot was planted to Pinot Noir and another site of 23 acres near Hopewell was added the following spring. Still more land was added to the holding in 1987 at the same time Wayne's brother Mickey became a partner. The large winery building was constructed in time for the 1990 vintage. Previous wines were made under contract at neighboring wineries.

A visit to Flynn Vineyards

Flynn Vineyards' tasting room is in a corner of the huge open winery, allowing visitors to take a look at the various pieces of equipment and stored wine while they taste. The tasting fee here should not be off-putting since you're afforded the opportunity of tasting the winery's sparkling Brut as well as the still wines.

The Wines

Winemaker Rich Cushman is the most experienced of any Oregon winemaker when it comes to making sparkling wine. His skill combined with the winery's top-of-the-line equipment adds up to quality and consistency in the sparkling wines. The still wines show the quality of the winemaking and the quality of the vineyard. Pinot Noir and Chardonnay, harvested from Flynn's Eola Hills sites make excellent quality varietals.

Honeywood Winery

1350 Hines St. S.E.
Salem, OR 97302
(503) 362-4111

Owner: Paul Gallick
Winemaker:
Sean McRitchie
First Year: 1934
Winery Capacity:
30,000 Gallons
1991 Production:
30,000 Gallons

Winery History

The historic Honeywood Winery in downtown Salem began as the Columbia Distilleries just after the repeal of prohibition in 1933. Production at that time was mainly fruit brandies and liqueurs, but soon the owners Ron Honeyman and John Wood decided to make fruit wines instead and the winery was born. Honeywood has operated continuously since that time with the current owner having been at the helm since 1973. With the increased availability of quality Oregon grapes for winemaking, the winery has increased production of premium varietal grape wines. Honeywood moved to its current location (from the original warehouse) in 1990.

Tasting Room Hours:
M-F, 9 AM - 5 PM,
Sat., 10 AM - 5 PM,
Sun. 1 - 5 PM

A visit to Honeywood Winery

Take the Highway 22 exit from I-5 and head west to Hines St. to find the Honeywood Winery just southeast of downtown Salem. Honeywood offers wine tasting every day along with an extensive selection of wine-related gifts in their gift shop / tasting room. A wide variety of wines - both grape varietal and fruit wines - are available for tasting.

The Wines

Honeywood continues to produce quality fruit wines from Willamette Valley harvests including Blackberry, Raspberry, Loganberry, Rhubarb, Plum and others. Varietals from Pinot Noir, Chardonnay, Riesling and Gewurztraminer are also made. A house specialty is white table wine (mostly Riesling) flavored with a small percentage of fruit juice.

Oak Grove Orchards Winery

6090 Crowley Rd.
Rickreall, OR 97371
(503) 364-7052

Owner & Winemaker:
Carl Stevens
First Year: 1987
Winery Capacity:
5,000 Gallons
1991 Production:
2,000 Gallons

Tasting Room Hours:
Tuesday thru Sunday,
Noon to 6 PM

Winery History

Carl Stevens has been making wine at home for 30 years using fruit that he grows in his orchard and vineyard. A portion of the original family homestead from the 1880s is home to orchards, vineyard and winery.

A visit to Oak Grove Orchards Winery

A reconstructed building originally at Camp Adair near Eugene serves as the tasting room for Carl Steven's winery. He moved the building and fixed it up for use both as a tasting room and as an inclement weather picnic site. Outside, picnic tables under the oak trees invite winery visitors to enjoy their repast on sunny days.

A note about weekday visits: Carl often has errands to run during the week and winery visitors come mostly on weekends, so if you're coming on a weekday, please call ahead to insure Carl will be there to welcome you.

The Wines

Carl's chosen varietals are two labrusca (concord) varieties popular in the New York wine growing regions. A Golden Muscat wine is made with 2% residual sugar and a true Concord is available in a dry or off-dry style. The winemaker recommends the dry Concord as a great accompaniment to a spaghetti dinner! Also crafted from estate-grown fruit is a unique Pie Cherry Wine that has a dedicated local following.

Oregon

Orchard Heights Winery

1991
WILLAMETTE VALLEY OREGON
GEWÜRZTRAMINER
ALCOHOL 12% BY VOLUME

6057 Orchard Heights
Road N.W.
Salem, OR 97304
(503) 363-0375

Owner: Ed Lopez
Winemaker:
Consultant
First Year: 1991
Winery Capacity:
10,000 Gallons

Winery History

This property began life as the Glen Creek Winery in the early 1980s but foundered as the decade drew to a close. Overgrown vineyards and a winery facility left dusty and unused made it hard for interested buyers to imagine a new life for the place. Along came Ed Lopez who heard about the site while seeking a horse ranch in the Eugene area. A real estate developer from Southern California, Lopez took a look at the property and had the vision of rebirth that others had not. Longtime Oregon winemaker Bob McRitchie joined up to blend the first releases from purchased wine and to get the winery in order. A short stint as winery partner ended when McRitchie decided to return to consulting instead of being tied to one operation.

A visit to Orchard Heights Winery

Find Orchard Heights just east of Oak Grove Road on Orchard Heights Road. Picnic facilities include trellised arbors shading inviting lawn on which to spread your blanket.

The Wines

Since the original Orchard Heights wines were vinted by others (and were sound examples of their style), it is difficult to judge how future bottlings will fare. The current owner is a good judge of wine and should be able to oversee a sound winemaking program.

Redhawk Vineyard

2995 Michigan City
Ave. N.W.
Salem, OR 97304
(503) 362-1596

Owner/Winemaker:
Tom Robinson
First Year: 1989
Winery Capacity:
10,000 Gallons
1991 Production:
4,500 Gallons

Tasting Room Hours:
May through Labor Day
Weekends, 12 to 5 PM

Winery History

Trained as a schoolteacher and possessing a great sense of humor, Tom Robinson now teaches visitors about wine in his tasting room at Redhawk Vineyard. Learning about wine himself during his days in the hot tub business in Portland, Robinson has chosen to create fanciful labels to help separate his quality table wines from the rest. Grateful Red, Chateau Mootom and Great White (complete with a shark on the label) are but a few of his humorous offerings of less expensive blended wines. The vineyard site was originally developed by Al Alexanderson (one of the founding partners in Hidden Springs Winery) and has the potential for excellent quality wines which Robinson sells as his regular Redhawk bottlings.

Tasting room art at Redhawk Vineyard includes this mural by Terry Pratt.

A visit to Redhawk Vineyard

The winery site is just above Highway 221 (Wallace Road) a few miles north of West Salem. The view across the vineyard to the Willamette River and the Cascades is breathtaking on sunny days. Tom pours wines in the winery tasting room with a tapestry backdrop that is the envy of all who visit. His deadpan sense of humor gives way to an occasional mischievous smile that intrigues even the most stoic winelover.

The Wines

While fame has come to Redhawk Vineyard through Grateful Red, it won't be long before the high quality Reserve Pinot Noir and Chardonnay push their way into the national reviews and bring well-deserved recognition to the winery. Limited quantities of Cabernet Franc, Pinot Blanc, Pinot Gris and Cabernet Sauvignon are also made.

Oregon

Schwarzenberg Vineyards

11975 Smithfield Rd.
Dallas, OR 97338
(503) 623-6420

Owners: Helmut &
Helga Schwarz
Winemaker:
Norbert Fiebig
First Year: 1987

Tasting Room Hours:
Mon.-Fri., 9 AM-5 PM
Sat., 10 AM to 5 PM
Sunday, 1 PM to 5 PM

Winery History

The Schwarz family planted their 50 acre vineyard in 1981 on their property overlooking the Basket Slough Wildlife Refuge west of Salem. The vineyard is planted to Chardonny and Pinot Noir - the two varieties which form the basis for the winery's production. The bonding of the winery in 1987 created an avenue to release wines made from the 1986 vintage harvested from the estate vineyard. Both the Chardonnay and Pinot Noir were well received by wine experts and consumers alike.

A visit to Schwarzenberg Vineyards

The Schwarzenberg winery is located northwest of the junction of Highway 22 and Highway 99W. You can turn onto Smithfield Road from either highway and the travel distance from highway to winery is about the same either way. The view of the wildlife refuge from the winery and vineyard inspired the artist's depiction of a Canada Goose on the Schwarzenberg Vineyard label.

The Wines

As mentioned above, Schwarzenberg concentrates on Chardonnay and Pinot Noir and offers the slogan "light and fruity and fun to drink" as the wines description. Red and white table wines are available from the winery with each version containing 100% varietal Pinot Noir or Chardonnay.

Serendipity Cellars

15275 Dunn Forest Rd.
Monmouth, OR 97361
(503) 838-4284

Owners:
The Longshore Family
Winemaker:
Glen A. Longshore
First Year: 1981
Winery Capacity:
8,000 Gallons
1991 Production:
5.550 Gallons

Tasting Room Hours:
Daily, Noon to 6 PM,
Closed Tuesdays
Winter, weekends only

Winery History

This tiny winery tucked away in a tiny valley near Monmouth is home to a dedicated winemaker and his family, striving each year to maintain an individuality in this era of winery 'sameness.'

Instead of limiting production to the typical varieties grown in Northwestern Oregon, Glen Longshore vinifies a grape called Maréchal Foch into a distinctive, fruity red wine. This grape comes from a family of 'French Hybrids,' genetic crosses between true vinifera grapes and other varieties bred to provide winter hardiness and resistance to phylloxera insects.

A visit to Serendipity Cellars

Follow Highway 99W south from Monmouth and turn west on Airlie Road. At the town of Airlie, turn south on Maxfield Creek Road to Dunn Forest Road. Up at the top of the hill on Dunn Forest Road

the winery is visible as the lower level of the Longshore home. As the need for more space increases, more home becomes winery. The tasting room features a selection of Serendipity Cellars' wines often poured by Glen's wife, Cheryl.

The Wines

Glen Longshore's hearty reds are touted as lacking the tannic roughness of traditionally made reds. The Marechal Foch, Zinfandel and Cabernet Sauvignon are made in small quantities and are often available only at the winery. Muller Thurgau and Dry Chenin Blanc are Glen's white varieties.

Silver Falls Winery

4972 Cascade Hwy. SE
Sublimity, OR 97385
(503) 769-9463

Owners:
  Ralph Schmidt,
  John Schmidt,
  Steve DeShaw,
  Jim Palmquist
Winemaker:
  Jim Palmquist
First Year: 1983
Winery Capacity:
  8,000 Gallons
1991 Production:
  8,000 Gallons

Tasting Room Hours:
Weekends, 12 to 5 PM

Winery History

The Silver Falls vineyard and winery have been operating since 1983-but 1988 was the first year that wines were widely released and promotion for the facility provided. The Palmquist family has grown Pinot Noir for many years and have sold the grapes as well as use them for the Silver Falls operation.

A visit to Silver Falls Winery

The location of Silver Falls Winery makes it a perfect destination for a weekend outing into the picturesque foothills of the Cascades. Only seven miles from Silver Falls State Park, the winery offers weekend tasting and tours as well as picnicing and a 1,200 sq. ft. social room available for parties or receptions. From Salem, follow State St., Hwy. 22 or Hwy. 213 to Cascade Highway.

The Wines

Wines produced at Silver Falls include Pinot Noir, Pinot Gris, Chardonnay, Riesling and Late Harvest Riesling.

Oregon

Stangeland Winery

8500 Hopewell Rd. NW
Salem, OR 97304
(503) 581-0355

Owners: Larry &
Kinsey Miller
Winemaker:
Larry Miller
First Year: 1991

Tasting Room Hours:
Tentatively open on
summer weekends.
Call ahead.

Winery History
Larry and Kinsey Miller planted their vineyard in the north Eola Hills in 1978. Selling grapes to other wineries, mostly Redhawk Vineyards, continues to support the vineyard, but Larry thought he would try his hand at winemaking as well.

A visit to Stangeland Winery
Located at the corner of Spring Valley Rd. and Hopewell Rd. (just 1/4-mile west of Hwy. 221), you'll find Stangeland Winery open most summer weekends from noon to 5 PM. Call ahead to make sure someone is there to meet you at other times.

The Wines
Small lots of Pinot Noir, Chardonnay and Pinot Gris are grown and produced at the Stangeland Winery.

St. Innocent Winery

2701 22nd SE
Salem, OR 97302
(503) 378-1526

Owner:
St. Innocent, Ltd.
Winemaker:
Mark Vlossak
First Year: 1989
Winery Capacity:
7,500 Gallons
1991 Production:
6,500 Gallons

Tasting Room Hours:
Memorial Weekend
and Thanksgiving
Weekend events only.
Other times by
appointment.

Winery History
A comfortable association with wine appreciation and a coincidental career move led to Mark Vlossak's winemaking career and St. Innocent Winery. As physician's assistant to Salem pediatrician Jim Lace, he was shown around the Eola Hills and became interested in the burgeoning wine industry of the early 1980s. Meeting local winemakers and vineyard owners was an important step with home winemaking and U.C. Davis short courses providing hands-on experience. Serving as assistant winemaker at Arterberry Winery in 1987 and 1988 springboarded Vlossak to bonding his own facility in 1989.

A visit to St. Innocent
Currently the winery offers visits only by appointment and on the Thanksgiving and Memorial Day weekend events.

The Wines
Mark Vlossak has earned a great reputation for high quality Pinot Noir, Chardonnay and sparkling wine. A believer in the importance of quality fruit to creating quality wine, he has carefully selected the vineyard sources for his bottlings. Chardonnay from Seven Springs Vineyard and Pinot Noir from O'Connor Vineyard have produced award-winning results. Mark's first love, sparkling wine, is carefully crafted with labor-intensive methods and great forethought put into each cuvée.

Willamette Valley Vineyards picnic area and view to surrounding countryside.

Willamette Valley Vineyards

8800 Enchanted Way SE
Turner, OR 97392
(503) 588-9463

Winery Owner:
Publicly Owned,
James Bernau, Pres.
Winemaker:
Dean Cox
First Year: 1989
Winery Capacity:
55,000 Gallons
1991 Production:
55,000 Gallons

Tasting Room Hours:
Daily, 11 AM to 6 PM

Winery History

"We knew many shared the dream of building and owning a world class winery in Oregon. As 2,620 wine enthusiasts, we pooled our resources to build Oregon's landmark winery and to produce the highest quality, premium wines." Indeed, these shareholders were the beginning of Willamette Valley Vineyards in 1989 and the success has come. Quality winemaking by winemaker Bob McRitchie (now handled by his son), quality management and a first-class facility have combined to create an example of what good planning can accomplish.

A visit to Willamette Valley Vineyards

Just of I-5 south of Salem (take exit 248), this beautiful facility stands out at the top of a hill covered in vineyards. A huge arch-gateway welcomes you from the frontage road and the winding driveway leads up to the stylish winery building and visitor center. A well-stocked tasting room invites your enjoyment of wines to sample as well as many gift items and foods to purchase. Terraces outside provide for picnicking with a great view.

The Wines

A wide range of varietals are made including Pinot Noir, Pinot Gris, Riesling, Muller Thurgau, Chardonnay and sparkling wines. Our Best of the Northwest panels nominated the Chardonnay and White Riesling for review.

179

Oregon

Witness Tree Vineyard

7111 Spring Vy. Rd NW
Salem, OR 97304
(503) 585-7874

Owner:
Douglas Gentzkow
Winemaker:
Gary Horner
First Year: 1987
Winery Capacity:
10,000 Gallons
1991 Production:
7,000 Gallons

Winery History

The Witness Tree Vineyard was planted in 1980 and is now producing commercial quantities of Pinot Noir and Chardonnay used by the winery constructed in 1987. The name of the winery and vineyard refers to a historic oak 'witness tree' that stands above the vineyard. This tree was used as a reference point by early surveyors platting this part of the Willamette Valley. A handsome tasting room was added to the winery building in 1992.

A visit to Witness Tree Vineyard

Just above Spring Valley Road, Witness Tree winery welcomes visitors to their cozy tasting room. Samples of Pinot Noir and Chardonnay are poured to interested wine lovers.

The Wines

The stated intention of Douglas Gentzkow is to "produce limited bottlings of classic Burgundian Pinot Noir and Chardonnay." The winery's current releases include barrel-fermented Chardonnay and a rich Pinot Noir aged in a variety of French oak cooperage.

Salem Area Accommodations & Dining

There are remarkably few choices in Salem for fine dining and even fewer for creative fine dining with knowledgeable wine pairing. However, there are some bright spots on the horizon. Accommodations are traditional motor inn chic with one or two exceptions.

Accommodations

Chumaree Comfortel, 3301 Market st. NE - (503) 370-7888, (800) 248-6723 Right off the Market St. exit from I-5. Of the motor inn choices, this is the most accommodating with helpful service and stress-free ambiance. Pool, sauna, jacuzzi, pets O.K. Ten minutes from downtown.

State House B & B, 2146 State St. - (503) 588-1340 Mike Winsett and Judy Uselmans handsome four bedroom B & B offers a beautiful back garden bordering on Mill Creek complete with hot tub and gazebo. Two regular rooms share a bath, two suites each have a private bath. Adjoining cottages have kitchenettes.

Dining

The Inn at Orchard Heights, 695 Orchard Heights Rd. NW - (503) 378-1780 In a converted home out in West Salem (across the river) this upscale continental restaurant has become a local favorite. Hans D'Alessio offers up a variety of seafoods and light meats in unique preparations. Pair your choice with selections from one of the area wineries.

Morton's Bistro Northwest, 1128 Edgewater in West Salem - (503) 585-1113 This neo-Northwest continental bistro offers creativity with each course. The chef is always finding new ways to use local ingredients and the wait staff is efficient yet unobtrusive. Although I personally haven't had the experience, it is claimed that Elvis has been seen here. Many local wines.

Salem Area and Eola Hills Activities for Young & Old

Silver Falls State Park, Highway 22, 20 miles east of Salem A not-too-long drive out to the country to enjoy waterfalls, hiking, bike riding, swimming and a deep woods picnic. Silver Falls Winery nearby is open weekends from 10 AM to 7 PM.

Minto Island Park - River Road South, Salem. A nice park along the Willamette for picnicing, bike riding and enjoying the river.

Brush College Park, West Salem off Wallace Road. Out in the general direction of the Eola Hills wineries , this little park has playground equipment and picnic tables along with trails and a softball field.

Willamette University, Salem
A stroll around this college campus may instill the values of higher education in your youngsters.

Dairy Queen - Wallace Road in Northwest Salem – A well-kept hamburger stand that cooks a custom burger in just about the same time it takes to wade through the line at McD's. Remember dipped cones and Dilly Bars?

Maud Williamson State Park - On the way north to Dayton, this pleasant park along the Willamette River offers a shady place to relax from a day of stressful wine touring!

Corvallis / Eugene Area Touring

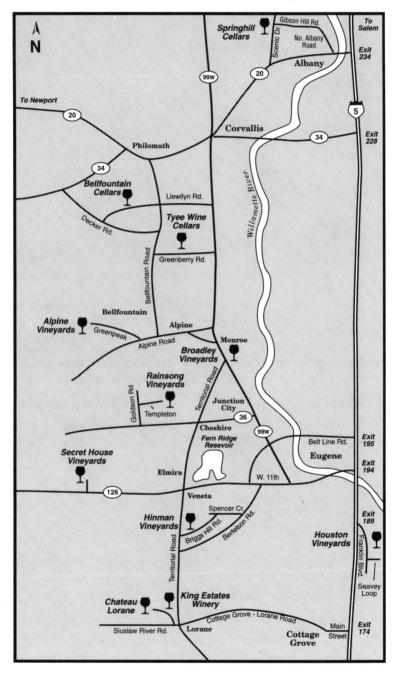

Corvallis / Eugene Area Touring

The area south of Salem is rich in soil, history and academics. The home of Oregon's two state universities is also home to many unique wineries. From north to south . . .

Head west on Llewlynn Road from 99W to find Bellfountain Cellars at the home of Rob and Jeanne Mommsen. Carved out of the foothills acreage, the winery occupies a little place in nature with surrounding forest and field. Bring your picnic to enjoy in the quiet woodland afternoon.

Head south on Highway 99W to find Tyee Wine Cellars on Greenberry Road. The Buchanan family along with Barney Watson and Nola Mosier have created a "quality not quanity" operation on the Buchanan's 100 year old farm. Margy Buchanan is your charming and informative tasting room hostess.

Farther down 99W, a right turn at the town of Monroe leads to Alpine Vineyards winery at the home of Dr. Dan Jepsen and family. Dan's medical responsibilities lie at the University of Oregon student health center but his creative outlet and exercise are the vineyard and winery. The towering oaks next to the winery provide shade for a tailgate picnic above the vineyard.

Weekend visitors can stop by Broadley Vineyards winery located right on Highway 99W at Monroe. Craig and Claudia Broadley opened for tourists in April of 1988 and have made them welcome with a tasteful tasting room and a picnic area out back along the Long Tom River.

Follow Territorial Highway south to Cheshire and turn west to visit Rainsong Vineyards off Goldson Road. Bring your lunch to enjoy by the pond or in the picnic area. Your hosts are owners Mike and Merry Fix.

West of Elmira, Forgeron Vineyard is apparently down for the count. Talk of bankers and lawyers persists but the winery ad tasting room are closed.

On Highway 126 (the coast road to Florence) you'll find Secret House Vineyards just west of the Junction with Territorial Highway. Ron and Patty Chappel, with their winemaker Gary Carpenter, are producing a delightful selection of wines including a delicious late harvest Riesling of special note!

Hinman Vineyards offers the peace and quiet of the countryside at their vineyard and winery on Briggs Hill Road. A scenic drive through forest and bucolic farmland precedes wine sampling and picnic opportunities at the winery. Follow Territorial to Briggs Hill or take the more complicated route from Eugene. This large facility offers a charming tasting room and a wonderful grassy amphitheatre for rollicking with the kids on a sunny day.

Chateau Lorane is just off Territorial on Siuslaw River Road and offers Oregon varietals and also unique wines not often seen in Oregon. Cabernet Franc, Durif, Grignolino, Zinfandel and Marechal Foche are joined by Melon, Pinot Meunier and Semillon to tempt the curious wine lover's palate. Enjoy a picnic by the private 24-acre lake.

Not open for tours or tasting, King Estate Winery is just north of Lorane. This large operation will be releasing the first wines in 1994 and plans distribution nationally as well as in the Northwest.

Tasting and tours by appointment are available at Houston Vineyards south of Eugene off I-5 exit 189. Franklin Blvd. leads to Seavey Loop Road and to Hoya Lane. Chardonnay is the preferred varietal of winery owners Steve and Jewelee Houston.

Oregon
Alpine Vineyards

25904 Green Peak Rd.
Alpine, OR 97456
Mailing address:
25904 Green Peak Rd.
Monroe, OR 97456
(503) 424-5851

Owner & Winemaker:
Dan Jepsen
First Year: 1980
Winery Capacity:
25,000 Gallons
1991 Production:
10,000 Gallons

Tasting Room Hours:
6/15 to 9/15, Daily
Noon to 5 PM
9/15 to 6/15, Weekends
Noon to 5 PM
Closed 12/25 - January

Winery History

When Dan and Christine Jepsen returned from two years in Africa working for the Peace Corps, they came to Oregon and planted a vineyard. An amateur winemaker throughout his years at medical school, Dan was attracted to the rural environment, the vigorous outdoor work involved and the prospect that somewhere down the line a winery might be in the works. The vineyard was planted in 1976 in a small valley between Corvallis and Eugene where 26 acres of vines now produce grapes for the Alpine Vineyards winery. The winery forms the ground level of the Jepsen's home which has a panoramic view of the vineyard and surrounding countryside.

A visit to Alpine Vineyards

A scenic seven mile drive from Highway 99W leads to Alpine Vineyards nestled in the Coast Range foothills northwest of Eugene. The vineyard - visible from the tasting room windows - produces all the grapes for Alpine's production. These estate bottled wines are poured for visitors by tasting room manager Christine Jepsen. A tour around the cozy winery is available for the asking and a picnic under the spreading oaks on a warm day is a delight.

The Wines

A strong believer in Oregon Chardonnay, Dan Jepsen's efforts with this wine have sold out year after year. Alpine Vineyards Chardonnay and Pinot Noir are worth seeking out, but be warned that a trip to the winery might be necessary to secure a supply from popular vintages.

Bellfountain Cellars

Winery History

In love with the idea of country life, Rob and Jeanne Mommsen traded in careers in the industrial east to forge a winery and home in the foothills of the Oregon Coast Range near Corvallis. With energy and enthusiasm they have built their home/winery, planted the first 10 acres of vineyard and established a reputation for quality wines.

25041 Llewellyn Rd.
Corvallis, OR 97333
(503) 929-3162

Owners/Winemakers:
Rob & Jeanne
Mommsen
First Year: 1989
Winery Capacity:
40,000 Gallons
1991 Production:
7,500 Gallons

Tasting Room Hours:
Weekends, 11 - 6 PM

A visit to Bellfountain Cellars

Turn west off Highway 99W on Llewllyn Road to find Bellfountain Cellars just past Fern Rd. The winery and vineyard are in a clearing in the pristine lowland forest with picnic tables and decks arranged to accommodate visitors. The owners encourage picnicking and strolling through the forest or along Bull Run Creek.

The Wines

Small quantities of Pinot Noir, Cabernet Sauvignon, Chardonnay, Sauvignon Blanc, Pinot Gris, Riesling and Gewurztraminer are produced.

Broadley Vineyards

265 South 5th
Box 160
Monroe, OR 97456
(503) 847-5934

Owners: Craig
& Claudia Broadley
Winemaker:
Craig Broadley
First Year: 1986
Winery Capacity:
5,000 Gallons
1991 Production:
4,500 Gallons

Tasting Room Hours:
May through Sept.,
Daily, 11 AM to 5 PM
October through Dec.,
Tues. - Sun., 11 to 4
January through April,
By appointment only.

Winery History

"City people" turned grape growers and winemakers is how Craig and Claudia Broadley think of themselves after nearly a decade of hard work learning the farming business. Originally involved in publishing and book distribution in San Francisco, the Broadleys found that Oregon was a perfect place to escape to their dream of winery ownership.

Their vineyard was planted beginning in 1980 and the winery building acquired in 1986 to accommodate the harvest of 15 acres of Chardonnay and Pinot Noir. Wines were first released in 1988.

A visit to Broadley Vineyards

The building now used as a winery for Broadley Vineyards was once a car dealership circa 1930. The large windows with a view of the Long Tom River allow the wine taster to appreciate nature along with a taste of nature's perfect beverage. A picnic area is outside for those longing to appreciate the view with their lunch.

The Wines

The Pinot Noirs and Chardonnays being produced by Craig Broadley follow his desire to craft Burgundian style wines that accompany food. Our Best of the Northwest panel found both the Broadley Reserve Pinot Noir and regular Pinot Noir quite exciting and of the highest quality. See reviews on page 17.

Oregon

Broadley Vineyards winery in Monroe, OR. (See text on preceding page.)

Chateau Lorane

27415 Siuslaw River Rd.
Lorane, OR 97451
(503) 942-8028

Owners: Linde &
Sharon Kester
First Year: 1992

Tasting Room Hours:
Summer weekends,
Noon to 6 PM

Winery History

Linde and Sharon Kester planted their 30-acre vineyard in 1984 and opened their winery and tasting room to the public in 1992. The beauty of the Coast Range foothills make their site something special a lake and forest setting.

A visit to Chateau Lorane

Travel down Territorial Highway to Lorane or follow the Cottage Grove-Lorane Road from exit 174 off I-5. The winery road is .2 miles west of Lorane on Siuslaw River Rd.

The Wines

A wide array of varietals are produced from the winery's vineyard and several more are made from purchased grapes. Pinot Noir, Chardonnay, Sauvignon Blanc, Riesling and Gewürztraminer are joined by Cabernet Franc, Durif, Grignolino, Zinfandel and others.

Forgeron Vineyards

89697 Sheffler Road
Elmira, OR 97437

Closed

Winery History

This winery was always a popular stop with visitors to the Eugene area who enjoyed the landscaped grounds, tidy tasting room and umbrella'd picnic tables by the fountain. So why did the place suddenly close in the summer of 1993? Rumors aboun but the truth eludes your humble author at presstime.

Hinman
Vineyards

27012 Briggs Hill Road
Eugene, OR 97405
(503) 345-1945

Owners: Doyle W.
Hinman, C. Chambers
Winemaker:
Joe Dobbes
First Year: 1979
Winery Capacity:
100,000 Gallons
1991 Production:
75,000 Gallons

Tasting Room Hours:
Daily, Noon to 5 PM

Winery History

Doyle Hinman realized a personal dream in 1979 when he bonded his winery just outside of Eugene, Oregon. Conceived as a stepwise investment, the winery started small with Doyle's friend David Smith providing assistance to the operation both financial and physical. Over the years, the winery has grown substantially and a new partner has replaced David Smith.

A visit to Hinman Vineyards

A 20-minute drive from Eugene, follow 11th St. (Hwy. 126) to Bailey Hill Rd. Turn left and follow this road for 5 miles, turning right on Spencer Creek Road for 2.5 miles. Turn left on Briggs Hill Road and travel the remaining 3.5 miles to the winery.

This large winery complex now encompasses several buildings including a tasting room and visitor center. Tasting and tours are offered daily.

The grassy amphitheatre adjacent to the winery is the site for concerts and other events.

The Wines

A wide selection of varietals is produced from both estate and purchased grapes. Pinot Noir, Chardonnay, Cabernet Sauvignon, Pinot Gris, Gewürztraminer, Riesling, Semillon and others are produced.

Houston
Vineyards

86187 Hoya Lane
Eugene, OR 97405
(503) 747-4681

Owners: Steven &
Jewelee Houston
1991 Production:
3,000 Gallons

Tasting Room Hours:
By appointment only.

Winery History

Steven and Jewelee Houston use only their own grapes in the production of their wine, but they have chosen to contract with an existing winery to produce wine according to their specifications. The term they use for their operation is a "custom crush grower" meaning that they have wine made from their grapes to their specifications.

A visit to Houston Vineyards

The Houston Vineyard lies along the Coast Fork of th Willamette River, next to the 2,300 acre Buford County Park off I-5 and just 2 miles east of Eugene. Wine tastings, sals and vineyard tours are available by appointment. Visitors are encouraged and welcome at the vineyard, please call ahead as hours of operation vary from day to day.

The Wine

Houston Vineyards are exclusive producers of Chardonnay.

An artist rendering of King Estate Winery near Lorane, Oregon.

King Estate Winery

80854 Territorial Road
Eugene, OR 97405
(503) 942-9874

Owner: King family,
Ed King, President
Winemakers: Brad
Biehl, Will Bucklin
First Year: 1992
Winery Capacity:
80,000 Gallons +
1992 Production:
40,000 Gallons

Winery History

Longtime Eugene resident Ed King is the head of this family-owned enterprise that is entering the Oregon wine industry in a big way. A large vineyard site southwest of Eugene is being planted and a huge winery building and aging cellar was constructed during 1992-93.

Vineyard manager David Michul, formerly at Bonny Doon winery, is undertaking the planting of 350 to 400 acres of vineyard utilizing a King Estate-owned, state of the art, vine propagation and nursery facility called Lorane Grapevines. Grafted cuttings are prepared for planting the King Estate vineyard and are also sold to other wineries.

The 100,000 square foot winery and aging cellar includes state of the art winemaking equipment, barrel aging cellar and winery offices.

A visit to King Estate Winery

No tourist facilities are planned for this large operation, but wines will be available nationally.

The Wines

King Estate crushed purchased grapes from the 1992 vintage and will be releasing Pinot Noir, Chardonnay and Pinot Gris. Future purchases of grapes are anticipated to provide greater comlexity in the wines.

Rainsong Vineyards Winery

92989 Templeton Rd.
Cheshire, OR 97419
(503) 998-1786

Owners/Winemakers:
Mike & Merry Fix
First Year: 1988
1990 Production:
2,000 Gallons

Tasting Room Hours:
June through Sept.,
Weekends, 12 to 5 PM

Winery History

Taking advantage of warm microclimates in the Coast Range foothills, Gary Carpenter and Mike Fix planted vineyards of classic Burgundian and Champagne varietals. Plantings in 1982 and 1985 have matured and are now fully producing. Award-winning wines have followed.

A visit to Rainsong Vineyards

Follow Highway 36 from Eugene through Cheshire. Turn right on Goldson Road and cross Hall Road to Templeton. The winery and tasting room are located on the edge of a small pond where a picnic area is available to visiting wine lovers.

The Wines

"Burgundian varietals" Pinot Noir and Chardonnay are the focus of this family run operation.

Secret House Vineyards

88324 Vineyard Lane
Veneta, OR 97487
(503) 935-3774

Owners: Ron and Patty Chappel
Winemaker:
Gary Carpenter
First Year: 1991
Winery Capacity:
5,000 Gallons

Winery History

Full-time entrepreneurs, Ron and Patty Chappel have a large vineyard to maintain, a tasting room to handle and a beautiful picnic area under Ponderosa pine trees to offer visitors. Retired from the business of importing fine arts from the Far East, the tasting room has touches of the orient as well as a beautiful gardenia bush in the corner that blooms as testament to Patty's green thumb.

A visit to Secret House Winery

Just two and a half miles west of Territorial Highway on Route 126, the winery is a convenient stop for those heading to the Oregon coast. Samples of several wines are offered and picnicking is encouraged on the winery grounds.

The Wines

Pinot Noir, Chardonnay, Riesling, Late Harvest Riesling and sparkling wine are produced here by winemaker Gary Carpenter.

Oregon

Springhill Cellars

2920 NW Scenic Dr.
Albany, OR 97321
(503) 928-1009

Owners: McLain
family, Gary Budd,
Merv Anthony
Winemakers: Mike
McLain, Gary Budd
First Year: 1988
Winery Capacity:
6,000 Gallons

Winery History

Shortly after Mike McLain planted his first acres of vineyard, he also expanded his real estate business to include vineyard land. The land values around Corvallis and Albany are much more reasonable than in the Dundee Hills and the suitability for vineyard is excellent. Gary Budd joined the enterprise in the late 1980s to help out as winemaker and Springhill's 1988 Pinot Noir won a gold medal and the Governor's award at the Oregon State Fair.

A visit to Springhill Cellars

A short jaunt off I-5 (take exit 234 and head west through Albany and north on N. Albany Rd.), the winery offers visitors a nice place to picnic and an enjoyable wine tasting experience.

The Wines

Mike McLain and Gary Budd are striving to make the very finest quality Pinot Noir, Chardonnay, Riesling and Müller Thurgau from the grapes harvested at the winery's Albany vineyard.

Tyee Wine Cellars

26335 Greenberry Road
Corvallis, OR 97333
(503) 753-8754

Owners:
Dave Buchanan,
Margy Buchanan,
Barney Watson,
Nola Mosier
Winemaker:
Barney Watson
First Year: 1985
Winery Capacity:
8,000 Gallons
1991 Production:
8,000 Gallons

Tasting Room Hours:
Daily, Noon to 5 PM
(May through Dec.)

Winery History

How many wineries can boast a one hundred year history of horse racing, sheep ranching and dairy farming? Grapes now grow where horses once thundered past the finish line and sheep pastures have been turned and planted with vineyards.

Tyee Wine Cellars began with homemade wine and a few grape vines but with vineyards growing and a winemaker on board the future looks promising. Dave and Margy Buchanan are the owners of the century-old farm that Dave's grandfather began back in the 1880's. Dave's home winemaking and grapegrowing led him back to his alma mater, Oregon State University, to look up Barney Watson, a U. C. Davis graduate hired by the school to do research for the Oregon wine industry. Barney liked the Buchanan's plans for a vineyard and winery and a partnership was born.

Most of the grapes for Tyee Wine Cellars current production has come from some of the area's best known vineyards. Estate-grown wines will

Tyee Wine Cellars near Corvallis, OR.

include Pinot Noir, Pinot Gris, Chardonnay and Gewürztraminer as soon as the young vineyards come into full bearing.

A visit to Tyee Wine Cellars

Rustic farm structures on the Buchanan farm have been remodeled to serve as winery and tasting room. New awnings have added a flair to the presentation while inside, Margy Buchanan offers samples of current releases for visitors. A very friendly welcome makes you feel right at home. Tyee offers several special events each year coinciding with the Memorial Day weekend and Thanksgiving weekend as well as their own July music event.

The Wines

Barney Watson's admitted fondness for Gewürztraminer has led the winery to great success with that varietal - a spunky style that accompanies Asian cooking and other spicy foods (see the **Best of the Northwest** review on page 29). Tyee's Pinot Gris has also been popular with wine judges and consumers at local enological events and was the favorite with our **Best of the Northwest** panel. See review of this delicious wine on page 27. Also produced at Tyee are Pinot Noir, Pinot Blanc, and Chardonnay.

191

Oregon

Corvallis /Eugene Accommodations & Dining

The Eugene and Corvallis areas offer some very sophisticated and enjoyable experiences that are an offshoot of their college town status. They have more popular restaurants and inns than Oregon's capitol city of Salem and offer a variety of activities appealing to young and old.

Accommodations
Corvallis

Towne House Motor Inn, 350 SW 4th - (503) 753-4496 A pleasant and modern motor hotel with restaurant, air conditioned rooms and convenient location to downtown and the OSU campus.

Madison Inn B & B, 660 SW Madison - (503) 757-1274 Adjacent to the delightful Central Park, Kathryn Brandis now welcomes guests to her childhood home to enjoy the spacious comfort of a 7 bedroom B & B. Sumptuous breakfasts and shady strolls in the park are the icing on the cake.

Eugene

Valley River Inn, 1000 Valley River Way, 97401 - (503) 687-0123 A getaway along the Willamette River offers rooms with river views, courtyards, secluded pool area and on-premises dining.

Eugene Hilton, 66 East 6th Ave., (503) 342-2000 One of the largest buildings in downtown Eugene, the Hilton borders on the Hult Center for the Performing Arts and offers great city views from many of its 271 rooms. Indoor pool, spa, game room.

Dining
Eugene

Cafe Central, 384 W. 13th, Eugene - (503) 343-9510 A very popular restaurant serving innovative and enjoyable fare for lunch and dinner. Extensive selection of wines, many from NW producers. Lunch, Mon. - Fri., dinner, Mon. - Sat.

The Excelsior Cafe, 754 East 13th Ave. (503) 342-6963 Choice local ingredients are prepared with style and creativity. A wide selection of menu offerings keeps the place crowded but excellent service helps keep pace. Local wines are well represented. Lunch and dinner daily.

Corvallis

The Gables, 1121 NW 9th St. (503) 752-3364 Local and regional ingredients are prepared to highlight freshness and true flavors. The menu leans toward the traditional American preparations that are popular in the country.

For Parents Only

Jogging and Bicycling - Eugene is acclaimed by runners and bikers as having the most runner/cyclist-friendly attitude of any Northwest city. Bike lanes stripe the roads and bike and jogging paths abound in parks.

Fern Ridge Resevoir - West of town on Highway 126, offers boating, fishing, water skiing, and more.

Skinner Butte Park, Spencer Butte Park - These two high points of the area offer great territorial views and profusions of flowers in the summer.

Van Duyn Candy Factory, near I-5 off Belt Line. What heartless parent would deny their child a visit to a candy factory?

Food and Wine Pairing with Northwest Varietals

	Chenin Blanc	Riesling	Gewurztraminer	Dry Riesling	Sauvignon Blanc	Semillon	Chardonnay	Pinot Noir	Lemberger	Merlot	Cabernet Sauvignon	Late Harvest Reisling	Port
	White Wines							Red Wines				Dessert Wines	
	Off Dry			Dry				Lighter		Heavier		Wines	
Mild Cheeses	●	●	●	●	●	●							
Strong Cheeses			●	●			●	●	●	●	●		●
Hors d'oeuvres	●	●	●	●	●	●	●						
Seafood													
Shrimp				●	●	●							
Crab, Lobster	●	●				●	●						
Oysters	Dry		Dry	●	●	●							
Clams, Mussels				●	●	●	●	●					
White Finfish		●		●	●		●						
Salmon				●			●	●	●	●			
Grilled Fish			●	●	●	●		●	●				
Fowl													
Chicken	●	●	●	●	●	●	●	●					
Duck, Goose			●	●				●	●	●			
Gamebirds				●	●			●	●				
Red Meat													
Pork & Veal			●	●	●		●	●	●				
Beef								●	●	●	●		
Lamb								●		●	●		
Game								●	●	●	●		
Asian Cooking	●	●	●	●		●	●						
Fruit Desserts	●	●										●	
Chocolate Desserts										●	●		●

193

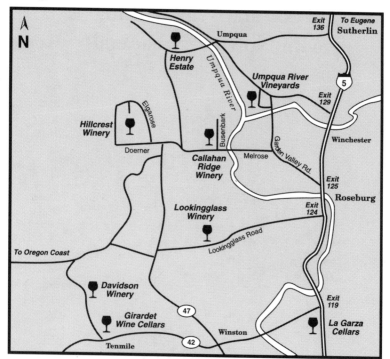

Umpqua Valley Touring

The extended valley of the Umpqua River winds through parts of Oregon rich in nature and rich in lore. The rushing stream of the Cascade Foothills offers up quiet corners for the fly fisherman to ply his trade. The likes of Ernest Hemingway and Zane Grey came here to enjoy the sport decades before a winery was conceived. Today the sport remains but several good wineries compete for the attention of lovers of the finer things in life.

The north part of this region finds Henry Estate Winery and Umpqua River Vineyards perched along the river. Henry Estate keeps regular hours and offers a broad range of varietals poured by family members in the tasting room. A call ahead to smaller Umpqua River winery insures an appointment.

In the middle part of the valley, the area known as Garden Valley, you'll find Callahan Ridge, home to some of Oregon's most appealing red wines. Pioneering Hillcrest Vineyard keeps regular hours with owner Richard Sommer on hand and Lookingglass Winery is open during the summer on weekends.

In the south part of the valley, close to the I-5 freeway at exit 119, the former Jonicole winery has been spruced up and reopened under the name La Garza Cellars. New wines, as well as an on-premise restaurant, rate a visit.

Two facilities operate northwest of the tiny town of Tenmile on Reston Road. Girardet Cellars is operated by former astro-physicist Philippe Girardet and his wife Bonnie. Their dedication to Umpqua-area winemaking and grapegrowing reached the decade milestone in 1993. The former Bjelland Winery, making wine since 1969, has been refurbished and refocused as Davidson winery by Guy and Sandra Davidson.

Callahan Ridge

340 Busenbark Lane
Roseburg, OR 97470
(503) 673-7901

Owners: Mary Sykes-
Guido, R. Mansfield
Winemaker:
  Richard Mansfield
First Year: 1987
Winery Capacity:
  27,000 Gallons
1991 Production:
  23,000 Gallons

Tasting Room Hours:
April through October,
Daily, 11 AM to 5 PM

Winery History

Callahan Ridge winery marked its sixth harvest in 1992. The winery was founded by Frank and Mary Guido along with Oregon native and German-trained winemaker Richard Mansfield. The wide selection of quality varietals produced at Callahan Ridge have helped establish the Umpqua Valley as one of Oregon's premier wine growing regions. Grapes from several sources including Elkton Vineyards (just 15 miles from the Pacific Ocean) and from Doerner Ranch at the base of the Callahan Range are used for the many varietals.

A visit to Callahan Ridge Winery

The 1878 building, constructed of hand-hewn beams, houses the tasting room for Callahan Ridge and is open for tours and tasting daily from April through October. Picnicking is encouraged in a shady field behind the winery.

The Wines

Among the many varietals produced at Callahan Ridge our **Best of the Northwest** panel found their Pinot Noir to be among Oregon's best. Also available are: Riesling, Dry Gewürztraminer, Cabernet Sauvignon, White Zinfandel, Sauvignon Blanc, Chardonnay and Select Harvest Riesling.

Davidson Winery

2637 Reston Road
Roseburg, OR 97470
(503) 679-6950

Owners: Guy &
  Sandra Davidson
First Year: 1969
Winery Capacity:
  20,000 Gallons
1991 Production:
  8,500 Gallons

Tasting Room Hours:
Daily, 11 AM to 4 PM
(summer months)

Winery History

The Davidson Winery operation is the new incarnation of what was once Bjelland Winery. Paul and Mary Bjelland were pioneers in the early days of Oregon winemaking. Guy and Sandra Davidson have taken over the facility and are producing rich and powerful wines of great character.

A visit to Davidson Winery

Follow Reston Road northwest from Tenmile (on Highway 42 from I-5) to find Davidson Winery in the shadow of the huge monolith that is a local landmark. Sandra Davidson is your host at the wnery tasting room. A satellite tasting room is located at Cabin Creek Wine Merch. in Oakland.

The Wines

Deep and intense Pinot Noir is the hallmark wine of Davidson Winery. The distinctive artist series labels are most unique. Chardonnay, Riesling and Rosé are also produced.

Oregon

Philippe and Bonnie Girardet and family.

Girardet Wine Cellars

895 Reston Road
Roseburg, OR 97470
(503) 679-7252

Owners: Philippe and
Bonnie Girardet
Winemaker:
Philippe Girardet
First Year: 1983
Winery Capacity:
40,000 Gallons
1991 Production:
14,000 Gallons

Tasting Room Hours:
Summer:
Daily, Noon to 5 PM
Winter: Saturdays only
Closed Christmas
season and January

Winery History

Although the 18 acre vineyard dates from the Girardet's arrival in Oregon in 1972, they were at first content to sell the output of their vineyard to other wineries. The winery began in 1983 and they hired enologist Bill Nelson to guide them through the first crush and to counsel them on proper selection of equipment.

A visit to Girardet Winery

The winery and tasting room are open daily during the summer. The vineyard is just outside the tasting room door and informal tours are available if time permits. Bonnie Girardet is your hostess.

The Wines

The blending of wines holds the key to success for Philippe Girardet who takes as much pride in his Oregon Vin Blanc and Oregon Vin Rouge as he does in his Chardonnay or Pinot Noir. Each of the blended wines includes generous portions of grape cultivars frequently referred to as 'French hybrids'. By blending these unusual varieties with Chardonnay and Pinot Noir (and other premium varietal wines) Philippe achieves a complexity and balance that serves as a fine accompaniment ot Northwest cuisine. Girardet Cabernet Sauvignon and Vin Rouge were well-received by our **Best of the Northwest** panels. See reviews beginning on page 15.

Henry Estate Winery

P.O. Box 26
687 Hubbard Creek Rd.
Umpqua, OR 97486
(503) 459-5120

Owners: Scott and
Sylvia Henry
Winemaker:
Scott Henry
First Year: 1978
Winery Capacity:
40,000 Gallons
1991 Production:
30,000 Gallons

Tasting Room Hours:
Daily, 11 AM to 5 PM
Tours available, tour
groups by appointment

Winery History

The science of engineering and the science of winemaking have come together many times in the evolution of Oregon's wine industry. Aeronautical engineer Scott Henry began his transition from drafting table and 'T' square to tractor and wine barrel in 1972 when he planted the first of 31 acres of vinifera grapes on the family ranch in the Umpqua Valley. Many family members are involved in the operation of the Henry Winery and vineyard. No fewer than four 'Scotts' can be found on the payroll including Scott Henry, Sr., Scott Henry, Jr. and a couple of other 'Scotts' related to the clan by marriage or friendship. Scott Henry's father is also a 'Scott' but he goes by his middle name, Cal (short for Calvin), to avoid confusion!

A visit to Henry Estate Winery

Cal Henry, Sr. sometimes takes the helm in the tasting room at Henry Estate and is very well-informed about the wines and winery. His long-time residency in the Umpqua Valley leads to intriguing stories of days past when famous authors used to fish the Umpqua River. Cal Henry remembers the days when he accompanied Zane Grey on such a trip.

Shaded picnic tables invite the visitor to enjoy an afternoon of food and wine alongside the Umpqua River. Tours of the winery and vineyard are available for those interested.

The Wines

The wines made at the Henry Winery include many 'estate bottled' selections produced from the Chardonnay, Gewürztraminer, Pinot Noir and Riesling grown at the Henry Ranch. The attractive and affordable Pinot Noir and Red Table Wine (also 100% Pinot Noir) have attracted the most attention among Northwest consumers and wine experts. The Estate Pinot Noir receives more skin contact and produces a heartier wine with greater aging potential. Recent vintages of Henry wines have seen less oak aging and are therefore more approachable at an early age.

Henry Estate Chardonnay and Select Cluster Riesling were favorites of **Best of the Northwest** panels with reviews on pages 24 and 34.

Oregon

Hillcrest Vineyards

240 Vineyard Lane
Roseburg, OR 97470
(503) 673-3709

Owner/Winemaker:
Richard H. Sommer
First Year: 1963
Winery Capacity:
41,000 Gallons
1991 Production:
11,000 Gallons

Tasting Room Hours:
Daily, 11 AM to 5 PM
Tours available
Tour groups welcome

Winery History

Richard Sommer is the original pioneer of the Oregon wine industry. More than a quarter-century has elapsed since he first planted grapes in the Umpqua Valley in 1961 after intensive study of the soils and climate of Western Oregon. The current 35 acres of estate producing vines are in the area that Sommer feels produce the finest Germanic Rieslings in the Northwest.

A visit to Hillcrest Vineyard

The winery offers picnic tables on an attractive deck for tasters to enjoy a lunch or snack with a sip of wine. Inclement weather has been allowed for with seating inside the tasting room also. Tours of the winery and vineyards are offered.

The Wines

Hillcrest White Riesling accounts for the majority of the winery's production. Each vintage produces slight nuances but the mature vineyards now have an unmistakable aroma and bouquet that are detectable each year. The Riesling is fermented to retain two to three percent residual sugar which complements the acidity producing a delightfully refreshing wine.

The Roseburg climate also embraces the production of Gewürztraminer, the spicy grape that is difficult to grow in warmer climates. The cool fall weather allows a spicy, but not bitter, wine to be made each vintage. The Cabernet Sauvignon and Pinot Noir from Hillcrest continue to astound winelovers with their long life and distinctive varietal character.

La Garza Cellars

491 Winery Lane
Roseburg, OR 97470
(503) 679-9654

Owners: Lenard and
Donna Postles
Winemaker:
Lenard Postles
First Year: 1975
Winery Capacity:
10,000 Gallons

Winery History

In 1969 Jon Marker came north from California with some friends and founded Jonicole Winery just off I-5 near Winston. A vineyard was planted in the early 1970s and a substantial winery was built on the site. A few vintages of quality wine were made then something went wrong. The winery succumbed to troubles of some sort during the early 1980s and laid abandoned until Donna Souza-Postles revived the property as La Garza Cellars with a group of investors in 1992. The winery is up and running again, vineyards are being restored and a restaurant has been opened on the premises! The

potential for this scenic corner of the valley has always been great and it is tremendous to see things shaping up.

A visit to La Garza Cellars

The winery and restaurant are open Wednesday through Sunday from 11 AM to 5 PM all year. Summer hours include operation seven days a week. Feel free to bring your own picnic or enjoy the tasty fare offered by the winery. Pleasant views of the vineyard and ponds make for a tranquil stop. Wines from other Oregon wineries augment the first efforts of La Garza at the tasting bar.

Lookingglass Winery

6561 Lookingglass Rd.
Roseburg, OR 97470
(503) 679-8198

Winery History

The Rizza family began their small winery operation in 1988 to craft wines in the style pioneered by their grandfather. Hearty Pinot Noir and Cabernet Sauvignon are offered.

A visit to Lookingglass Winery

The Rizza family winery is a substantial building, dug into the hillside and constructed of stone with ornamentation of tile and stained glass. Find the winery by taking exit 124 from I-5 then traveling west 4.5 miles on Lookingglass Road to the winery. Tasting room hours are noon to 5 PM daily during the summer only.

Umpqua River Vineyards

451 Hess Lane
Roseburg, OR 97470
(503) 673-1975

Owner/Winemaker:
Greg DeNino
First Year: 1988
Winery Capacity:
3,000 Gallons
1991 Production:
1,500 Gallons

Winery History

The DeNino family has opened up their winery on the banks of the Umpqua River in the Garden Valley section of Roseburg. Wines are made from grapes harvested at the family vineyard and from some purchased at Safari Vineyards.

A visit to Umpqua River Vineyards

Take exit 129 from I-5 and follow Del Rio Road to the Old Garden Valley Road then head south to Hess Lane. Nearby River Forks Park is a nice stop to run the kids. The winery tasting room is open weekends only from noon to 5 PM, April through October.

The Wines

Greg DeNino crafts hearty Cabernet and Merlot red wines and Sauvignon Blanc, Semillon and Chenin Blanc from white grapes.

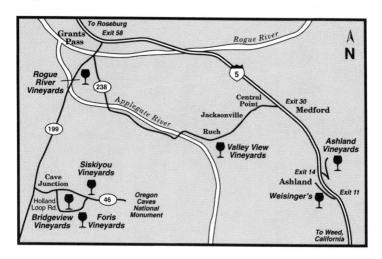

Southern Oregon Touring

This part of Oregon is such a wonderland of recreational possibilities that wine lovers often recreate first and think wine tasting second. However, if you've made it this far down I-5, it would be a shame not to enjoy the hospitality of the fine wineries located here.

Closest to Grants Pass is Rogue River Vineyards where Bill Jiron oversees a communal winery dedicated to providing the wines that the customers want. A special bottling line was added so that carbonated wine coolers could be made.

A half hour down Highway 199 you can stop in the Bridgeview Winery tasting room in the town of Kerby. Although the working winery and vineyard are located a few miles away, the owners encourage visitors to try the wines at the tasting room where the grape arbors shade the deck and you can relax from your drive. Those venturing to the winery during the winter months will find it a delightful stop with decks overlooking a large pond and a cosy tasting room.

Six miles east of Cave Junction on the Oregon Caves Highway you'll find Siskiyou Vineyards. The winery's lakeside nature path is the site of the Southern Oregon Wine Festival each June. Nearby, off Holland Loop Road, Foris Vineyards winery is open daily from 11 AM to 5 PM.

Backtrack up Highway 199 to pick up Highway 238 for a scenic drive along the Applegate River to Valley View Vineyards. The places where the road crosses the river offer some pretty views and some tempting glances at swimming holes in hot weather. Valley View is just south of the town of Ruch.

In the town of Jacksonville you'll find a pioneer spirit and another tasting room for Valley View Vineyards. Further south in Ashland, Weisinger's and Ashland Vineyards are each just a short drive from Interstate 5.

Ashland Vineyards

2775 E. Main
Ashland, OR 97520
(503) 488-0088

Owner: Bill Knowles
Winemaker:
 Andrew Swan
First Year: 1988
Winery Capacity:
 12,000 Gallons
1991 Production:
 10,000 Gallons

Tasting Room Hours:
Daily, 11 AM to 5 PM

Winery History

Pilot Bill Knowles combined his love of flying with his love of wine by planting his vineyard and building his winery just a few blocks from the Ashland airport. The production of several varietals that due well in Southern Oregon's warm summer climate complement traditional cooler weather wine.

A visit to Ashland Vineyards

The graceful swans on this winery's label also appear in the pond out behind the winery and tasting room. Take care not to picnic too near the water as these birds sometimes belie their beauty by pan-handling for your lunch.

The Wines

Cabernet Sauvignon and Merlot are joined by white varietals Chardonnay, Sauvignon Blanc, Riesling and Müller Thurgau.

Bridgeview Vineyards

4210 Holland Loop Rd.
Cave Junction, OR
97523 • (503) 592-4688

Owners:
 Robert & Lelo Kerivan
Winemaker:
 Laurent Montalieu
First Year: 1986
Winery Capacity:
 110,000 Gallons
1991 Production:
 60,000 Gallons

Tasting Room Hours:
Tasting room in Kerby -
May - October, 11 AM
to 5 PM; Winery Oct. -
May, Noon to 5 PM

Winery History

One of Oregon's largest wineries, Bridgeview Vineyards has earned a reputation for fine wines and consistent quality. The 74-acre vineyard surrounding the winery just east of Cave Junction includes Riesling, Gewürztraminer, Müller-Thurgau, Chardonnay, Pinot Gris, Sylvaner, Muscat, Pinot Noir and other varietals.

Talented winemaker Laurent Montalieu received his formal training at the Bordeaux Institute of Enology and worked at Chateau La Tour Blanche and at Domaine Mumm in California before joining Bridgeview in 1988.

A visit to Bridgeview Vineyards

The Bridgeview winery owners have established a tasting room - The Oregon Wine Barrel - in nearby Kerby on the well-traveled Highway 199. Special events and the large outdoor deck draws tourists to sample wine and purchase gifts and deli-style meals in the summer sun. Visits to the Bridgeview winery five miles east of Cave Junction are offered during winter months.

Continued on next page.

Oregon

The Wines of Bridgeview Vineyards

Bridgeview Vineyards offers Pinot Noir, Pinot Gris and Chardonnay along with the winery owner's favorites - Germanic varietals of Riesling and Gewürztraminer. Our tasting panels for **Best of the Northwest** applauded Bridgeview Chardonnay, Pinot Gris and Gewürztraminer. Reviews begin on page 15.

Foris Vineyards

654 Kendall Road
Cave Junction, OR
97523 • (503) 592-3752

Owners:
Meri & Ted Gerber
Winemaker:
Sarah Powell
First Year: 1987
Winery Capacity:
16,000 Gallons
1991 Production:
11,000 Gallons

Tasting Room Hours:
Daily, 11 AM to 5 PM

Winery History

The history of Foris Vineyards is the history of grape growing in the Illinois Valley - the farming area east of Cave Junction. The first five acres of vines were planted back in 1973 - about the same time that the Willamette Valley wineries were just starting up. Ted Gerber brought his family to Oregon to escape the urban lifestyle and fast pace of California - a farm and vineyard seemed the perfect choice. The first Foris varietals were fermented at a nearby winery but since 1987 wine has been made at the Foris winery facility at the vineyard.

A visit to Foris Vineyards

Wine tasting is offered in the cozy Foris tasting room adjacent to the winery. Meri Gerber's craft of weaving grape vines into fanciful wreaths and baskets is on display and many items are for sale. Tours of the winery are available by appointment.

The Wines

Ted Gerber recognizes the importance of Pinot Noir to Oregon's wine scene and he makes a very fine version. Chardonnay, Gewürztraminer and Early Muscat are other favorites.

Rogue River Vineyards

3145 Helms Road
Grants Pass, OR 97527
(503) 476-1051

Winemaker: Bill Jiron
First Year: 1984
Winery Capacity:
28,000 Gallons

Tasting Room Hours:
Daily, 10 AM to 5 PM

Winery History

The partners at Rogue River Vineyards spent four years working two jobs to build their commune-like winery operation in the clean air of Southern Oregon. Commuting from the Lodi area of California they built their dream piece by piece.

Winemaker Bill Jiron (pronounced 'he - roan') can now relax from the frantic pace as he and the other winery partners are established with their families at the winery site. Spouses and children all pitch in to handle the responsibilities associated with a winery that operates independently.

A visit to Rogue River Vineyards

A variety of interesting souvenirs produced in the winery wood shop, pinicking on the deck and a chance to sample Rogue River wines are the draw.

The Wines

Unique varietal interpretations and spritzy wine coolers are offered for tasting and for sale. Friendly hosts and hostesses smile and pour . . .

Siskiyou Vineyards

6220 Oregon Caves Hy.
Cave Junction, OR
97523 • (503) 592-3727

Owner: C. J. David
Winemaker:
  Donna Devine
First Year: 1978
Winery Capacity:
  8,500 Gallons
1991 Production:
  8,500 Gallons

Tasting Room Hours:
Daily, 11AM to 5 PM

Winery History

A location on the Oregon Caves Highway has helped Siskiyou Winery gain popularity and renown but they couldn't make it on the location alone. Owner C. J. (Suzi) David has a strong will to succeed and has surrounded herself with talented, determined people who can get the job done.

The winemaker at Siskiyou is such a person. Donna Devine came to the winery in 1980 after a brief exposure to the wine industry through newspaper reporting. Now a seasoned veteran of the Southern Oregon wine scene, Donna has gained the respect of her enological peers by producing many first-rate wines from Siskiyou's 10-acre vineyard near the winery.

A visit to Siskiyou Vineyards

The winery and tasting room at Siskiyou are friendly and comfortable. The tasting room staff know the wines and are eager to help novice wine drinkers gain an appreciation for finer qualities of varietal wines produced here. A view of the working winery is available from a balcony just outside the tasting room. Each June Siskiyou Winery holds the Southern Oregon Wine Festival featuring music, food, crafts and lots of fun all on the banks of Suzi David's two acre trout lake.

The Wines

Cabernet Sauvignon, Pinot Noir, Zinfandel, Chardonnay and La Cave Red, White and Melange (blush) are produced.

Oregon

The historic pole barn that was converted to Valley View Vineyard's winery.

Valley View Vineyards

1000 Applegate Road
Jacksonville, OR 97530
(503) 899-8468

Owners: The
  Wisnovsky Family
Winemaker:
  John Guerrero
First Year: 1978
Winery Capacity:
  55,000 Gallons
1991 Production:
  23,000 Gallons

Tasting Room Hours:
Daily, 11 AM to 5 PM

Winery History

Encouraged by the success of other Southern Oregon grape growers, the Wisnovsky family planted Valley View Vineyard in 1972. The vineyard site near the scenic Applegate River offered a micro-climate suitable for production of Cabernet Sauvignon and Merlot in addition to Chardonnay. The vineyard and winery were named after a small winery pioneered by Peter Britt in the 1850s.

The 26 acre vineyard matured slowly leading to the winery's bonding in 1978. That first year produced an astounding Cabernet that beat several first growth Bordeaux in a blind tasting.

A visit to Valley View Vineyards

Valley View operates two tasting rooms to promote their wines in the Rogue River Valley. The winery tasting room near the town of Ruch on Highway 238 welcomes visitors to taste the wine and tour the winery facility and visit nearby picnic grounds along the Applegate River. "The Tasting Room" in downtown Jacksonville is an appropriately named purveyor of wines.

The Wines

Valley View's reputation for fine red wines is well-deserved. Merlot and Cabernet are made in a ripe, toasty style and offer plenty of power for current consumption or aging. Chardonny, Sauvignon Blanc and proprietary blends round out the line. Valley View Merlot and their Jazz Label Sauvignon Blanc appear in the **Best of the Northwest** reviews beginning on page 14 of this guide.

Weisinger's of Ashland

3150 Siskiyou Blvd.
Ashland, OR 97520
(503) 488-5989

Owners: John and
Sherita Weisinger
Winemaker:
Donna Devine
First Year: 1988
Winery Capacity:
10,000 Gallons

Tasting Room Hours:
Summer: Daily, 11 AM
to 6 PM; Winter and
Spring: weekends only

Winery History

John and Sherita Weisinger founded their winery on a hill southeast of Ashland with a beautiful view of the Rogue Valley and the Cascade Mountains. A small vineyard is on the property but wine is made mostly from purchased grapes.

A visit to Weisinger's of Ashland

Not far from I-5, take exit 14 if you're southbound and head southwest on Tolman Cr. Rd. to Siskiyou Blvd., turn left. Northbound take exit 11 directly on to Siskiyou. The winery is dressed up in Alpen half-timbered style and continues the theme in the tasting room. Weisinger's offers an "Italian" red blend named Mescolare as a specialty of the house and also a great selection of locally made foods and souvenirs. The tasting room is closed during January and February.

The Wines

Cabernet Sauvignon, Chardonnay, Gewürztraminer and Cabernet Blanc are offered in addition to the "Mescolare."

Umpqua and Southern Oregon Accommodations

Roseburg

Best Western Garden Villa, 760 NW Garden Valley Blvd. - (503) 672-1601, (800) 547-3446 (OR), (800) 528-1234 (U.S.) West of I-5 near the Garden Valley Shopping Center. Pool, spa, air conditioned. Restaurant nearby.

Windmill Inn, 1450 NW Mulholland Dr. - (503) 673-0901, (800) 452-5315 (OR), (800) 547-4747 (U.S.) An attractive chain of motor inns in Southern Oregon. Pool, spa, sauna, air conditioned, CTV, restaurant/lounge.

Grants Pass

Paradise Ranch Inn, 7000-D Monument Dr. - (503) 479-4333 A complete resort complex on 300 acres near Grants Pass. Swimming pool, tennis, hiking-biking-jogging trails. Relax in the hot tub, fish in one of the lakes on the property or sharpen your golf game on the putting green. Some units with fireplaces.

Lawnridge House B & B, 1304 NW Lawnridge - (503) 479-5186 Air conditioned cool in summer, cozy fireplace blazing in winter. Two bedrooms plus Bridal Suite. Full breakfast.

Ashland

Morical House B & B, 668 N. Main St. -(503) 482-2254 Each room has private bath and air conditioning.

Winchester Inn B & B, 35 South 2nd- (503) 488-1113 Seven air conditioned rooms with bath, close to theater. Excellent dining room with good wine list and superb cuisine.

Oregon

Umpqua and Southern Oregon Accommodations

Steamboat

Steamboat Inn, Hwy. 138, Steamboat, OR 97447, (503) 498-2411, This fly-fishing camp is where the legends came to practice the gentlemanly art of using the Tonkin cane rod. Cabins and cottages are set among the woods and delightful meals are offered by reservation in the lodge.

Jacksonville

Jacksonville Inn, 175 E. California St., (503) 899-1900. This fabulous restaurant also offers a place to rest your head in the upstairs guest rooms with private baths. A full breakfast is included with lodging. The restaurant is among the finest in Oregon and the wine list details a superb collection.

Umpqua and Southern Oregon Dining

Oakland

Tolly's 115 Locust St., exit 138 off I-5, (503) 459-3796 Highly recommended by all the local wineries, Tolly's offers the standard steak and seafood dishes preferred in the area but also gets creative with some specials for visiting city folks. Open for lunch and dinner every day.

Grants Pass

Riverside Inn, 971 SE 6th - (503) 476-6873 At the popular local hotel, a nice view dining room overlooking the Rogue River as it courses through downtown Grants Pass.

Ashland

Ashland is so full o unique and enjoyable restaurant experiences that you should really dine out for every meal. Two of the best are:

Chateaulin, 50 E. Main - (503) 482-2264 The best wine list in Ashland accompanies excellent French preparations of veal, seafood and other delights. Near theater.

Winchester Inn, 35 S. 2nd St. - (503) 488-1113 The Winchester offers excellent culinary experiences drawn from many cultures, including Oregon. Outstanding wine list.

For Parents Only

Wildlife Safari - Just outside Roseburg you can drive through a game farm with all manner of wild beasts and pretend you're really in Jurassic Park when you fake a stalled car.

Indian Mary Park - NW of Merlin - Camping and fun times along the Rogue River near Hell Gate Canyon.

Valley of the Rogue State Park, Hwy. 99 East of Grants Pass (I-5 exit 45) Camping, picnicing and fishing along the Rogue River.

Oregon Caves National Monument - Kids have to be 6 or older to take the tour through the caves. The nearby Oregon Caves Chateau offers lodging, dining and child care during the summer months.

Fishing - Both the Rogue and Umpqua Rivers are known for excellent fly-fishing (see listing for Steamboat, above). Check with the locals to find out where the fish are biting.

Jet Boat Trips - A hair raising, high speed ride on a wild river really has a way of taming a cranky adolescent.

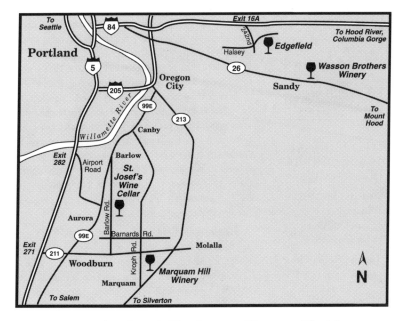

East Portland and Clackamas County Touring

The Clackamas County area east and southeast of Portland has a few wineries tucked away for winelovers to visit on a weekend jaunt from the Rose City. This area of Oregon has many different faces, those of agriculture sometimes take a back seat to developments of condominiums and industrial parks but take heart, all the wineries here are doing great!

In this age of recycling, the McMenamins (of brewpub fame) reclaimed the local poor farm and created Edgefield, a unique collection of restored buildings that include a lodge (like a B & B), theater, pub, restaurant and winery. Almost to Troutdale off the Wood Village exit from Interstate 84.

Wasson Brothers Winery in Sandy, near Mount Hood, is on the skiers and hikers route to and from the mountain. Grape wines as well as fruit and berry wines are the draw. Look for the storefront winery right on Highway 26.

Mount Hood Winery (see Columbia Gorge touring section) is up the road apiece at Government Camp.

Joe Fleischmann of St. Josef's Wine Cellar in Canby makes a very nice Zinfandel from grapes purchased near The Dalles. Chardonnay and Pinot Noir are also available as well as Riesling and Gewürztraminer. The winery offers picnic tables for your enjoyment out by the lake and vineyard.

Not far from St. Josef's, Marquam Hill Vineyards offers a similar rural experience with vineyard, lake and expansive picnic area that is available for receptions, reunions and weddings.

Edgefield

2126 S.W. Halsey St.
Troutdale, OR 97060
(503) 669-8610

Owners: McMenamins
Winemaker:
 Rich Cushman
First Year: 1990

Tasting Room Hours:
Daily, Noon to 8 PM

Winery History

Edgefield Manor, built in 1911, served for several decades as the Multnomah County Poor Farm. The farm, dairy, cannery and meat packing plant employed many in a self-sufficient system. As the Poor Farm was phased out in the late 1940s, the main lodge was used as a nursing home until 1982.

The McMenamin clan purchased Edgefield in 1990 from Multnomah County and began a remarkable restoration project. The complex now contains Bed and Breakfast-style accommodations in the main lodge and Administrator's House. The Edgefield Winery and Brewery were two of the first parts of the restoration to be completed (the McMenamins are, after all, Oregon's pre-eminent brew-pub entrepreneurs!).

A visit to Edgefield

Head east from Portland on I-84 to Troutdale and take the Wood Village exit #16A. Follow 238th Dr. S. to the first light and turn left on Halsey St. for one-half mile. The Edgefield complex has something for everyone including its own theater, pub, restaurant, etc. The winery offers it's own candlelit cellar for tasting and relaxing.

The Wines

A wide variety of wines are produced here. Sample Rieslings, Nouveau Pinot Noir, Cabernet Sauvignon, Pinot Gris, Sauvignon-Chardonnay, Port and sparkling wine.

Marquam Hill Vineyards

35803 S. Hwy 213
Mollala, OR 97038
(503) 829-6677

Owners:
Joe & Marylee Dobbes
Winemaker:
 Joe Dobbes
First Year: 1989
Winery Capacity:
 6,000 Gallons
1991 Production:
 2,000 Gallons

Tasting Room Hours:
Daily, Noon to 6 PM
Winter, weekends only

Winery History

Joe and Marylee Dobbes discovered an idyllic life in the rural countryside near the foothills of the Cascades. A small family winery, making wine from grapes grown on the property, welcoming visitors for tasting – it all seemed like just the thing to enhance a nearly perfect location.

A visit to Marquam Hill Vineyards

A half-hour drive from I-5 through Woodburn and on toward Mollala leads to Hwy. 213 and a left turn to Marquam Hill Vineyards. The Dobbes' 8-acre lake, expansive vineyard plantings and woodsy clearings are a wonderful place for a family outing and a relaxing picnic.

The Wines

Joe Dobbes crafts Pinot Noir, Chardonnay, Riesling, Gewürztraminer and Müller Thurgau from grapes grown in the 19-acre estate vineyard. The Marquam Hill Chardonnay impressed the **Best of the Northwest** panel and is reviewed on page 24.

St. Josef's Wine Cellar

28836 South Barlow Rd.
Canby, OR 97013
(503) 651-3190

Owners:
Fleischmann Family
Winemaker: Joe &
Kirk Fleischmann
First Year: 1983
Winery Capacity:
35,000 Gallons
1991 Production:
11,000 Gallons

Tasting Room Hours:
Daily, Noon to 5 PM
Winters: weekends only

Winery History

Joe Fleischmann traded in his baker's apron and the smell of rising bread dough for the rubber boots of a winemaker and the smell of fermenting wine. The success he achieved in baking is a local legend but the family winery is also making its mark.

Joe and his son Kirk produce their wines from their ten-acre vineyard and from Zinfandel purchased from The Dalles. When the Zinfandel grapes are just right they make a red wine - big and bold like the Egri Bikaver of their Hungarian ancestors. When the Zin is not as ripe, they make a delicious White Zinfandel.

A visit to St. Josef's Weinkeller

A short four mile drive out Barlow Road from Highway 99E leads you into the Clackamas farm country and to the vineyards and winery of St. Josef's. The winery has facilities for receptions and banquets as well as their cozy tasting room and gift shop. A special attraction for visitors is the magnificent picnic area by the Fleischmann's spring-fed lake behind the winery.

The Wines

Pinot Noir, Cabernet, Zinfandel, Riesling, Gewürztraminer and Chardonnay are produced.

Oregon

Wasson Brothers Winery

41901 Highway 26
Sandy, OR 97055
(503) 668-3124

Owners:
  Jim & John Wasson
Winemaker:
  Jim Wasson
First Year: 1982
Winery Capacity:
  10,000 Gallons
1991 Production:
  6,000 Gallons

Tasting Room Hours:
Daily, 9 AM to 5 PM
Tours available, tour
groups welcome.

Winery History

Jim Wasson and his twin brother John have been part-time farming in Clackamas County since the 1960s including winegrapes since 1978. In the early 1980s they took up amateur winemaking and became so good at it that Jim quit his plumbing job and opened a winery. Their winery building is right on Highway 26 between Portland and the Mt. Hood recreation areas. A perfect stop for tired skiers on their way home from the slopes!

A visit to Wasson Brothers Winery

When you drive up to the Wasson Brothers Winery a mile east of Sandy, Oregon you might think you've found a wild west saloon. The tall, false-facade of the building and the wide, covered veranda echo the boardwalks of earlier times. But there's plenty of parking and the signs are friendly enough so why not swagger on in?

The first thing you notice is that the boardwalk is new concrete and the building is no relic from another century, things are up-to-date and ship-shape when the winery opens each day for business at 9 AM. Wines are available for tasting and wine-related gifts await your perusal.

If you'd rather make your own, the Wasson Brothers will be happy to set you up with home winemaking equipment from the supply shop right in the tasting room. You say you'd rather make beer? Well step over to this counter here! A great place to stop and some really friendly people!

The Wines

Production at the Wasson Brothers winery is split about half and half between fruit and berry wines and varietal grape wines. Seems like the local folks prefer the tasty Loganberry, Blackberry and Rhubarb while the skiers and city folks like the Pinot Noir, Riesling and Chardonnay. Who says you can't please all of the people, all of the time?

Jim Wasson's gold medal efforts with Pinot Noir haven't gone unnoticed by wine consumers or by wine judges. He has developed a style that is enjoyed by all and offers classic Pinot Noir nuances. Other grape varietals are equally promising.

Oregon Coast Touring

Was it Mark Twain who said, "The mildest winter I ever spent was summer in Tillamook."? So what if there are nine foggy days out of ten in the middle of June on the Oregon Coast. The beaches are still beautiful, the people are friendly and the wine tasting rooms are numerous.

If you are anywhere near Astoria you simply MUST stop by Shallon Winery for a visit with Paul van der Veldt. This fellow is such a hospitable gent that his unusual selection of wines doesn't bother even the snobbiest wine snob. Trust me on this one, you'll have a good visit.

South of Astoria on Highway 101 you can visit Nehalem Bay Winery near Mohler. Owner/winemaker Pat McCoy has a wide variety of fruit and grape wines to try and an interesting selection of gifts to browse. The winery is east of Highway 101 about one mile.

No other operating wineries are located on the coast but many inland wineries have tasting rooms in the larger tourist meccas. The cities of Seaside, Tillamook, Lincoln City, Newport, Florence and Gold Beach have all had satellite tasting rooms at one time or another. They come and go with each summer season, so check the rack at the local information center for this year's offerings. Also see listings under accommodations and dining on page 213.

Nehalem Bay Winery

34965 Highway 53
Nehalem, OR 97131
(503) 368-5300

Owner & Winemaker:
Pat McCoy
First Year: 1973
Winery Capacity:
15,000 Gallons
1991 Production:
12,000 Gallons

Tasting Room Hours:
Daily, 10 AM to 5 PM

Winery History

Tucked into a converted cheese factory, circa 1909, Nehalem Bay Winery has been serving Oregon Coast tourists for two decades. Owner and winemaker Pat McCoy is a big civic booster for the Nehalem area and the winery is home to numerous events. Originally, only fruit wines were offered – in an age when hardly anyone knew about Oregon Pinot Noir – but now the winery produces mostly grape wines from their own Willamette Valley vineyard source.

A visit to Nehalem Bay Winery

The turn from Highway 101 is marked both with a sign to the winery and a state highway sign to the town of Mohler. Drive east one mile then look for the winery in its half-timbered splendor on the right. Weekdays you may find yourself alone when you first enter the tasting room. Give a shout and manager Ray Shackelford will return from his chores to pour your samples and have a chat. Weekend business is more brisk and you'll no doubt have company for sipping the samples.

The Wines

Pinot Noir, White Riesling, Bay Blush, Loganberry, Cranberry and Methode Champenoise Sparkling Wine are produced.

Oregon

Paul van der Veldt serves some of his unusual wines to winery visitors.

Shallon Winery

1598 Duane St.
Astoria, OR 97103
(503) 325-5978

Owner/Winemaker:
 Paul van der Veldt
First Year: 1978
Winery Capacity:
 2,000 Gallons
1991 Production:
 500 Gallons

Tasting Room Hours:
Daily, "Noonish" to
6 PM

Winery History

A most unusual man is at work in Astoria making some of Oregon's most unusual wines. Paul van der Veldt will serve you a wine reminiscent of berries and cream, and one that takes you back to mom's kitchen and her delicious lemon meringue pie. His latest creation is chocolate orange wine is a thick style you can eat with a spoon! These are the legacies of a retired construction company manager who transformed an Astoria car showroom and meat locker into Shallon Winery.

A visit to Shallon Winery

The winery is located right in downtown Astoria about two miles east of the bridge to Washington and a few blocks up the hill from Highway 30 on Duane St. Insist on a tour. The winery part of the building and laboratory are fanciful creations just like the master's wine. Imagination was the driving force behind both. Return to the tasting room to sample the wines about which Paul quips, "It's not that they're so great, they're just unique!"

The Wines

Fruit wines are a specialty here including Blackberry, Peach and Apple, but the piece de résistance are the three wines not duplicated in this world – or any other. Enjoy Cran du Lait (made from cranberries, and whey from the local cheese factories), Lemon Meringue Pie wine (with sweet cracker accompaniment to simulate crust), and the latest Pots de Creme, chocolate/orange wine.

Oregon Coast Accommodations & Dining

The Oregon Coast is famous for cool weather and a warm welcome. Genuine hospitality is the order of the day and fine food is the rule rather than the exception. The only drawback is that several thousand other people are planning their vacation right now. Crowds can affect the atmosphere.

Accommodations

One listing for each major stop is all we have room for. Sorry.

Astoria

Franklin House B & B, 1681 Franklin Ave., 97103 (503) 325-5044 Astoria's seafaring heritage goes back over 180 years and this Victorian B & B seems right at home in any decade. Park-like grounds in quiet location.

Cannon Beach

The Argonauta Inn, 2nd & Larch, 97110 (503) 436-2601 Cottages with beach access and an Oregon Coast-chic decor feature TV, fireplace and most have kitchens. Very popular.

Lincoln City

Shilo Inn, 1501 NW 40th Pl. 97367 (503) 994-3655 North of town This modern accommodation includes indoor pool, kitchens, fireplaces and all right on the beach! Great family place.

Newport

Embarcadero Resort Marina, 1000 SE Bay Blvd. 97365 (503) 265-8521 An upscale complex of condo-style rooms with magnificent views of Newport Bay. Indoor pool, spa, kitchen units have fireplaces.

Waldport

Cliff House B & B, Adahi Rd. off Hwy. 101, 97394 (503) 563-2506 Whale watch from your room high above the water. Elegant accommodations and just-right service. Gourmet breakfast features regionally local produce in season.

Dining

Seek out the satellite winery tasting rooms and wine shops for your dining-in or select one of these guaranteed good meals.

Astoria

The Ship Inn, #1 Second St. on the waterfront (503) 325-0033 Your English hosts have brought their talents for tasty fish & chips and Cornish pasties. Enjoy the view of river activity with your pint of English ale.

Lincoln City

Chateau Benoit Tasting Room & Cafe, Factory Outlet Mall Creative sandwiches, salads, soups and snacks are joined by a wine tasting bar and a nice selection of wine and food gifts. Coastal hospitality at its best.

Gleneden Beach

Salishan Lodge Dining Room, Highway 101, (503) 764-2371 The chefs at this landmark culinary establishment turn out the finest in continental-Northwest cuisine and sommelier Phil Devito presides over a wine list numbering to 1,000 selections with over 30,000 bottles in storage. The wine cellar may be toured by appointment.

Newport

The Whale's Tale, 452 Bay Blvd. (503) 265-8660 On the waterfront and offering every meal of the day, every day of the week (in summer). Owner Dick Schwartz brags on his delicious breakfast choices as well as his superb seafood offerings and desserts at dinnertime.

A Mileage Chart for Planning Your Northwest Wine Tour

Wine touring around the Pacific Northwest can involve a fair amount of driving time. While reading flowery and romantic descriptions of wineries, restaurants and bed-and-breakfasts, one often forgets the four or five hours behind the wheel to achieve these far-off delights. Below is a chart of common wine country destinations for all three Northwest states which will help you plan your trip with greater accuracy.

One note of caution, the mileage calculations have been based on the shortest possible route given the best, mid-summer driving conditions. If you are traveling to Yakima or other east-of-the-Cascades location from a western starting point, keep a weather eye out for pass conditions. Snoqualmie Pass (Interstate 90) is kept open all year except for rare extreme conditions that close the road for hours at a time. Chains are required infrequently, but studded tires (approved traction devices) are often mandatory during winter travel.

	Seattle	Portland	Yakima	McMinnville	Tri-Cities	Salem	Spokane	Eugene	Walla Walla	Roseburg	Hood River	Sequim	Boise
Seattle		175	140	225	222	223	277	289	281	362	239	77	524
Portland	175		228	50	220	48	372	114	239	187	64	228	431
Yakima	140	228		238	82	234	206	300	141	375	122	217	384
McMinnville	225	50	238		270	20	422	86	289	159	114	165	442
Tri-Cities	222	220	82	270		268	152	334	59	407	156	299	302
Salem	223	48	234	20	268		420	66	287	139	112	276	422
Spokane	277	372	206	422	152	420		486	160	559	308	354	379
Eugene	289	114	300	86	334	66	486		353	73	178	342	433
Walla Walla	281	239	141	289	59	287	160	353		426	175	358	252
Roseburg	362	187	375	159	407	139	559	73	426		251	415	506
Hood River	239	64	122	114	156	112	308	178	175	251		292	367
Sequim	77	228	217	165	299	276	354	342	358	415	292		601
Boise	524	431	384	442	302	422	379	433	252	506	367	601	

Idaho & Montana Wine Touring

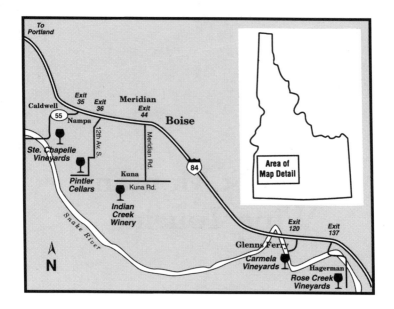

Idaho Wine Touring

Most of the Idaho wine industry is located in the southwest part of the state where the climatic influence of the Snake River provides excellent growing conditions for grapes. Water from the river for irrigation has long made this part of Idaho an agricultural oasis.

Ste. Chapelle Winery is one of the largest in the Northwest with a huge capacity and multiple buildings housing tanks, equipment and a first-class tourist facility. The French cathedral-inspired visitor center offers views of the surrounding vineyards. A tour of the facility is offered after a tasting selected wines.. A grand selection of gifts and snacks is available.

A view picnic area and an informative wine tasting and winery tour await the visitor to Pintler Cellars south of Nampa. This family operation ovffers a soft, lush lawn, picnic tables and an unbeatable view of the Snake River Valley.

Nearby, Bill Stowe of Indian Creek Winery offers tastings of his bottlings at the winery near Kuna.

Petros Winery in Boise does not have a tasting room but the wines are poured at many regional festivals and other wine events.

A drive of almost two hours through the sagebrush east of Boise is rewarded by a visit to Carmela Winery at Glenn's Ferry and Rose Creek Vineyards winery in Hagerman. The golf course and restaurant attached to Carmela Winery provide a constant source of customers for the winery tasting room. Rose Creek offers tastings at their winery in the lava-rock cellar of a historic local building.

Northern Idaho wineries include Camas Winery in Moscow (open most days) and Pucci Family Winery near Sandpoint (open by appointment).

Camas Winery

110 S. Main St.
Moscow, ID 83843
(208) 882-0214

Owners:
Stuart & Susan Scott
Winemaker:
Stuart Scott
First Year: 1983
Winery Capacity:
4,000 Gallons

Tasting Room Hours:
Tuesday thru Saturday,
Noon to 6 PM

Winery History

Camas Winery traces its name back to the original inhabitants of Northern Idaho, the Nez Perce Indians. A staple food among these tribes was the root of the Camas Lily that grew wild as waving fields of blue flowers throughout the Palouse. Today, replaced by wheat and other crops, the Camas Lily is found only in secluded hollows and on the label of Camas Winery!

The Camas Lily gained another appreciative consumer when early settlers of Northern Idaho found their pigs rooting up the Camas bulbs and going "hog wild" over them. This corner of the Palouse thus became known in those early days as "Hog Heaven." In honor of this historic reference to their winery's namesake, Stuart Scott blended a pair of special table wines with the names Hog Heaven Red and Hog Heaven White. Even more popular than the wines themselves are the outrageous Hog Heaven T-shirts and sweatshirts. The whimsical porcine imbibers are portrayed dancing around a bottle and glass of Camas wine, obviously enjoying more than the root of the flower.

A visit to Camas Winery

Co-owner Sue Scott is your charming hostess at the winery tasting room in downtown Moscow. A blended wine, Vandal Gold, pays tribute to the local college mascot and to the festive college-town atmosphere.

The Wines

The wines are all family-made from grapes grown in the nearby Columbia Valley of Washington State and include a selection of dry to semi-sweet whites and a flavorful Cabernet Sauvignon. Lemberger, Mead and other proprietary creations round out the line.

Idaho

Carmela Vineyards

795 West Madison
P.O. Box 290
Glenns Ferry, ID 83623
(208) 366-2313

Owner: Jim &
Carmela Martell
Winemaker:
Scott Benham
First Year: 1990
Winery Capacity:
14,000 Gallons
1992 Production:
11,000 Gallons

Tasting Room Hours:
Daily, 11 AM to 5 PM

Winery History

Wow! Finally a winery with its own restaurant and 9-hole golf course! Jim and Carmela Martell are true entrepreneurs with their own idea of fun and success in the Idaho wine business. Trading on their experience working for larger phone companies, they now own the Rural Telephone Co., specializing in providing service to isolated communities in their area. Vineyards seemed like a good idea in the 1980s and they now have 48 acres of quality varietals in production. A winery followed and a deli-restaurant was added to fill up some of the extra space in the winery building. A golf course was built using equipment already on hand for the other ventures. Bring your sticks when you visit Carmela Vineyards!

A visit to Carmela Vineyards

The winery is located two miles south of I-84. Exit at one of the two Glenns Ferry exits and follow signs for Three Islands State Park, you'll go right by the winery. Stop in for a visit seven days a week.

The Wines

The owners of Carmela Vineyards hired talented Scott Benham in August of 1992 to handle their winemaking duties. Scott is busy producing a wide range of varietals including Cabernet Sauvignon, Merlot, Chardonnay, Riesling, Muscat, Semillon and Cabernet Franc.

Cocolalla Winery

E. 14550 Bunco Road
Athol, ID 83801
(208) 683-2473

Owner: Donald &
Vivian Merkeley
Winemaker:
Donald Merkeley
First Year: 1986
Winery Capacity:
2,000 Gallons

Winery History

Donald Merkeley has been experimenting with methode champenoise sparkling wine with the first commercial release due out soon. No vineyard is owned as grapes are purchased from Taggares Vineyard in Othello. The winery is located just northeast of Spokane off Highway 95 N. Winery visits are by appointment only at this time.

Indian Creek Winery

Rt. 1, 1000 N.
McDermott Rd.
Kuna, ID 83634
(208) 922-4791

Owner: Bill Stowe
and four other partners
Winemaker: Bill Stowe
First Year: 1987
Winery Capacity:
16,000 Gallons
1991 Production:
7,000 Gallons

Tasting Room Hours:
Call for current hours

Winery History

When Bill Stowe re-enlisted in the Air Force, he made the military promise they would station him in Idaho. He wanted to prepare for his retirement and had considered farming to be a possibility in the area near Mountain Home Air Force Base.

Bill's brother Mike is a schoolteacher in Davis, California. By taking parttime classes across town at U.C. Davis, he was able to learn quite a lot about grape farming and become a valuable ally to his brother. The two men shared knowledge and Bill planted 20 acres of varietals near Kuna in 1983. Winemaking from his own grapes and those of neighboring growers was the next step and Indian Creek Winery was born.

A visit to Indian Creek Winery

The winery is located a few miles southwest of Boise near the town of Kuna. Take the first exit west of Boise (Meridian Road) and drive south to Kuna, then turn right (west) on Kuna Road to the winery.

The Wines

A consistent medal winner has been Bill Stowe's rich and fruity Pinot Noir. Also produced are Riesling, Chardonnay and White Pinot Noir.

Petros Winery

264 N. Maple Grove Rd.
Boise, ID 83704
(208) 322-7474

Owner: Pete Eliopulos
Winemaker:
Mickey Dunn
First Year: 1987

Winery History

The late 1980s saw some wild times in the Idaho wine business. In 1986 Bill Broich had left Ste. Chapelle Winery and had found new partners to begin the Winery at Spring Creek. His questionable operating practices caused concern with major investors and his interest was purchased. Pete Eliopulos took the helm and tried to steer the winery to safety under the new name Petros. The name survived and some wine survived but the winery became the property of a local bank. The Petros brand is now supported by winemaking at other facilities.

The Wines

Wines produced currently for release at Petros include Chardonnay, Riesling, Cabernet Sauvignon and others. Awards have been forthcoming for the quality efforts supported by regional distribution.

Idaho
Pintler Cellars

13750 Surrey Lane
Nampa, ID 83651
(208) 467-1200

Owner: Pintler Family
Winemaker:
  Brad Pintler
First Year: 1988
Winery Capacity:
  15,000 Gallons
1991 Production:
  11,000 Gallons

Tasting Room Hours:
Friday, Sat., Sunday;
Noo to 5 PM

Winery History
Several generations of the Pintler family have farmed the fertile plateau that stretches south to the Snake River from Nampa. Crops were usually sugar beets - easy to grow and a stable market for the final commodity. In the early 1980s the success of neighboring Ste. Chapelle and other area wineries led the Pintlers to plant a vineyard on their land to accompany the other crops. As the vineyard came into bearing in the late 1980s, a winery was constructed and visitor amenities were added.

A visit to Pintler Cellars
The attractive winery building, picnic area and gazebo make a nice stop for any wine odyssey and the view across the Snake River Valley is superb. Wines are often poured by members of the Pintler family and the winemaking operation is explained to those interested. The hardest part of finding Pintler Cellars is navigating through downtown Nampa. Exit 36 from I-84 leads you southbound on Franklin Ave. Turn right on 11th Ave. and jog over to 12th Ave. at 3rd St. S. Follow 12th Ave. S. south to a right turn on Missouri Rd., a left on Sky Ranch and finally a right on Surrey Lane to the winery.

The Wines
A wide range of varietals is produced at Pintler Cellar and they have done very well in competitions and with consumers. Chardonnay, Dry Riesling, Johannisberg Riesling, Semillon, Cabernet Sauvignon and Pinot Noir are produced.

Pucci Winery

1055 Garfield Bay Rd.
Sandpoint, ID 83864
(208) 263-5807

Owner/Winemaker:
  Skip Pucci
First Year: 1982
Winery Cap: 6,000 Gal.

Winery History
The Pucci Winery is in scenic Bonner County Idaho near Lake Pend Oreille and the tourist-oriented community of Sandpoint. The tall evergreens that surround the Pucci home and winery building are often the roosts for osprey and other birds of prey that feed on fish from the lake.

Skip Pucci makes his wines according to family tradition going back six generations. Much of the equipment used by Skip is homemade – replicas of wine equipment from earlier times.

A visit to Pucci Winery
A short drive off Highway 95 leads through the pristine forest to the Pucci home and winery. Call ahead for an appointment.

Rose Creek Vineyards winery in downtown Hagerman.

Rose Creek Vineyards

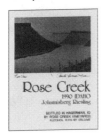

111 West Hagerman
Box 356
Hagerman, ID 83332
(208) 837-4413

Owners: Jamie, Susan
& Stephanie Martin
Winemaker:
Jamie Martin
First Year: 1984
Winery Capacity:
15,000 Gallons
1990 Production:
13,500 Gallons

Tasting Room Hours:
Daily, 11:30 AM to
5:30 PM

Winery History

The three-foot thick lava walls of the Rose Creek Vineyards winery hold secrets going back over 100 years to the settlement of Southern Idaho and the beginnings of agriculture along the winding Snake River. The building, whose upper floor houses the Idaho State Bank, is on the National Register of Historic Places and originally served as a dry goods store for early Idaho settlers.

In the cool dark of the lower level, tanks and barrels have been installed to produce the wines from nearby vineyards and from other purchased grapes. The Martins have dedicated themselves to the success of Rose Creek Vineyards as Susan handles the tasting room in downtown Hagerman while Jamie works in vineyard management for other Idaho grape growers.

A visit to Rose Creek Vineyards

The long drive from Boise to Hagerman is worthwhile once you turn down into the Hagerman Valley. Located in a rimrock canyon, the town and nearby landmarks share a rocky environment of great beauty. At the winery you can enjoy samples of the latest Rose Creek wines and browse the crafts and gift items, some of which are locally made.

The Wines

Riesling, Chardonnay, Cabernet Sauvignon, Basque Red, and Pinot Noir are produced.

Idaho

Ste. Chapelle Winery

14068 Sunnyslope Rd.
Caldwell, ID 83605
(208) 459-7222

Owner: Symms Fruit
Ranch, Inc.
Winemaker:
Mimi Mook
Asst. Winemaker:
Kevin Mott
First Year: 1976
Winery Capacity:
325,000 Gallons
1991 Production:
300,000 Gallons

Tasting Room Hours:
Mon. - Sat., 10 AM to
6 PM, Sunday, noon to
5 PM

Winery History

Ste. Chapelle has come from a small, back-country winery to be one of the five largest wineries in the Pacific Northwest. Each vintage sees a greater production of Idaho wines and continuing success in national and international wine competitions. The challenge of marketing over 100,000 cases of wine each year has been met with the creation of a top flight marketing organization that has placed the wine in 25 states and overseas in several foreign countries.

The creation of consumer-oriented wines like the bulk process 'champagnes' has allowed Ste. Chapelle to keep low prices on popular varietals like Chardonnay and Riesling. This affordability has made the brand popular with restaurants and also with grocery chains who now offer expanded wine departments in many Northwest markets.

A visit to Ste. Chapelle Vineyards

For the winelover who doesn't mind a little driving, a trip to Ste. Chapelle is a treat. The attractive winery, designed in the style of the Paris cathedral for which it is named, provides the visitor a warm welcome complete with a tour of the facility and tasting of the winery's latest releases.

Jazz concerts are held each Sunday in July to the delight of local music and wine afficionados. Wine and food are available as the music wafts through the vines and orchards.

Take exit 35 from Interstate 84 and follow Highway 55 south about 13 miles. The winery is on your left.

The Wines

Ste. Chapelle Director of Winemaking Mimi Mook and winemaker Kevin Mott produce a broad range of wines to please every palate. From fresh and fruity Riesling, Chenin Blanc and Blush to buttery Chardonnay and crisp Fumé Blanc to hearty Cabernet Sauvignon and Merlot, you can find a wine you like. Sparkling wines are produced by both methode champenoise and the bulk method known as Charmat. All are of high quality. Dry Riesling, Fumé Blanc and two sparkling wines impressed our panelists for **Best of the Northwest** selection. Reviews begin on page 14.

Winemaker Kevin Mott and Director of Winemaking Mimi Mook at Ste. Chapelle Winery near Boise.

Mission Mountain Winery

P. O. Box 285
U. S. Highway 93
Dayton, MT 59914
(406) 849-5524

Owners: Dr. Thomas J. Campbell
Winemaker: Tom Campbell, Jr.
First Year: 1984
Winery Capacity: 15,000 Gallons
1991 Production: 11,500 Gallons

Winery History

Back in the early 1980s Tom Campbell planted vineyards near Flathead Lake in Northwestern Montana on property owned by he and his father, T. J. Campbell, a Missoula physician. Early efforts were troubled by frost but frost-hardy varieties were selected and overhead sprinklers were installed to combat the problem. Montana grapes are now harvested and vinted into methode champenoise sparkling wine. Mission Mountain Winery received Montana's first winery bond. Winemaker Tom Campbell, Jr. owns Horizon's Edge Winery in Zillah in Washington's Yakima Valley.

A visit to Mission Mountain Winery

The winery tasting room is open daily, May through October, from 10 AM to 5 PM. You'll find it just off Highway 93 near Flathead Lake.

The Wines

Our **Best of the Northwest** sparkling wine panel found Mission Mountain Pale Ruby Champagne to be among the very best in the Northwest. Also produced are Riesling, Chardonnay, Cabernet Sauvignon, Muscat Canelli and Blush.

Idaho

Idaho Accommodations & Dining

Idaho is most famous for its beautiful, unspoiled wilderness and recreational opportunities. Many visitors to Idaho prefer to camp of bring along their RV, but the accommodatiosn below are excellent choices for the less adventurous.

Accommodations

Moscow/Pullman

Cavanaugh's Motor Inn, 645 Pullman Rd., Moscow - (208) 882-3560, Large indoor spa, restaurant and lounge, suites with jacuzzi.

Boise

Shilo Inn Riverside, 3031 Main St. (exit 49 off I-84) - (208) 343-7662 Located on the Boise River, indoor pool, exercise room, pets O.K.

University Inn, 2360 University - (208) 345-7170 Restaurant and lounge, kids stay free, air conditioned, free continental breakfast. Moderate.

Boisean Motel, 1300 S. Capitol Blvd., (208) 343-3645 Pool, restaurant, kitchens available, parks and museums are closeby.

Idaho Heritage Inn B & B, 109 W. Idaho (83702), (208) 342-8066 This former home of Idaho Governor Chase Clark and Senator Frank Church is on the National Register of Historic Places.

Nampa

Shilo Inn Nampa Suites, 1401 Shilo Dr. (exit 36 off I-84) - (208) 465-3250 Larger rooms with refrigerators, microwaves. Indoor pool, sauna, exercise room, some kitchens, restaurant.

Hagerman

Cary House B & B, 17985 U.S. 30, Hagerman - (208) 837-4848 Exquisitely restored turn-of-the-century farm house. Gourmet breakfast, near hot springs and Snake River.

Rock Lodge Motel, Route 30, Hagerman - (208) 837-4822 Air conditioned, kitchens, hot mineral spas, year 'round trout fishing on property.

Coeur d'Alene

Coeur d'Alene Resort, I-90 exit 11, (208) 765-4000 The dazzling resort of northern Idaho with 338 lakeside rooms, golf, fireplaces, pools, beach, gourmet dining at Beverly's.

Dining - Boise

Renaissance Ristorante Italiano - Main at 5th (208) 344-6776 Dinner served daily with emphasis on Northern Italian cuisine with innovative selections as well as traditional offerings. Wine list includes local bottlings.

Dining - Nampa/Marsing

Sandbar River House - Main at 5th (208) 344-6776 Just south of the Idaho wine country, this steak and seafood house on the banks of the Snake River offers delicious food and an excellent selection of local bottlings.

For Parents Only

Balancing Rock - Impress your brood with this natural wonder south of Hagerman.
Shoshone Falls - Larger than Niagara on the Snake River.

Skiiing - Great skiing near Boise at Bogus Basin or how about Sun Valley?
Birdwatching - The Snake River Birds of Prey natural area south of Kuna is a world-renowned Raptor habitat.

A Guide to Northwest Microbreweries

Ever since Grant's Ale and Red Hook burst onto the Northwest suds scene in the early 1980s the region has seen at least one new microbrewery open each year. Fiercely independent, these brewers prefer to carve a niche in the marketplace for their product by sheer force rather than change their personal formula to suit broader tastes. Thus we have a wide variety of ales and lagers produced in small quantities for the consumption of only a small percentage of U. S. beer drinkers.

As the number of micros spirals upwards, quality and consistency continue to improve and the variety of unique brews becomes ever greater. The drop-out rate has been amazingly small as almost every micro-brewed product seems to attract a stalwart group of appreciative beerdrinkers who keep each brand afloat.

From the smallest brewpub, offering its wares to a neighborhood clientele, to the largest regional producers with product in bottle as well as barrel, beer lovers find ecstacy in discovering new brews and places to enjoy them.

We have room only to list the largest regional producers which includes all the original microbrewers who began the Northwest Real Beer revolution a decade ago. Here they are, as of presstime, alphabetically:

Bridgeport Brewery

1313 NW Marshall
Portland, OR 97209
(503) 241-7179

Brewer:
Team Brewing Effort

Brewpub:
Open Tuesday - Sunday

Brewery History

Dick Ponzi of Oregon winemaking fame revived the Cartwright Microbrewery in downtown Portland much to the delight of NW beerdrinkers in 1984 and with the assistance of his able brewmeister Karl Ockert has succeeded where others before him had failed. The copper Bridgeport Ale and full-bodied winterbrew have gained a reputation for quality and character. The Golden ale is very popular and the new Bridgeport Blue Heron Bitter has gained an immediate following.

As a co-sponsor of the first Oregon Brewers Festival in July of 1988 the Bridgeport folks established themselves as one of the leaders in the Oregon microbrewery scene. The event will take place each summer in Portland - call the brewery for details.

Brands Offered:

BridgePort Ale, BridgePort Blue Heron Pale Ale, BridgePort Coho Pacific Light Ale, BridgePort XX Stout, BridgePort Old, Knucklehead Ale.

Deschutes Brewery & Pub

1044 Bond St.
Bend, OR 97701
(503) 382-9242

Brewer: Mark Vickery
Brewpub Hours:
M-Th: 11AM-11:30PM
Fr, Sa: 11AM-12:30 PM
Sun: 11 AM - 10 PM

Brewery History

The mighty heat of a Central Oregon summer and the cold of winter make the brews from Deschutes even more tasty. Begun in 1988, the brewery and pub are located right in the heart of Bend and offer terrific soups, sandwiches, chili and other specialties. The large pub is a favorite with local beer lovers and with the many tourists who come for the skiing in winter and the golf , tennis and horseback riding in summer. A full range of brews is produced with at least two from the regular lineup and several special or seasonal beers on tap. All pours are offered in small tasters for free sampling. Some of the beers are distributed on draught regionally.

Brands Offered:

Cascade Golden Ale, Bachelor Bitter, Black Butte Porter, Bond Street Brown Ale, Obsidian Stout and Jubelale (hearty brown ale for autumn). Other seasonal beers are brewed.

Full Sail Brewing Co.

506 Columbia St.
Hood River, OR 97031
(503) 386-2281

Brewer:
James Emmerson
Brewpub Hours:
Th-Su, Noon to 7 PM
Summer months the pub is open daily.

Brewery History

With a view of the operating brewery through one window and a view of the Columbia River windsurfing action through the other, Full Sail Brewing and it's WhiteCap Brewpub in the old Diamond Fruit Cannery is a hit. The first ale released was a copper-colored 'golden ale' brewed malty and hoppy for real ale lovers. During 1988 three new ales were introduced. Expansion of sales into bottled product complements regional distribution of draught so that this operation is now one of the Northwest's largest. A great visit when you're in the Gorge.

Brands Offered:

Full Sail Golden Ale, Full Sail Amber Ale, Full Sail Pilsner, Main Sail Stout, Top Sail Porter, Full Sail Brown and Wassail (seasonally).

Hale's Ales

105 Central Way,
Kirkland, WA 98033
(206) 827-4359
410 N. Washington St.
Colville, WA 99114

Brewer: Mike Hale
Brewpub Hours:

Brewery History

Mike Hale established his first microbrewery in Eastern Washington in 1983, but conquered the Seattle market by constructing a brewery in downtown Kirkland. Moss Bay Amber Ale is served at the Kirkland Roaster and Ale House next door. Visits to the brewery to see the operation under way are by appointment. The commitment to producing British style ales goes back to Hale's 11 months study in England working with some of the craft brewers there to learn their brewing secrets of old.

Brands Offered:

Moss Bay Amber Ale, Pale Ale, Stout, Special Bitter, Celebration Porter, Wee Heavy.

Hart Brewing
Pyramid Ales

110 Marine Drive
Kalama, WA 98625
(206) 673-2121

Brewer: Jack Schaller,
Clay Biberdorf

**Brewery Tours
& Tasting:**
Weekdays: 10 AM-4 PM
Saturdays (May-Sept):
10 AM - 4 PM

Brewery History

Pyramid Ales were among the first to gain acceptance in the NW beer marketplace and they now are old standbys in many a Real Ale pub. The original brewery occupied a storefront in downtown Kalama. Today the proud, glassed-in brewhouse is visible from I-5 standing above the Kalama Marina just north of the grain elevator. Tours of the facility are capped with a tasting of the products available at the time. Pyramid ales are among the few Northwest versions that have kept the styles brewed from the very beginning (although several new brews have been added to the line). The Wheaten Ale and Pale Ale have are Northwest classics in craft brewing and should be on every beer lover's "must taste" list.

Brands Offered:

Pyramid Pale Ale (called Special Bitter when offered on draught), Pyramid Wheaten Ale, Pyramid HefeWeizen (with yeast remaining), Pyramid Best Brown Ale, Pyramid Amber Wheat Beer, Sphinx Stout, Snow Cap Ale (seasonal barleywine style), an Wheaten Bock (seasonal spring beer).

Maritime Pacific Brewing Co.

1514 NW Leary Way
Seattle, WA 98107
(206) 782-6181

Brewer:
George Hancock

Brewery Tours:
Sat: 11 AM - 6 PM

Brewery History

Maritime Pacific is a family-owned enterprise that began in 1990 after 10 years of planning and organization. Located not far from the Ballard Locks and Fishermen's Terminal, Maritime Pacific salutes the tall ships that once plied the waters of Puget Sound and the men who sailed them. The signature of the Maritime brews is the flavor of wheat malt that is included in all the recipes. The brewery is just west of the Ballard Bridge on Leary Way and offers tours on Saturdays to interested beer lovers. The product is mostly available on draught at Seattle-area pubs and restaurants and the several seasonal brews have won a consistent following.

Brands Offered:

Flagship Red Ale (amber-style ale), Clipper Gold Wheat Ale, Islander Pale Ale, Nightwatch Ale (dark amber, Oktoberfest style), Windjammer Dark Wheat Ale (Sept./Oct.), Windfest (October), Navigator Dark Ale (wheat bock beer brewed in Nov./Dec.), Bosun's Black Ale (Jan.-Mar.) and Maybock (May).

Pike Place Brewery

1432 Western Ave.
Seattle, WA 98121
(206) 622-1880

Brewer: John Farias

Brewery Hours:
M-Sat, Noon - 6 PM

Brewery History

Merchant du Vin president Charles Finkel and Liberty Malt Supply owner John Farias began this enterprise with consultation from NW brewer Vince Cottone as a microbrewery downstairs from the historic Seattle Pike Place Market. Located in the space next to Liberty Malt on the Western Ave. hillclimb, the brewery scheduled its first product release for January of 1989.

Sample pours of products on hand are dispensed through Liberty Malt Supply and tours of the brewery are just a poke-your-head-in-the-door and look around the space. Both the Pale Ale and Stout are available for take-out purchase. The ales are brewed under license for east coast distribution by Catamount Brewing in Vermont and in the midwest by The Indianapolis Brewing Co.

Brands Offered:

Pike Place Pale Ale and Pike Place Stout.

Portland Brewing Co.

1339 NW Flanders
Portland, OR 97209
(503) 222-7150

Technical Director:
Matt Muñoz

Brewpub Hours:
11:30 AM to 11 PM,
Fr, Sa til Midnight

Brewery History

Begun in 1986, Portland Brewing Co. once brewed Grant's Ale products under license for Portland distribution in addition to original beers. Today, their own line of flavorful brews is all they make and the small brewpub continues to quench the thirsts of Portlanders and tourists alike. A large new brewery opened in a location nearby the brewpub in 1993 expanding the production capacity by a factor of 10 over the small brewery that occupied the back of the pub. Liberal weekend hours at the pub assure beer aficionados adequate time to enjoy their brew in a relaxed atmosphere. The Oregon Honey Beer and McTarnahan's Scottish Ale are currently the operation's best sellers.

Brands Offered:

Portland Ale, McTarnahan's Ale, Oregon Honey Beer, Winter Ale, Portland Porter, Portland Stout and Mount Hood Beer.

Redhook Ale Brewery

3400 Phinney Ave. N.
Seattle, WA 98103
(206) 548-8000

Brewermaster:
Doug MacNair

Brewpub Hours:
M-Th: 8:30 AM - 11 PM
Fr: 8:30 AM - Midnight
Sat: Noon - Midnight
Sun: Noon - 7 PM

Tours:
Weekdays: 3 PM
Sat/Sun: 1:30, 2:30,
3:30, 4:30

Brewery History

Redhook started a lot of the hoopla over microbrewing when they opened their brewery in Seattle in 1981. Paul Shipman and the other principals involved got things up and going with a minimum of fuss and are now a brewing success story. Bottling of Redhook products began in 1987 and with the Redhook and Ballard Bitter ales in distribution. The original draft Redhook Ale earned the moniker "banana beer" due to its fruity/estery character. That product is now occasionally brewed as a seasonal ale with the Extra Special Bitter replacing it in the draught and bottled lineup.

The big news of 1988 was the opening of the new Redhook Brewery in Fremont complete with a computerized brewhouse and an outstanding new on-premise pub. The Trolleyman - named after the restored building's original tenant, the Seattle Electric Railway - opened with a rousing celebration on October 7 of 1988. Another major expansion will be completed by fall of 1994 on a site across from Chateau Ste. Michelle Winery in Woodinville.

Brands Offered:

Redhook ESB, Ballard Bitter, Blackhook Porter, Winterhook (seasonal) and Wheat Hook.

Rogue River Brewery

31-B Water St.
Ashland, OR 97520
(503) 488-5061

Bayfront Brewery
Bay Boulevard
Newport, OR
(503) 265-3188

Brewmasters: Gregory
Kebkey, John Maier

Brewery History

In 1988 several Portland-area executives (some from Nike) were looking for an investment in the microbrew arena. They found their brewer in a talented young man working for the McMenamin's chain of brewpubs and founded their brewery in Ashland to cash in on the built-in traffic from the Shakespeare Festival. This plan met with less than the desired level of success and regional distribution to draught accounts became the new focus.

In 1990 they added a second brewery and pub on the main street in downtown Newport on Oregon's highly touristed coast. Greater success in this location has come from the restaurant/pub format.

Brands Offered:

Rogue Pale Ale, Rogue Golden Ale, Rogue Amber Ale, many seasonal and specialty brews.

Thomas Kemper Brewing Co.

22381 Foss Rd. NE
Poulsbo, WA 98370
(206) 697-1446

Brewer: Rande Reed

Brewpub Hours:
Daily, 11 AM - 6 PM

Brewery History

Will Kemper and Andy Thomas got together in 1984 to make a hobby into a business by leaving an environmental consulting firm for the uncertain future of starting a microbrewery. In 1987 the brewery moved to Poulsbo where a 8,000 square foot refrigerated stone building looked mighty good as a brewery. The new facility catapulted the brand to greater recognition and success and as business often goes, the founders departed to pursue new dreams. Their original goal of producing traditional draft-style Bavarian lagers remains, however, and is being handled admirably by brewer Rande Reed and his staff. In addition to the original lagers, Thomas Kemper now produces a wide variety of specialty and seasonal brews.

A delightful tap room and beer garden are available for visitors to relax and enjoy the product, along with snacks and light meals.

Brands Offered

Pale Lager (the original Helles), Poulsbo Pilsner (more hoppy), Hefe Weizen, Weizen Berry (raspberry-flavored wheat beer - delicious!), Integrale (Vienna-style amber lager), Rolling Bay Bock (Feb.-May, bock style), Oktoberfest, Winterbrau (Nov.-Feb., hearty winter brew).

Widmer Brewing Co.

929 North Russell St.
Portland, OR 97227
(503) 281-2437 (bier)

Brewers: Kurt & Rob
Widmer, Frank
Commanday, others

Brewery Tours:
Sat: Noon and 1 PM
Brewpub: B. Moloch/
Heathman Bakery &
Pub, 901 SW Salmon

Widmer's NW Portland brewery produces fine German-style beers by the season. Lighter beers for warmer months, heavier beers for colder months. The Altbier is a year 'round favorite as is the refreshingly zippy Weizen. Pass the lemon slices.

Kurt and Rob Widmer located their original brewery in Portland's micro-brewery district in 1985 producing their Altbier for draught sales to taverns. An increase in the number of beer varieties dictated more brewing space and a building was bought and renovated with an investment of over $1 millon. The Heathman Bakery and Brewpub is the usual place to sample Widmer beers although the brewery has two tours on Saturdays and pours "whatever is on tap in the employee break room."

Brands:
Altbier (available all year, a hoppy, rich style), Weizen, Hefe Weizen, Oktoberfest, Fest, Bock and Doppelbock.

Yakima Brewing & Malting Co.

REAL ALES

25 N. Front St.
Yakima, WA 98901
(509) 575-1900
Pub 575-2922

Brewer & Founder:
Herbert L. (Bert) Grant

Brewpub Hours:
Mon-Thur:
11:30 AM - 11 PM,
Fri & Sat til 1 AM,
Sun til 9 PM

Brewery History
Bert Grant began his operation in the old Yakima Opera House in 1982 and found immediate success with his draught Scottish Ale. Other brews were less successful but still viable in their market niches. The tiny pub tucked into a corner of the brewery space was abandoned to move across the street to the old Yakima Train Depot. The space was enlarged and a small demonstration brewery was installed in a glassed-in enclosure. The pub is busy every lunchtime, has customers all day, and is slammed on weekend evenings. It's a great place!

Almost all of Grant's products are available now by the bottle throughout the Northwest. The Russian Stout seems to have taken the least harm from bottling. I still prefer Grant's Scottish Ale on draft by far. As Bert Grant's advertising said at the time bottled product was released, "Bottled Under Protest!"

Brands Offered:
Scottish Ale, Imperial Stout, Wheat Beer, India Pale Ale, Yakima Cider (production temporarily suspended), Celtic Ale, seasonal Spiced Ale.

Index to Northwest Wines & Wineries

Index to Northwest Wines & Wineries

Index to Northwest Wines & Wineries

Enjoy the Fine Food and Wines of the Pacific Northwest

Food and Wine Northwest Style

By Gilda Barrow-Zimmer & Chuck Hill

- Over 100 Tempting Recipes
- Wine Selections for Each Entree, Appetizer and Dessert
- Detailed Recipes – Easy for Beginning or Experienced Cooks

Special Offer for Autographed Copies